GW01162356

ŚAṄKARA SOURCE-BOOK

VOLUME II

ŚAṄKARA ON THE CREATION

Errata

Page 85, Extract 10. End of first paragraph should be: 'like the appearance of a snake in a rope.'
Pages 130-131. Delete the last sentence 'And thus it is.. '
Page 232, Extract 3, second paragraph, end of last sentence, should read: 'as if they were saying a father were born from his son.'

ŚAṄKARA ON THE CREATION

A ŚAṄKARA SOURCE-BOOK

VOLUME II

by

A.J. ALSTON

SHANTI SADAN
LONDON

First Edition 1980
Reprinted 1983

Second Edition 2004

Copyright © Shanti Sadan 2004
29 Chepstow Villas
London W11 3DR

www.shanti-sadan.org

All rights reserved.
No part of this publication may be translated, reproduced or transmitted in any form or by any means without the written permission of the publisher.

ISBN 0-85424-056-X

Printed and bound by
J W Arrowsmith Ltd., Bristol BS3 2NT

PREFACE TO SECOND EDITION

The present work is the second volume in a series of six aiming to bring before the reader all the most important texts of the great Indian Teacher, Śaṅkara, on the various themes of religious philosophy, collected together from their scattered position in his commentaries and presented in systematic form under topics. If the texts of the first volume, *Śaṅkara on the Absolute*, treated of the Absolute as it is in its true nature, those of the present volume explain how it appears when viewed in relation to the world-appearance. Of its three chapters, enumerated V, VI and VII within the Source-Book as a whole, the first brings together the important texts on God or the Lord (Īśvara) as creator, controller and inner ruler of the world, the second discusses the nature and composition of the world, and the last reveals the nullity of the Creation in the final metaphysical analysis.

Though forming part of a series intended to cover Śaṅkara's teaching in its totality, the book has a unity of its own. Texts have been chosen with a view to exhibiting with precision how Śaṅkara conceived Māyā, and what rôle it played in his system. Further groups of texts show what emphasis he placed on the theory of material causality known as Sat-kārya Vāda, and how he handled and developed the teaching, taken over from the Brahma-Sūtras, that the material and the efficient cause of the world are ultimately one and the same. Texts are quoted to show the importance for Śaṅkara of the upanishadic concept of Name and Form (nāma-rūpa) and how he distinguished between a manifest and an unmanifest state of Name and Form. Name and Form in their unmanifest state were for him indeterminable (anirvacanīya) as either identical with or different from the Absolute, and it was from unmanifest Name and Form that the whole world-appearance arose.

PREFACE

Other sections of the book cover Śaṅkara's treatment of some typical Hindu cosmological doctrines, such as those of the five Great Elements corresponding to the five sense-organs, of World-Periods or Kalpas, and of the rôle of the gods (deva) as presiding over the forces of Nature while being themselves no more than manifestations of one great cosmological principle, the Cosmic Vital Energy (prāṇa). Finally, texts are included which bring out how the whole teaching about Creation must be viewed in the wider context of transcending all plurality through realization of one's identity with the non-dual Self.

My obligations have already been indicated in the previous volume. The present one, like its predecessor, is dedicated with the deepest reverence to the late Hari Prasad Shastri, to whom it owes its existence.

A. J. ALSTON
LONDON 2003

CONTENTS

page

Preface v

Sanskrit transliteration ix

Chapter

V. The Absolute as Creator and Controller

1. The Absolute as Creator and Controller of the World 1
2. The Absolute as the Lord 13
3. The Absolute as the Material and Efficient Cause of the World 16
4. The Absolute as Inner Ruler 45
5. The Absolute as the Lord of Māyā 66

Notes to Chapter V 95

VI. The World and its Presiding Deities

1. Sat-kārya Vāda 110
2. Name and Form: Indeterminability 136
3. World-periods and Theory of the Elements 164
4. The Presiding Deities 178

Notes to Chapter VI 198

CONTENTS

Chapter		*page*
VII. The Acosmic View		
1.	The Creation-texts as a Device to teach Non-Duality	213
2.	Nothing can come into being	228
3.	The Argument from Dream	244
	Notes to Chapter VII	261
List of General Abbreviations		271
Bibliography		274
Conspectus of the Śaṅkara Source Book		293

The General Index and the Index to Texts Cited are published at the end of Volume VI, *Śaṅkara on Enlightenment*.

TRANSLITERATED SANSKRIT WORDS

The following table gives the most elementary indications of the value of the vowels that are variable in English (but regular in Sanskrit) and of the unfamiliar symbols and groupings of letters found in transliterated Sanskrit words. It is not intended as an accurate guide to correct pronunciation, for which see M. Coulson, *Sanskrit* (Teach Yourself Books), 4-21.

a	=	u in but
ā	=	a in father
ai	=	uy as in buy
au	=	au in audit (or French au)
c	=	ch in chant
ch	=	ch aspirated (said with extra breath)
ḍ	=	d in drake
e	=	ay in hay (better, French é elongated)
h	=	immediately after a consonant aspirates it without altering the value. (bh, ph, etc.)
ḥ	=	strong h
i	=	i in hit
ī	=	ea in eat
jñ	=	ja or gya (as in big yard)
ṃ	=	m before b, p, v, y and at the end of a word; elsewhere = n
ṅ	=	n in king
ṇ	=	n in tendril
ñ	=	n (except in jñ, q.v.)
o	=	o in note
ṛ	=	ri in rich
s	=	s in such
ś	=	sh in shut
ṣ	=	sh in shut
ṭ	=	t in try
u	=	u in put
ū	=	oo in boot

CHAPTER V

THE ABSOLUTE AS CREATOR AND CONTROLLER

1. The Absolute as Creator and Controller of the World

The doctrine of creation has to be considered initially as a theological and not a philosophical one. The mind cannot mount up unaided from a consideration of causality as it operates in the phenomenal world to appreciate the relation of the world to the Absolute from which it proceeds. And if it could, matter would be an eternal reality and the Absolute would be limited and conditioned by it and so not the Absolute. But once the ear has heard the sacred texts proclaiming that the world was projected by an omniscient and omnipotent Being, then reason can compare the texts and reflect on them to discover their deeper meanings, and the understanding can be applied constructively to the data of experience to discover analogies to strengthen one's faith in the revealed teaching.

We have already seen that the texts teach the existence of the Absolute as 'that from which all this comes forth'. But did they imply that this Being is actively involved in the creation and control of the world, or is it merely conceived as an actionless divine ground on which the world manifests through nescience? Śaṅkara's answer is that from the standpoint of the highest truth there is no plurality and no world and no Creator, and only the divine ground exists, if even the notions of existence or ground can be applied to it. But from the standpoint of nescience the world of duality is a fact. And from that standpoint it is a grievous error to believe that the world-process goes on through the operation of any blind force and without the conscious support and control of an omniscient and omnipotent Lord. To correct this error, the upanishadic texts speak occasionally of the Lord (īśa, etc.) and imply that He is the efficient and material cause of the universe, the Inner Ruler and Divine Magician who spreads forth the whole world-appearance under His own conscious control as a mere illusion. In the present chapter we shall be considering Śaṅkara's evaluation of the texts which posit the existence of the Absolute as the Lord and Controller of the phenomenal world. In the chapter to follow we shall be occupied with the texts which, taking for granted the presence of the Absolute in and behind the world as its Inner Ruler and support, describe the way in which the phenomenal world evolves under its control. And in the chapter following after that (Chapter VII) we shall see how, after all, the whole Vedic doctrine of creation is only part of that larger process of false-attribution-to-be-followed-by-subsequent-denial which we have seen to be the theological method of the school to which Śaṅkara belonged. A few further points concerning Śaṅkara's Īśvara-conception will emerge from his criticism of the theism of the Pāśupatas and Pāñcarātras to be given in Volume IV.

The present section will bring forward a group of Extracts in which it is clear that the 'Lord' spoken of in the ancient texts is nothing but the Absolute associated with the external adjunct (upādhi) of name and form set up by nescience. The doctrine of name and form will be discussed in more detail at Chapter VI, section 1, below. The Extracts of the present section bring out how the Absolute is not a 'Lord' or 'Controller' in its true nature, as in its true nature it alone exists and there is nothing for it to rule and control. Yet they grant that nescience sets up a world of multiplicity, and that the ancient texts, the Upanishads, Gītā and Brahma Sūtras, concur in teaching that the world of multiplicity, though a mere appearance, contains too much order, harmony and complexity to be ascribed either to the handiwork of the individual soul or to the unguided collective results of the deeds of living beings or to blind chance. From our ignorant standpoint, we are compelled to assume the existence of a conscious Creator and Controller. And since those who realize their identity with the Absolute in immediate intuition are very rare, and those who can meditate on the Absolute in abstract impersonal form are comparatively rare, the conception of the Absolute as the Creator and Controller of the world, endowed with omniscience, omnipotence, compassion and other excellencies in superabundant measure, is for most people the best that is available.

In any case, the worst error is to allow the instinctive demands for sense satisfaction to efface all memory of the revealed teaching that both the world and the individual soul are but finite expressions of a principle that is infinite, immortal and divine. To prevent this, the student is initially taught that the Self, as the Lord, first projected from Himself the 'elements' or 'deities' that compose and guide the matter of the world, and then entered them to 'unfold name and form'. The present group of Extracts proceeds from this starting point and is concerned with the correction of some initial misunderstandings that may follow from such teaching. The first Extract guards against an over-literal acceptance of the doctrine. The world and the individual soul are both, as such, mere appearances. The Absolute does not literally project them from itself and then stand over against them in eternal opposition. The Absolute is their true nature. It is not intrinsically the omniscient and omnipotent Creator, Lord and Ruler of the world and the individual, but appears to be such due to the external adjunct of name and form set up by nescience. The external adjunct (upādhi) has been defined as 'that which, standing near (upa) anything, imparts (ādhadāti) to it (the appearance of) its own qualities'.[1] The external adjunct is that which, *from the standpoint of an observer*, appears to limit or qualify something, though not in fact determining or affecting its real nature in any way.

The example given in our first Extract is that of pots and space. A big pot, say, and a small pot, each enclose a separate parcel of air conforming in size and shape to the contours of the pot in which it is contained. It will be moved or carried about inside the pot when the latter is moved or carried about. It also appears to natural uncritical observation that a certain parcel of space or of the subtle element called ether (ākāśa) is enclosed in each pot in the same way, although it is clear to mature reflection that no parcels of space are in fact enclosed within a pot and that no parcel of space can be moved about by moving a pot. The Absolute is related to the finite forms set up by nescience in the same way as the apparently enclosed parcels of space relate to the pots. It appears to be confined within them and to be separate in each, and to act and move when they act and move. When we reflect that the degree of order, harmony and complexity in our experience is inexplicable without a first cause and conscious controller, we are then unable to prevent ourselves from conceiving the Absolute as the omniscient and omnipotent Creator and Controller of the world. And although this is not its real nature from the standpoint of the highest truth, it is nevertheless a most important truth from the standpoint of nescience, and neglect of it is a source of error and suffering.

In the second Extract Śaṅkara argues that there is no question of the individual soul creating the universe. It is in fact the work of the Absolute (brahman), which, from the standpoint of nescience, is omniscient and omnipotent, and which, as we shall see in the following section, was by Śaṅkara virtually equated with Īśvara. The Vedic texts show that the Absolute is, in one sense, different from and greater than the individual soul, as it is that being 'free from grief and hunger, whose will is always realized, which has to be sought by the individual soul'[2] (and is therefore in some sense different from it). From the standpoint of nescience it appears to be different from the individual soul, even though from the standpoint of the highest truth it is not different, just as the universal ether seems to be something different from the small parcel of ether apparently enclosed within a pot, though mature reflection reveals them as identical. True, the whole purpose of the Advaitin's discipline is to realize his identity with the supreme Self. But until this intuitive realization is attained, it is an error to disbelieve in the existence of a power greater than the individual soul, who manifests as the world and who also upholds and controls his manifestation. Variety and difference in unity is the law of manifestation, and Śaṅkara cites from the three great realms, the mineral, vegetable and animal kingdoms, examples to prove this law.

Extract No.3 deals with the same Chāndogya text and presents us with an objector who takes it in a very literal sense to mean that the individual soul creates his own world of name and form. Against this, Śaṅkara declares that the individual soul has not the power to organize this vast cosmos in which we appear to exist, and that those exalted deities who do have this power receive it from the Lord. Alternatively, even if the individual soul could fashion the world, the individual soul itself is nothing but the supreme Self in conditioned form, so that it would be the supreme Self at work in the end, and the supreme Self, as we shall see in the next section, was something Śaṅkara did not differentiate from the Lord.

Extract No.2 contains one phrase that seems to attribute omniscience and omnipotence directly to the Absolute. Extract No.4 insists once more that all finite forms are appearance and not reality and are due to external adjuncts set up by nescience. But it does also contain a hint of how the passages in which Śaṅkara seems to attribute finite characteristics to the Absolute can be explained. For it declares that the whole realm of appearance, the finite, is 'indeterminable as the Absolute or as anything different from the Absolute', while the Absolute is 'other than it'. The Advaita Teacher (ācārya) has realized in immediate intuition that all is the non-dual Self and knows that any differentiation is due to nescience and unreal. But he goes on living a kind of twilight existence in the empirical world till the fall of the body. If he did not do so there would be no teaching and no living spiritual tradition. From this 'twilight' standpoint he can attribute empirical characteristics to the Self, because the world is still in some sense 'there' for him, and yet he is not deluded by belief in its reality. He sees the objects of the world, but he sees them as nothing other than the Absolute, while at the same time seeing that the Absolute is different from them.

TEXTS ON THE ABSOLUTE AS CREATOR AND CONTROLLER

1. Thus the Lord conforms to the external adjuncts formed by name and form set up by nescience in the same way that the ether conforms to external adjuncts such as the clay pot and the (differently shaped) coconut water vessel, etc. And within the realm of human experience, He rules over the conscious beings called individual souls (jīva), who are in truth nothing but his own Self, but who assume the limitations of body, mind and senses in the same sense in which the ether assumes the shape of the pots in which it is apparently enclosed. But the body, mind and senses are (not real, being) wrought of name and form which are set up by nescience. Hence the 'Lordship' of the Lord, as well as his omniscience and omnipotence, exist only in relation to external conditions (upādhi) which are (illusory because they are) of the nature of nescience.

From the standpoint of ultimate truth, there can be no talk of any dichotomy between a Lord and His subjects, or of qualities such as omniscience, etc., in the Self. For (from the standpoint of the highest truth) no external conditions exist in the Self, in the true nature of which all external cognitions stand negated through knowledge....

On the other hand the Veda does speak of the conception of a Lord and his subjects obtaining in the realm of empirical experience... The author of the Brahma Sūtras, too, when he says (in the present Sūtra) 'non-different from the Absolute', is speaking from the standpoint of the final truth. But when he is speaking from the standpoint of ordinary experience, he says, 'Let it be as in the world'[3] and speaks of the Absolute as comparable to the great ocean (assuming modification in its waves). And here he does not refute this conception, but resorts voluntarily to the doctrine that the world as a manifold effect is a transformation (pariṇāma) of the Absolute. For such a view will be needed later in passages dealing with meditations on the Absolute as associated with qualities.[4]

❖

2. That which we designate as the Creator of the Universe is the Absolute (brahman), omnipotent, omniscient, ever pure, enlightened and free by nature. He is superior to the individual soul and different from it. One cannot in his case raise objections like saying that He could not be the Creator of the world because such an action would not further his own interests. For in his case (unlike that of the individual soul) there is no good that has to be achieved and no evil that has to be removed, for He is ever free by nature. Nor is there any obstruction either to his knowledge or to his power, for He is omniscient and omnipotent. The individual soul, it is true, is not of this nature. And in his case the argument that he could not be the creator of the world because it would not be in his

interest to create it (since it would involve him in trouble) does indeed apply. But we do not speak of the individual soul as the Creator of the Universe. For, as the author of the Sūtras puts it, 'The Vedic teaching is that there is a difference'.[5] The Veda shows that the Absolute exists (from the standpoint of nescience) as a being superior to the individual soul by teaching that there is a difference between them. This is shown in the (implicit) reference to subject and object in such texts as 'The Self, indeed, is to be seen, etc....'[6]

Perhaps you will object that complete non-difference between the individual soul and the Absolute is taught in such texts as 'That thou art',[7] and it is not possible to justify the self-contradictory notion that they are both different and non-different. But there is nothing wrong in our position here. For we have already shown on various occasions how both difference and non-difference are possible (from different standpoints) on the analogy of the universal ether and the ether 'enclosed' in a pot.

Moreover, when one becomes awake to the non-difference of the individual soul and the Absolute through such texts teaching their non-difference as 'That thou art', this puts an end to the notion that the individual soul is suffering transmigration and also to the notion that the Absolute is a World-Creator. For all empirical notions of distinction, which are introduced by error, are cancelled and eradicated by right knowledge. How then could there be any creation? And how could there be such defects (in the Absolute) as failure to fulfil its own self-interests?[8] We have already explained many times how the condition of transmigration and failure to fulfil one's own self-interest are mere erroneous notions arising from failure to distinguish one's true nature from its external adjuncts, the body and its organs, which are themselves but effects of name and form, set up by nescience. And this state of transmigration, typified by the conviction that one has been cut off from and rendered different from the Self through physical birth and death, has no real existence whatever. But before the empirical notion of difference has been annulled, the conviction that the Absolute is greater than the soul, derived from such texts implying difference as 'He must be sought, He must be enquired into',[9] serves to dismiss the idea that the Absolute is affected by such defects as inability to encompass its own good.

And the author of the Sūtras adds that the objections are also without force 'on account of the example of stones, etc.' Stones, to take an example from worldly experience, have the common property of consisting of the element earth. But some, like diamonds and quartz, are precious. Others, like the sun-stone, are of comparatively lesser value, while there are others only good for throwing at dogs and crows. Thus stones, taken as a whole, exhibit variety and difference. Or take the case of seeds. They all in common depend on earth. Yet they manifest variety as flowers, fruit, scent, sap and so forth, and this even in such opposed examples as the sweet sandalwood tree and the bitter kimpāka tree. And again, from the same one source of the juices of eaten food, there arise such different products as the blood on the one hand and the hair of head or chest on the other. In the same way, it is quite intelligible that the effects arising from the single entity, the Absolute, should manifest variety, and that the individual soul and the Self in its form as pure Consciousness (prājña) should be different.[10]

3. Here (at Chāndogya Upanishad VI.iii.2) the doubt might arise whether it was the individual soul who was the agent in unfolding name and form or the highest Lord. Why? Because of the specification (about entering) 'with this living self (jīva)'. It could be, for instance, as in the world when a king might say 'Let me enter the enemy's army by means of a spy and calculate his strength'. In such a manner of speaking, the king attributes to himself, as the ultimate causal agent, the activity of calculation that belongs properly to the spy, and says 'Let me calculate', using the first person. In the same way, because He is the ultimate causal agent, the deity (Being) (uses the first person and) attributes to Himself the activity of unfolding name and form which belongs properly to the individual soul. Moreover, it is seen that the individual soul does in fact unfold name and form, as for example in the case of the invention of personal names such as Ḍittha or (his descendant) Ḍavittha and (in fashioning) such forms as pots and dishes. So this unfolding of name and form was performed by the individual soul.

In face of this preliminary assertion, the author of the Sūtras replies, 'But the fashioning of name and form...' With the word 'but' the author shows that a thesis is being rejected. The 'fashioning' refers to the unfolding of name and form (at the time of creation, spoken of in the Chāndogya text in question). This fashioning of name and fashioning of form in the case of fire, sun and lightning, as also in the case of grasses, reeds and foliage, of tame animals and wild beasts and human beings and so forth, extending to every individual of every species, can only be the work of the highest Lord, the Creator of fire, water and food (the deities affirmed in the text in question to constitute the three worlds)... But would it not be right to say that the text lays down that the individual soul was the agent, on account of the specification 'with this living self (jiva)?' Not so. For the words 'with this living self' stand in immediate proximity to the phrase 'Let Me enter these' and so qualify that and not 'Let Me unfold'. For if it were the individual soul who was the subject of the verb 'unfold', then the deity 'Being' would be the subject only in a figurative sense (after the manner of the king and the spy). But we reject this. For the individual soul, who is not, as such, the Lord, has not the power to unfold names and forms[11] in all their variety, including mountains, oceans, rivers and the rest. And even those (exalted beings like Brahmā) who do have this power derive it from the Lord alone.

On the other hand the individual soul is not completely different from the highest Lord, like the spy is from the king. This is already clear from the specification 'with My living self', and also because the very existence of an individual soul is only due to the Self being associated with an external adjunct (in the form of the individual's body and organs). Hence, even if the unfolding of name and form had been performed by the individual soul, it would still, in the last resort, have been performed by the highest Lord alone.[12]

❖

4. But will it not be a contradiction for the one propounding the doctrine that the Self is the eternal, changeless Absolute (brahman) to speak of the Lord (īśvara) as cause, when, on account of perfect unity (i.e. unity without even internal differentiation), there cannot be any dichotomy between a

Lord and that over which He holds control? No, because the omniscience of the Lord depends on His unfolding the seed of name and form which are of the nature of nescience. 'Verily, the ether came forth from this very Self (ātman)'.[13] It is clear from such texts as this that the projection, maintenance and dissolution of the world proceed from the omniscient, omnipotent Lord, eternal, pure, enlightened and free by nature, and not from the non-conscious 'Nature' of the Sāṅkhyas or from any other such hypothetical principle (such as the atoms of the Vaiśeṣikas or the Fate of non-Vedic theoreticians of earlier times)...

But how can we deny that we are saying anything contradictory when we speak (at the same time) of the perfect unity and non-duality of the Self? Listen. Name and form, imagined through nescience as if they were the very nature of the omniscient Lord, themselves indeterminable either as the real principle itself (tattva) or as anything different (anyatva), the two seeds of the whole complex world of transmigratory experience, are spoken of in the Veda and the Smṛti as the power of illusion (māyā-śakti) and the Nature (prakṛti) of the omniscient Lord. The omniscient Lord Himself is other than these two. This we know from such texts as 'The ether, verily, brings to manifestation name and form; that which stands within them is the Absolute'... and 'Who makes the one seed into many'.[14]

2. The Absolute as the Lord

In Śaṅkara,[15] the terms 'Īśvara' (the Lord) and 'Parameśvara' (the supreme or highest Lord) are virtually interchangeable terms. The notion of 'the Lord' or 'the highest Lord' is also usually identical with that of the Absolute (ātman, brahman), though in certain contexts it may be distinguishable. The only positive characteristic which Śaṅkara attributes to the Lord is that of Consciousness. He seldom attributes the character of 'bliss' either to the Absolute or to 'the Lord' and he certainly never associates the latter with the 'bliss sheath' in the manner of his followers.

From the Lord's nature as Consciousness other characteristics follow. He is omnipresent (sarva-gata).[16] Hence He is in the body of the individual, but that body does not limit Him.[17] He is eternally self-evident from beginningless time.[18] As He is Himself perfectly identical with the Absolute, He is often characterized by negatives. He has no body,[19] He is not an agent,[20] enjoys not a whiff (gandha) of individual experience[21] and has no defects or sins. As He identifies Himself with no body, He does not experience the feeling 'I suffer'.[22] He is eternal and raised high above all change (kūṭastha-nitya) like the highest Self,[23] He has no form (rūpa),[24] He is imperceptible (adṛśya)[25] and needs no support (ādhāra). He cannot be known through the secular means of knowledge, and for this very reason His nature is revealed as the final import of the meaning of the Veda.[26] He is not subject to transmigration (asaṃsārin) and His Lordly power (aiśvarya) knows no limits. These and similar texts show that for Śaṅkara 'the Lord' (īśvara) and 'the Absolute' (brahman) are essentially one and the same thing.

Śaṅkara often declares that the Lord and the individual soul are different.[27] He also distinguishes, from the standpoint of nescience, between the Absolute and the individual soul.[28] On the other hand, at other places he identifies the individual soul with the Lord,[29] with the highest Self (paramātman),[30] and with the Absolute (brahman).[31]

The differences, of course, are not real. They are conditioned by external adjuncts set up by nescience.[32] The essential identity of the individual soul with the Lord is hidden (tirohita) by the association of the latter with the body, its illusory adjunct. The distinction between the individual soul and the Lord, however, is set up by wrong-knowledge and is not real.[33] It is through the influence of nescience that the highest Lord appears to undergo 'pluralization'.[34]

In the interests of strict non-dualism, Śaṅkara is obliged to modify the statement at Brahma Sūtra II.iii.43 that the individual is a part (aṃśa) of the Lord by the insertion of the word 'as if' (iva).[35] The real nature of the individual soul is the highest Lord.[36] Nevertheless, their natures are not 'exchangeable'. The Lord has not the nature of the individual soul, even if the soul in its true nature is the Lord.[37] The individual soul, indeed, may loosely be spoken of as having the potentiality (sambhava) of acquiring or 'realizing' the characteristics (dharma) of the highest Lord.[38] Nevertheless, the Lord is something more than the embodied soul if the latter is considered *qua* embodied. He is the real Self.[39]

The highest Lord, we have seen, can properly bear only one predicate. His nature is Consciousness. All other affirmations in regard to Him reduce Him below His real stature. Such affirmations can, however, occur. They occur when the Lord is considered in His capacity as 'Lord' specifically in relation to the world or to the individual soul, or when He is taken as an object of meditation. There are just a few passages in which, considered in such contexts as these, the Lord is actually differentiated from the Absolute (brahman), though even in these contexts the Lord and the Absolute are normally identified. The Lord may be called, in relation to the world over which He is 'Lord', its projector (sraṣṭṛ)[40] or its maker (kartṛ)[41] or the one who fashioned (akalpayat) the universe,[42] or the cause (kāraṇa) of the universe.[43] He is the unmoved mover.[44] He is omniscient[45] and is often called omnipotent (sarva-śakti). He exists in everything as its essence, and, despite the mention of subordinate deities, it is He ultimately who witnesses and presides over the evolution of all forms even after they have come into manifestation. When the texts speak of various subordinate deities, they imply that all are the one deity Īśvara viewed under different external adjuncts.[46]

In the passages dealing with creation, the words 'the Lord', 'the Absolute' and even 'the Absolute in its highest form' (para-brahman) remain, in general, interchangeable terms. Perhaps the only exception to this lies in the statement that the 'Lordship' (īśvaratva) of the Lord is illusory.[47] One cannot find Śaṅkara saying that the nature of the Absolute as Absolute (its 'brahmatva') is illusory. But apart from this, the predicates of Īśvara that appear in the teachings about creation are likewise predicable of the Absolute in the same context. The Absolute (brahman) is projector (sraṣṭṛ),[48] maker (kartṛ),[49] and the cause (kāraṇa) of the universe.[50] As such, the Absolute (brahman) is intelligent (īksitṛ),[51] and can also be called omniscient and omnipotent.[52]

The relationship between the Absolute and the Lord is in some ways paralleled by that between the individual soul (jīva) and the highest Self (paramātman). Just as the 'Lordship' of the Lord is not absolutely real, so is the 'individualized form' of the individual soul, its 'jaivam rūpam' or 'jīvic form', not absolutely real. But it is noteworthy that whereas the term 'the Lord' can always and everywhere be substituted for the term 'the Absolute' (brahman), the term 'individual soul' (jīva) can never be substituted for the term 'the highest Self' (paramātman). Thus the use of the term jīva, and similar terms such as śārīra and vijñānātman, to designate the individual soul *always* implies that the individual soul is being considered under its illusory aspect. On the other hand the use of the term 'the Lord' only occasionally implies that the Lord is being thought of in association with some illusory adjunct. It may do, but it need not, and in the vast majority of cases it does not.[53]

3. The Absolute as the Material and Efficient Cause of the World

The Extracts in the present section are given largely in the order in which they occur in the Brahma Sūtra Commentary. In the first Extract it is argued that one cannot take full account of the upanishadic texts without admitting that the Absolute is both the efficient and material cause of the universe. Śaṅkara maintains, in conformity with the language of the Brahma Sūtras, that the Absolute undergoes transformation (pariṇāma) to assume the form of the objects of the world as well as of the mental representations through which they are known, the latter being conceived, as we shall find in Chapter VIII, as reflections of Consciousness in the more subtle phase of matter that constitutes mind. Extract 2 explains how the Absolute undergoes transformation without the aid of any external efficient cause in virtue of the knowledge-power and activity-power inherent in it. The 'transformation' is more akin to the power of projection enjoyed by gods and certain exalted seers (ṛṣis) than to the physical transformation undergone by non-conscious substances such as, say, milk when it transforms into curds. Extract 3 affirms that the Absolute remains distinct from the primordial stuff of the world (prakṛti). It is only the latter that undergoes modification, while the Absolute in its true form remains immutable. The Vedic and Smṛti texts which affirm that the Absolute undergoes modification are not to be taken as stating the ultimate truth about the causality of the Absolute. As will be explained in detail at Vol.V, Chapter XII, section 2, below, Śaṅkara only regarded a text as an authoritative source of information as to fact if it generated certain and fruitful knowledge. The texts apparently attributing causality to the Absolute did not for him fall into this category,[54] so they had to be interpreted as teaching some deeper truth behind the surface meaning of the words. It turns out that the Absolute is not, in the last resort, a cause. But the hearer, blinded by nescience, sees causality everywhere, and the texts predicating transformation of the Absolute are really concerned with affirming the existence of the Absolute in terms that a hearer blinded by the appearance of causality would understand. A sign that the real concern of the texts is only with the existence of the Absolute is that it is a knowledge of the existence of the Absolute, and not of its causality, that brings 'fruit', the fruit, namely, of immortality.

Extracts 4-6 bring the expected declaration that even the statements about the Absolute being equipped with creative powers are only made from the standpoint of nescience. The nearest analogy in the world to the activity of the Absolute in creating the world is that of sport, though the process is not in fact intelligible to the human mind. Extract 6 again emphasizes that the creation texts are not concerned with recording historical facts, a theme which will be taken up again in the Extracts of the first section of Chapter VII. Extract 7 discusses more elaborately the objection that if the Absolute were the material cause of the world it ought to be non-conscious like the objects of the world. The objection represents the position of the Sāṅkhyas, who maintained that the material cause of the world was non-conscious Nature. The further point is made that, while the effect is non-different from its material cause, the material cause is different from and superior to the effect. Extract 8 shows how the dissolution of the objects of the world of plurality back into the Absolute need not be regarded as contaminating the purity, homogeneity and unity of the latter. Extract 9 confronts the objection that the presence of subject-object duality in experience renders the view that all proceeds from one material cause untenable. The answer is by appeal to the analogy of water. Waves and bubbles are mutually distinct, and yet both are non-different from water.

TEXTS ON THE ABSOLUTE AS MATERIAL AND EFFICIENT CAUSE

1. The Absolute has been defined as 'That from which proceed the origin, (maintenance and dissolution) of this (world).'[55] And since a definition of that kind might be regarded equally as covering the material cause, such as the clay or the gold in the case of pots or bracelets, or the efficient cause, in these cases the potter or the goldsmith, an enquiry is opened to decide what the exact nature of the causality of the Absolute might be.

At a first glance it might appear that it was only the efficient cause. For there are texts saying that the agency of the Absolute in creation was preceded by thought, as for example 'He took thought' followed by 'He projected the Cosmic Vital Energy'.[56] And agency preceded by taking thought is found only in efficient causes such as potters and the like. Actions are found in the world to arise and produce results only when there is the co-operation of a variety of factors (amongst which the material and efficient causes are separate), and it is but right to extend this law to the case of the creation of the world.

Moreover, the Absolute is frequently called the Lord. And 'lords', such as kings and beings like Vaivasvata (i.e. Yama, the ruler of the kingdom of the dead) who preside over recognized realms, are conceived as efficient causes only and not as the material causes of the realms over which they preside. So, by analogy, the highest Lord, too, must be a mere efficient cause.

And there is a further reason. This world, considered as an effect, is composed of parts and is non-conscious and impure. Its material cause must have these same characteristics likewise, as the material cause and its effects are seen to be invariably of like nature (e.g. clay in clay-pots). But we know that the Absolute is not of this nature, for we have such texts as 'Partless, actionless, without blemish, tranquil, pure'.[57] Hence there is nothing left but to accept the traditions of the Smṛti (here meaning the dualistic form of the Sāṅkhya system, granted Smṛti status because conceived by its adherents as emanating from the ṛṣi Kapila) that the material cause of the world is something other than the Absolute, (namely, non-conscious Nature) which has these qualities of impurity and the like. For when the Veda speaks of the Absolute as the cause it means specifically the *efficient* cause.

To this suggestion we reply as follows. The Absolute has to be accepted as both the material cause — termed by the author of the Sūtras the 'prakṛti' or primary matter — and the efficient cause, and not as the efficient cause alone. Why? Because, as he puts it, this is the way to avoid contradicting the preliminary affirmations (pratijñā) and supporting examples (dṛṣṭānta) given by the Vedic texts. For example, there is the preliminary affirmation implicit in the text 'Did you ask for that teaching whereby that is heard which was not heard before, that is thought which was not thought before, that is known which was not known before?'[58] From this we conclude that there is something through knowing which all else becomes known, even though it was not known before. It is only when one knows a material cause that one can know everything else through knowing that, for effects are non-different from their material causes. On the other hand, an efficient cause is invariably distinct from the effects he produces, as is the case with an architect who produces a house. And the supporting example given in this upanishadic text refers only to the material cause when it says, 'Just as, my dear one, by (knowing) one clod of clay all that is made of clay is known, the modification being only a name arising from speech, while the truth is that it is just clay...'[59]

On the other hand we also have to conclude that the Absolute is the efficient cause of the universe on account of the absence of any other being subjecting it to control. In the world, we find that material causes like clay and gold only function as such (material causes) when there are potters and goldsmiths subjecting them to control. But the Absolute, although the material cause of the world, is not subject to external control in this way. For it is affirmed that before the creation of the world the Absolute alone existed, one only, without a second...[60] Because we have (in the Chāndogya text under consideration) independent action preceded by a declaration of intent, we must admit the presence of an agent. And because the declaration of intent to become many refers to the inmost Self in the words 'Let Me become many', we must conclude that the Self is also the material cause of the universe.

And there is a further reason why it must be the material cause. The texts speak of the springing forth of the universe from the Absolute and its dissolution back into it... That from which anything springs forth and into which it dissolves back is universally recognized to be its material cause, as in the case of rice and barley and other crops which spring forth from and dissolve back into the earth. The author of the Sūtras specifies the Absolute as the ultimate cause which presupposes no further material cause of its own...

And there is yet another reason why the Absolute is the material cause. In a section dealing with the Absolute, we hear 'That (the Absolute) itself made itself (into the world)',[61] a text which predicates both agency and objecthood of the Self, the second occurrence of the term 'itself' signifying objecthood and the first agency. But how can that which is already established as the agent be itself the object of an act of making? 'Through transformation (pariṇāma)' says the author of the Sūtras. Although the Self was already established as existent, it transformed itself through particular modifications (vikāra). Transformation in the form of assumption of modifications is found in material causes like clay. And because of the first specification 'itself', we know that it was (itself the efficient cause because) non-dependent on any external efficient cause...

As for the objection that agency preceded by conscious intent is in the world only found in efficient causes like potters (who are different from the material causes on which they are operating) and not in the material causes themselves, to that we reply that the causation of the Absolute is not strictly comparable with worldly causation. This is not a matter within the province of inference.[62] And because it belongs to the province of revelation, it has to be conceived just as the revealed texts say.[63]

❖

2. *Objection:* The statement made earlier that the conscious principle, the Absolute, one without a second, was the cause of the world, could not be right. For (where conscious causes are at work) we invariably notice the assemblage of materials and instruments. Here in the world, potters and weavers and so on proceed to their respective tasks only after they have possessed themselves of various materials and instruments, such as the clay and the wheel and the (potter's) stick and the cotton threads. How can the Absolute proceed to the act of the creation of the world if He has no auxiliaries, as you maintain, and if He does not assemble His means and instruments? The truth is, then, that the Absolute, as you conceive it, is not the cause of the world.

Answer: There is nothing wrong in our position here. For it is intelligible as being due to the peculiar nature of the causal substance, as in the case of milk. For we find in ordinary experience that milk and water transform themselves of their own accord into curds and ice respectively, without recourse to any means or instruments. And the same can very well be the case with the Absolute.

Objection: How can you say such a thing? Milk and the like do depend on external means for transforming themselves into curds and so on. They depend on heat and other such factors.

Answer: This is no objection. It is the nature of milk itself that determines the kind and extent of the transformation: heat and other external factors can do no more than hasten the transformation into curds. And if the milk did not itself have the propensity to turn into curds, it could not be forced to do so by heat or any other external factor. The wind and the ether, for instance, are not forced by heat to turn into curds. The auxiliary factors merely enhance the capacity of milk to transform itself into curds. But as the power of the Absolute is already infinite, nothing can enhance it in any way.

And there is the Vedic text, 'It has no body and no sense-organs. It has no equal and no superior. Its supreme powers are spoken of in the Veda as multifarious, as natural to it, as consisting in a power of knowledge and a power of activity'.[64] Thus because the Absolute, though one, is possessed of a multifarious power, it can undergo multiform transformation (pariṇāma) on the analogy of milk transforming itself into curds.

Objection: Very well. Let us grant that non-conscious substances like milk become transformed into curds, etc., without recourse to external means and instruments, as this is actually seen to be the case. But conscious agents, on the other hand, such as potters, are seen to produce their various effects only after first resorting to the appropriate means. How can a conscious principle like the Absolute act without auxiliaries?

Answer: Like the gods and other such beings, we reply. In the world, the gods, the departed ancestors (pitṛ), the immortal sages (ṛṣi) and the like, beings of great spiritual power, though conscious, are found to materialize large numbers of bodies of different kinds and different consistency, vast palaces, chariots and the like, and all quite spontaneously and without resort to any external means or instruments, and solely through thought-power as associated with their possession of supernormal faculties. Of this, the texts of the Vedas, Brāhmaṇas, Epics and Purāṇas are a proof.[65]

Moreover, the spider projects its web quite spontaneously. Cranes become pregnant without receiving seed. The lotus spreads from lake to lake without any means of conveyance. And in the same way, the Absolute, though a conscious principle, projects the world without recourse to any external means or instruments.

Our opponent might object here and say that these gods, etc., who have been cited as examples to illustrate the causality of the Absolute, are not in the same category as the Absolute. For example, in producing supernormal manifestations, the gods, etc., have the service of their non-conscious bodies as material cause, whereas the Self does not. And the spider's web consists of a solidified form of the spittle derived from eating yet smaller creatures. Even the female crane only conceives 'spontaneously' when it hears the sound of thunder.[66] And the lotus, though conscious, creeps across from one lake to another by means of its non-conscious body, like a creeper crawling along to a tree. Thus the lotus is (a conscious being using its non-conscious body as an instrument and) not a non-conscious being somehow moving about from lake to lake spontaneously.[67] So these examples will not do to illustrate the causality of the Absolute (as occurring without the help of external instruments).

Against this, we should reply that we see nothing wrong in our position. For all that was meant was to show that the causality of the Absolute was different from that of the potter, etc., (mere efficient causes). The class exemplified by potters and the class exemplified by gods are alike in respect of being conscious, and yet the potters and the like need external materials and instruments before they can produce their effects, whereas gods and the like do not. And thus it is intelligible that the Absolute, though conscious, should create without recourse to external materials and instruments. That is all we wish to explain by citing the example of the gods and the rest. So no general rule can be established that causality must in every case follow any particular example of it that we may happen to have seen.[68]

❖

3. It is not true (as the opponent suggests) that our position implies that the *whole* of the Absolute undergoes modification (pariṇāma). Why not? 'Because of the Vedic texts', says the author of the Sūtras. For just as the Vedic texts declare that the world arises from the Absolute, so do they also describe the Absolute as without modification (vikāra). For they refer to it as distinct both from the primordial stuff (prakṛti) of the world and from the modifications (vikāra) which that stuff assumes. We find such texts, for example, as 'Come, let Me enter these divinities (fire, water, food) and unfold name and form' and 'His divine power comprehends all this (empirical world), but in Himself the Self is greater. All these creatures constitute one quarter of Him: three quarters of Him is immortal in heaven'.[69] And we draw the same conclusion from the statement that He has His dwelling-place in the heart[70] (which suggests that the Self is partless because the ether in the heart is partless) and the mention of reaching pure Being (in dreamless sleep). And if the *whole* of the Absolute had

passed over into the effect, then the specification about dreamless sleep occurring in the text 'Then, my dear one, he unites with Being in dreamless sleep'[71] would be inexplicable. For he would only be uniting with a modified Absolute (and he is already united with that in waking experience) and no Absolute free from modification would exist. We also conclude that the Absolute does not undergo modification from the denials that it lies within the range of the senses. For any modification (vikāra) of the Absolute would fall within the range of the senses. Therefore the Absolute is free from modification.

On the other hand there is no question of our being allowed to contradict the texts which speak of the partlessness of the Absolute either, for partlessness is accepted from the mere fact of its being taught in the Veda. And moreover, the Absolute is, as the author of the Sūtras puts it, 'rooted in the Veda', that is, it is knowable only through the Veda and not through the empirical means of knowledge such as perception and the rest. Consequently, it must be accepted to be just what it is said to be in Vedic revelation. And Vedic revelation teaches about the Absolute *both* that it is partly involved in modification *and also* that it is partless. Even in the domain of things pertaining to secular experience such as gems, magic formulae and herbs, powers are found which produce a number of contradictory effects amid all the permutations of time, space and secondary causes. Even these powers (belonging to the world of ordinary secular experience) cannot be understood by bare reasoning unless one has received precise inside information of the form 'This object possesses such and such powers which depend on such and such auxiliaries and can be used on such and such objects for such and such purposes'. How much less, then, can the unfathomable nature of the Absolute be understood without the help of Vedic revelation. And thus we hear in the Purāṇas,[72] 'Infathomable indeed are these beings. One should not apply logic to try to understand them. The definition of the unfathomable is "That which lies beyond the natural sphere".' Therefore right knowledge about what transcends sense-perception depends on revelation.

Objection: Something inherently contradictory cannot be conveyed even by revelation. Consider the proposition 'The partless Absolute undergoes modification (pariṇamate), but not completely'. If the Absolute were partless, either it would not undergo modification at all, or else it would undergo modification completely. And if you say that it undergoes modification with one form and remains unchanged with another, then any such assumption about different forms would imply parts.

In regard to action, when one is confronted with contradictions such as 'In performing the "overnight" ritual one takes up the Ṣoḍaśin Soma-vessel' and 'In performing the "overnight ritual" one does not take up the Ṣoḍaśin Soma-vessel', one may get round the contradiction by regarding the two texts as allowing an option, because the performance of any action is subject to the will of man (so that there can be alternative ways of doing it or a choice of not doing it, etc.).[73] But in the present context (i.e. the context of the presence of two contradictory *metaphysical* statements about the Absolute) there is no possibility of getting round the two views as optional, because metaphysical reality is not subject to the will of man (so that the possibility of option does not arise). So your position is hard to make out.

Answer: There is nothing wrong in our position, because differences of form are accepted as being imagined through nescience. The real is not thereby invested with parts if it shows distinctions of form that are (only) imagined through nescience. The moon does not in fact become many when seen as if many by an eye afflicted with the disease called timira. But the Absolute becomes subject to modification and to all empirical experience through distinctions consisting of name and form, manifest and unmanifest, which are imagined through nescience and are indeterminable either as being the reality itself or as being anything different.[74] But in its ultimately true form it remains beyond all empirical experience and not subject to modification (pariṇāma). Because name and form, imagined through nescience, are 'mere results of the activity of speech'[75], the partlessness of the Absolute is in no way affected by them.

Nor are the texts affirming that the Absolute undergoes modification concerned with teaching modification as a historically true fact, for no 'fruit' is mentioned in connection with such knowledge.[76] The real purpose of these texts is to proclaim that the Absolute, beyond all empirical experience, is one's own Self, for in the case of that knowledge a fruit *is* mentioned. For the passage which begins 'This Self indicated through the words "Not thus, not thus"' concludes 'Verily, Janaka, thou hast attained the fearless state'.[77]

❖

4. It has been said that the variegated universe of plurality and modification can proceed from the Absolute, though the latter is a perfect unity, because it is associated with a variety of powers. But how can we be sure that the Absolute really is associated with a variety of powers? To this question the author of the Sūtras replies that the Absolute is 'equipped with everything (necessary to produce the world), as we see to be the case from the revealed texts'. And it is a fact that we have to accept that the supreme Deity is equipped with all powers. Why? Because of the texts. That the supreme Deity is equipped with all powers is shown by such texts as 'Encompassing all worlds, containing all desires, containing all odours, containing all tastes, encompassing all this world, without speech, without concern',[78] 'Whose desires and purposes invariably attain fulfilment',[79] 'He who is omniscient or all-knowing'[80] and 'Verily, at the command of that imperishable, O Gārgī, the sun and the moon stand in their respective positions'.[81]

Very well. But there are Vedic texts which teach that the supreme Deity is bereft of organs, such as 'Without eyes, without ears, without voice, without mind'.[82] How then could He accomplish any action, even if He were equipped with all powers? The gods and other conscious beings, even though they possess all (necessary) powers, are known to accomplish this or that deed only as equipped with the appropriate body and organs. And how, indeed, could a Deity of whom all particular characters are negated in the formula 'Not thus, not thus'[83] even be possessed of all powers?

The answer to all this, says the author of the Sūtras, has already been given above.[84] The Absolute in all its profundity can be fathomed through Vedic revelation alone, not through the considerations of logic. Nor is there any rule that the potency of one thing must behave in the same way as the potency of another. Even the statement that the Absolute, though bereft of all particular characters, can be associated with all powers, is made only through attributing to the Absolute distinctions that are imagined through nescience. And it is in the same sense that the Veda teaches that the Absolute is equipped with all powers, even though void of organs of action, in the words 'He is swift without feet, He takes without hands, He sees without eyes, He hears without ears'.[85]

❖

5. It is through My presence, as Overseer, O son of Kuntī, that this whole universe with all that moves and all that is fixed, that includes both a manifest and an unmanifest state, is able to unfold[86] and assume its various phases. Every course of action in the world must necessarily be first conceived as the means to the fulfilment of some end before it can begin. And such action is directed towards, and finds fulfilment in, further conscious experience, as is shown by (the invariable accompaniment of) such feelings as 'Let me experience this', 'I see such and such', 'I hear such and such', 'I feel happy', 'I feel miserable', 'I will do this for the sake of that' or 'I want to know such and such'. And there are Vedic verses that confirm the notion (which this rational reflection suggests) that there stands a conscious Controller behind the world...

Yet if there is no other conscious principle apart from the one Divinity, the Overseer of all, who is but bare

Consciousness and unconcerned with individual enjoyment and experience in any form, then it is out of place to raise or attempt to answer the question 'What was the purpose of creation?' For in this connection we have such verses as 'Who knows aright, or who has declared, whence arose this creation?'[87] And the Lord Himself has declared, 'Knowledge is overlaid with ignorance, whereby these creatures are deluded'.[88]

❖

6. The opponent raises a further difficulty about the Creator of the world being a conscious being. If the supreme Self were a conscious being, he says, He could not contrive to create this spherical universe. Why not? Because all who initiate any action must have a purpose. In the world, for instance, intelligent persons are not seen to initiate even the most casual actions unless they redound to their own advantage, what to say of actions of weight and consequence. And the Veda repeats this well-known truth in the words, 'Everything, indeed, that is pleasant to a person is pleasant to him not for everyone's sake but only for his own sake'.[89] And to initiate the construction of this whole world-sphere, high and low, is an undertaking of no mean order.

If the initiation of this activity (the opponent continues) were assumed to be in the self-interest of the supreme Self, this would contradict the Vedic teaching that He (already) enjoys perfect satisfaction. If, on the other hand, no interest of His were to be served, He would not have initiated the activity. Perhaps you will say that lunatics, though conscious, are seen to act without the prompting of self-interest, from sheer weakness of mind. And you may claim that the initiation of action by the supreme Self is of the same kind. But if this were so, it would contradict the Vedic teaching about the omniscience of the supreme Self. So it follows that the notion of creation proceeding from any conscious principle cannot be maintained (and the world must proceed from the non-conscious Nature taught by the Sāṅkhyas).

By the use of the word 'but' the author of the Sūtras shows that he rejects this objection. The action of the Lord in initiating the world proceeds from His own nature without the least self-interested end in view, and is of the nature of a sport. It is like the notion of some king or great minister who has realized all his desires and initiates some sports in the pleasure-gardens without any practical motive. Or again, it is like breathing in and out which just proceeds naturally and without any consciously maintained end in view. For no one can point to any practical end that the Lord could possibly have in view, either on the basis of reason or of Vedic revelation, and no one is in a position to interrogate Him personally about His nature either.

To us it might appear that the creation of the world-sphere would be a very huge undertaking. But to the supreme Lord it is mere sport, as His powers are infinite. In the world, indeed, one can think up various subtle ends to explain even sport, but one cannot do so in the case of the activity of the supreme Lord, as He is spoken of in the Veda as having all His desires fulfilled.

Nor can you say that He does not create the world, as there are texts saying that He does. Neither can you say that

He acts like a lunatic, as there are texts saying that He is omniscient.

Yet the texts teaching that there was a creation are not concerned with proclaiming the ultimate truth. For their subject-matter falls within the realm of practical experience consisting of name and form imagined through nescience, and their ultimate purpose is only to indicate how one's true Self is the Absolute. This is a point which should never be forgotten.[90]

❖

7. *Objection:* Your statement (says a philosopher of the Sāṅkhya school) that the Absolute, a conscious being, is the cause of the world in the sense of being its primary matter, will not hold. For if this were so, the modification (i.e. the world) would have been different in nature from the primary matter from which it was composed (which is impossible). For this world, which you suppose to be a modification (vikāra) of the Absolute, is seen to be non-conscious and impure and hence essentially different from the Absolute. And the Absolute is known on the authority of the Vedic revelation to be conscious and pure and hence different from the world. We know of no examples where one thing is both different in nature from another and at the same time a modification of it. Gold ornaments and other gold products are not modifications of clay, neither are clay dishes modifications of gold. On the contrary, effects invariably associated with clay proceed from clay only, effects invariably associated with gold proceed from gold only.

This world is non-conscious. It is pervaded throughout by

the three constituents (guṇa).[91] It can be an effect only of non-conscious Nature, composed of the three constituents, not of the upanishadic Absolute as the Vedantin conceives it, which is different in nature. That this world is different from the Absolute is clear, because the former is found to be non-conscious and impure. It is impure because it is composed of the three constituents, as is evident from the fact that it gives rise to joy (sattva guṇa), misery (rajas guṇa) and despondency (tamas guṇa), as also from the fact that it is differentiated into high and low, exemplified by heaven and hell. That it is non-conscious is clear from the fact that it is found to supply instruments for consciousness in the form of body and senses. If consciousness and the world were of the same nature, they could not stand to one another as employer and instrument, any more than two lights can be of service to one another mutually.

It will not do (for the Advaitin) to invoke here the example of master and servant to show that two beings alike in point of being conscious can stand as employer and instrument. For even in the case of the master and servant, it is really only the non-conscious element (in the servant) that stands as instrument to the conscious element (in the master). For it is only *what is possessed by* one conscious being, the mind and body and other instruments, that can be of service to another conscious being. One conscious being cannot, as such, be of service to another conscious being, or harm him either. For we Sāṅkhyas hold that souls, as units of pure consciousness, are transcendent and do not act. Therefore, the instruments of action are non-conscious. We have no proof that wood or clods of earth are conscious. Yet there is a distinction current in the world between the conscious and the non-conscious. Hence we must conclude that the world cannot have the Absolute for its primary matter, as it is essentially different in nature (being non-conscious).

It might be contended against my position (continues the dualist Sāṅkhya opponent) that because the Veda teaches that the Absolute forms the primary matter of the world, we must accept on the authority of this revelation that the whole world is in fact conscious. For we see that the nature of the primary matter invariably characterizes its evolved effects. That we do not apprehend this (it might be argued) must be due to some peculiar modification which consciousness undergoes. For example, the human soul is clearly conscious, but in dreamless sleep and some other states (such as swoon and trance) consciousness is not apprehended. So we should conclude that it is in some such way as this that consciousness is present in wood and clods of earth, but not perceived. And even though the souls, as conscious beings, and their instruments, such as body, mind and senses, are all fundamentally consciousness, yet a distinction between an 'employer' and his 'instruments' is intelligible on the basis of this very distinction between consciousness clearly perceived as such and consciousness not clearly perceived as such, as also between consciousness without name, form and activity and consciousness as associated with these appendages. Human flesh on the one hand, and food such as broth and rice on the other, are both fundamentally derived from the earth-element, yet they can stand respectively as beneficiary and auxiliary on account of particular distinctions in their nature, and the same principle applies in the case of the soul and its instruments. And this would explain the familiar distinction between the conscious and the non-conscious.

But all this, says the dualist opponent in conclusion, could at best explain how the Vedantic Absolute could be the cause of the world even though the latter was non-conscious. It fails entirely to explain how the Vedantic Absolute could be the cause of the world though it is pure (homogeneous) and the world impure (composite, composed of the three constituents and including varieties of quality and degree, etc.).

Answer: But in the words 'And we know this to be so from the Veda' the author of the Sūtras replies to this whole position by showing that not even the other distinction (i.e. the distinction that the world is non-conscious and its cause conscious) can be refuted. No one in the world has any real knowledge that the entire universe is conscious in nature, and the notion that it is so is a mere idle fancy. Because the Veda speaks (in some places) of the material cause of the world as conscious, Vedic authority is invoked in favour of this idle fancy (*viz.* that the whole universe is conscious in nature), whereas in fact Vedic teaching emphatically contradicts it. That is why the author of the Sūtras says that we know that the world is distinct in nature from the Absolute, its cause, 'from the Veda, too'. The Veda itself, in the text 'It becomes both the conscious and the non-conscious',[92] teaches that a certain part of the world is non-conscious and that the non-conscious part is distinct in nature from the Absolute....

Nor is anyone entitled to object that texts like 'The earth spoke, the waters spoke'[93] show that the elements and the sense-faculties are conscious by nature, for such texts refer to the deities presiding over the elements. It is conscious beings, the deities presiding over elements like earth and sense-faculties like speech, to which the texts attribute speaking and other activities characteristic of conscious beings, and not to the mere elements or sense-faculties as such.

And why is this so? Because, as the author of the Sūtras puts it, of the 'distinctions' and 'presences' found mentioned in the texts. We have already explained the distinction between the souls as conscious experiencers on the one hand and the elements and sense-faculties as non-conscious beings on the other. If everything were conscious, this distinction could not be maintained. Moreover, the Kauṣītakī Upanishad deliberately uses the word 'deity' in the course of the conversation among the (personified) sense-faculties, to indicate that the conscious beings presiding over the functioning of the organs, and not the organs themselves, were the beings taking part in the conversation....[94]

As for the 'presence' of the presiding deities everywhere in the elements and sense-faculties, it is taught in the Vedic hymns, the eulogistic passages of the Veda, and also in the Epics and Purāṇas... Hence this world must be taken as distinct from the Absolute....

It has been asserted (by the opponent) that this perceptible world cannot have the Absolute (brahman) for its material cause (its 'prakṛti') because it is different from the Absolute in nature. But the argument that the material cause is non-different from the effect is faced with exceptions. For we see in the world that hair, nails and other (non-conscious) products rise from men, who are regarded as conscious beings. And conversely, scorpions and other conscious creatures rise up from non-conscious matter such as dung.

Objection: The real material causes of the non-conscious hair and nails are the non-conscious *bodies* of men; likewise it is the non-conscious *bodies* of scorpions and the like which rise from non-conscious dung and the like.

Answer: Even so, there *is* an element of difference between the material cause and effect, namely, that part of the non-conscious (piece of dung, etc.) becomes the seat of consciousness (in becoming the body of the scorpion) while the rest does not. And this implies a change of nature, because men and such other (conscious beings) are quite different in nature from hair and nails and the like (which are non-conscious). And the same consideration applies to the case of the dung and the scorpion. And if the material cause and its modification (as effect) were *absolutely* identical, it would imply the loss of their (distinct) nature as material cause and modification respectively.

The opponent might perhaps claim that there was a common element of identity, consisting in a certain 'earthiness' of nature, between men and their hair and nails on the one hand, and again between dung and scorpions on the other. But this will not harm our case, as it is seen that the world of effects, beginning with the ether, has in common with the Absolute the quality and nature of existence (sattā). Further, we would ask the following question of the one who wishes to refute the view that the Absolute is the material cause of the world on the ground that it is different in nature from its effect. Are we to say that the Absolute is different in nature from the world (and so deny that it can be its material cause) merely because the latter *falls short of complete identity* with the Absolute? Or is it because it is *different in every way without exception?* Or is it because the world *lacks the characteristic of consciousness?*

On the first supposition, there could be no material cause or modification anywhere whatever. For there cannot be a material cause and its modification unless there is some superiority in the cause (as distinct from the effect).[95] On the second supposition, the opponent's thesis would be outright untenable. For it has already been said that the character of the Absolute as existence is actually perceived as accompanying the objects of the world beginning with the ether.[96] On the third supposition, the opponent can bring forward no example to damage our case. For he would require to produce against us, the Absolutists (Brahma Vādins), an example of something (that could be shown on our own principles) not (to be) accompanied by consciousness and so not having the Absolute for its material cause. But how can he do so, since we maintain that the entire realm of objects has the Absolute for its material cause? That the opponent's teaching contradicts the revealed teachings of the Veda is perfectly obvious (and so requires no elaboration here).[97]

❖

8. Here an objection is raised that takes the following form. If the Absolute of the Upanishads were really the material cause of an effect that was gross, composed of parts,

non-conscious, limited and impure, then, at the time of cosmic dissolution at the end of the world-period (pralaya) the effect would be withdrawn into the cause and would become identical with the latter. But it would infect the cause with its imperfections. During the period of the cosmic dissolution the Absolute, as cause, would be impure and have the other imperfections associated with the world, its effect. And this would invalidate the upanishadic doctrine that the Absolute, as cause of the world, was omniscient... If you tried to maintain that at the time of cosmic dissolution, too, this world remains distinct from the Absolute, then that would amount to saying that the cosmic dissolution was impossible. And as there can be no such thing as an effect that is not distinct from its cause, the whole Vedanta position is untenable.

To this we reply that we do not admit that there is anything untenable in our system. To begin with, the criticism that if the effect dissolves into the cause it will infect the latter with its qualities is no criticism at all. Why not? Because, says the author of the Sūtras, no example can be brought in favour of the argument. Consider the case of dishes and other products formed from clay. As separate from the original lump, they have varying values and can be classed as good, bad and indifferent. But when they are dissolved back into clay, they do not infect the latter with their erstwhile qualities. Nor do the ornaments and the like, when melted back into gold, infect the latter with their particular properties. Living bodies of the four classes (born from the womb, from the egg, from sweat or through fissure) proceed from the great earth-element (from which they draw their sustenance in the form of food), but do not infect the earth-element with their individual peculiarities when they at length dissolve back into it after death.

And the opponent's view that the effect infects the material cause with its own peculiar qualities when it dissolves back into it cannot be supported by any example. If the individual effect still retained its peculiar qualities after it had returned back into the cause, it could not be *dissolved* into the latter. Though cause and effect are non-different, it is the effect that has the nature of the cause while the cause does not have the nature of the effect,[98] as we shall explain in commenting on Sūtra II.i.14 below.

Moreover, in saying that at the time of dissolution the effect infects the material cause with its peculiar qualities, the opponent said very little. For if this contention were true at all, it would hold when the world was in manifestation, for we hold that the effect and the cause are non-different throughout. That the effect is non-different from the cause in past, present and future is proclaimed in such texts as 'All this is the Self....'[99] And again, since the effect and its properties are merely imagined through nescience they do not affect the cause in any way. And the same argument disposes of the difficulty about the world-dissolution.[100]

❖

9. *Objection:* There is a perfectly well-known distinction in ordinary life between the experiencer and the objects of his experience. The experiencer is the conscious soul dwelling in the body. The objects of his experience are sound and the other great elements (of the classical Hindu physics, *viz.* water, fire, wind and earth) that go to make up the world. As,

for example, there is Devadatta, the enjoyer (eater), and rice, the object of his enjoyment. If either the experiencer were to become an object of experience, or the objects of experience were to become the experiencer, this perfectly well-known distinction would collapse. The doctrine that these two are both non-different from the Absolute as supreme cause, however, implies that they are mutually identical. And to have a doctrine that contradicts such a well-known distinction cannot be right. Moreover, we have to assume that the distinction which we see now between the experiencer and the objects of his experience must also have held throughout the past and will hold throughout the future. Hence it follows that the Vedic doctrine that the Absolute is the cause of the world cannot be right, as it would abolish the well-known distinction between the experiencer and the object of his experience.

Answer: In face of any objection like this, says the author of the Sūtras, one must reply, 'The distinction can be maintained, as in the world'. That is to say, the distinction between object and subject can be maintained on our world-view, because we can produce a parallel from worldly experience. For it is a matter of experience that such products of water as foam, ripples, waves and bubbles, though non-different from the water of the sea, are mutually distinct and join one another and enter into other such mutual relations. And though they are non-different from the water of the sea, these products of water, foam, waves and the rest, are not mutually identical. And though they are not mutually identical, this does not affect the fact that they are non-different from the sea. In the same way, in the case under consideration, the experiencer and the objects of his experience need not be mutually identical, though they remain non-different from the Absolute. It is true that the experiencer is not exactly a product of the Absolute, as the Veda declares in the text 'Having created that (the world), He entered into it'.[101] This means that it is the Creator Himself, not subject to modification of any kind, who enters into his effect as the (ultimate) experiencer. Nevertheless, when He has entered into the effect (the world), distinctions (i.e. apparent distinctions) are set up through external adjuncts, like the apparent distinctions arising in the ether through such external adjuncts as pots. Hence we maintain that there can very well be the distinction into experiencers and objects of experience, even though neither are different from the Absolute, just as in the case of the sea and its waves, etc.

The author of the Sūtras refuted the objections of the opponent in the words 'The distinction can be maintained, as in the world' on the basis of accepting the distinction between the experiencer and the objects of his experience familiar from ordinary dealings in the world. But from the standpoint of ultimate truth this distinction does not exist, as we hold to the non-difference of cause and effect. The effect is the pluralistic universe, beginning with the element called ether. The cause is the Absolute. The effect is not in the truest sense admitted to exist except as non-different from the cause. Why not? As the author of the Sūtras puts it, 'Because of such texts as the one proclaiming that modifications are only an activity of speech....'[102]

The gist of the passage is as follows. Through one lump of clay, everything made of clay is known, whether pots, dishes or buckets, because all are identical in point of consisting of clay. This is so because a modification is a mere activity (i.e. suggestion) of speech, the giving of a name. That is to say, the modification exists and comes into being through the activity of speech. By 'modification' is meant the pot, dish or bucket. And there is no real transformation (pariṇāma) whatever. It is the mere giving of a name, nothing real. The truth is, there is only clay.

This is the traditional example given in the Veda to illustrate the causality of the Absolute. And from this Vedic text giving an example of 'a mere activity of speech' we conclude that, in the case of the point illustrated by the example, this whole effect (i.e. the world) has no existence except as the Absolute. Later in the same passage, the text first declares that fire, water and food are effects of the Absolute (conceived as material cause) and then proclaims that the effects of fire, water and food (the world in its totality) are nothing apart from fire, water and food, and says 'Fire (i.e. the empirically perceived worldly fire) is seen to lose its quality of being fire. A modification is a mere activity of speech, the giving of a name. The truth is there are only three forms (i.e. the three root-elements fire, water and food in their elemental form as divinities)....'

And the fact (also referred to in the Chāndogya Upanishad passage in question) that all can be known from the knowledge of one principle (as when we know everything made of iron when we know one pair of iron nail-scissors) is not explicable in any other way. The ether apparently enclosed in the pot and the ether apparently enclosed in the coconut water-vessel are not really distinct from the universal ether. The water of the mirage is nothing other than the barren soil of the desert, since it does not exist when not seen and has no permanent intelligible nature. And one should realize that in just the same way this pluralistic universe, consisting of experiencers and their objects of experience, is nothing other than the Absolute.[103]

4. The Absolute as Inner Ruler

The following are some of the main passages in which Śaṅkara argues that the authority of the Veda and of the Smṛti and also our own experience of ourselves and of the world about us compel us to acknowledge the existence of a moral order and so of an omniscient Lord as its Overseer and Controller.

Śaṅkara had to establish this position against the Pūrva Mīmāṃsakas. The author of the Brahma Sūtras (who could hardly himself have been Bādarāyaṇa) contrasts the view of the ancient authority, Bādarāyaṇa, which allows scope for the presence of an omniscient deity presiding over the distribution of the fruits of ritualistic action, with that of Jaimini, the reputed author of the Pūrva Mīmāṃsaka system, who did not. It is a historically interesting point that Śaṅkara seems to attribute belief in God to Jaimini, but not belief in an active God who presides over the distribution of the fruits of action. This may have been the view of Upavarṣa too,[104] though from Śabara onwards the Mīmāṃsakas tended to deny the existence of Īśvara in the interests of preserving the sovereign and automatic efficacy of ritual. We cannot, however, pursue this historical enquiry here, but must invite the reader instead to go through the Extracts collected below, where he will find an important aspect of Śaṅkara's Īśvara-conception gradually taking shape and emerging to view.

Extract No.1 is concerned with the main upanishadic text proclaiming the existence of an 'Inner Ruler' (antaryāmin). Though without a body and organs, He possesses a body and organs in a certain sense in virtue of the fact that He lies immanent within the world. As the material cause from which all the powers and energies in the world spring, He may be conceived as possessed of them. Extract No.2 affirms that He is the unknown Knower in every living being. No.3 argues that there must be an omniscient Lord to distribute the fruits of deeds. Nos.4 and 5 add further arguments to substantiate this position, mostly based on the argument from design. No.6 denies that the Lord is cruel on the ground that He acts responsibly and with due regard to the deeds of creatures.

TEXTS ON THE ABSOLUTE AS INNER RULER

1. There is an upanishadic text[105] which begins, 'He who stands within this world and the world beyond and within all creatures and controls them from within' and which proceeds 'He who inhabits the earth, who stands within the earth, whom the earth does not know, whose body is formed by the earth, who controls the earth from within, He is your Self, the Inner Ruler, the Immortal'. Here the Veda teaches that there is a certain Inner Ruler (antaryāmin) who abides within the realm of the gods, the realm of the Vedas, the realm of sacrificial ritual, the realm of macrocosm and the realm of the microcosm.[106]

The term 'Inner Ruler' is a special technical term peculiar to this passage,[107] and hence one might wonder if it was some deity that identified itself with various realms or whether it was some yogin who had acquired mastery of the various occult powers treated of in the Yoga Sūtras, or whether it was the supreme Self or whether it was yet again some other principle.

Should we, for instance, suppose that because the term is unfamiliar, that which it signifies must be something unfamiliar too? Even if we did, we could not admit that it was significant and yet had some wholly inexplicable meaning. Moreover the phrase 'Inner Ruler' is not altogether unfamiliar as meaning 'that which rules from within'. So let us assume that the Inner Ruler is some god who identifies himself with the earth and other principles. There are Vedic passages in line with such an assumption, as for instance the passage 'Whose abode is the earth, who sees through fire, whose light is the mind'.[108] A deity (devatā) of this kind, being equipped with a body and organs, could very well abide within the earth and other principles and control them. Or it might be that some yogin with occult powers had entered into everything to control it. But it could not be the supreme Self, as the latter has no organ or instruments.

To all this we reply that the Inner Ruler declared by the Veda to be within the various realms, such as that of the gods, is the supreme Self and no other. Why? Because, replies the author of the Sūtras, his attributes are mentioned. The supreme Self can very well have the attribute of 'Controller' in the sense of abiding within this whole complex of modifications (i.e. the universe), differentiated into the various realms such as that of the gods, and subjecting it to his control. For that which is the material cause of all modifications can very well be thought of as possessed of all powers. And the qualities of being the Self and being immortal, mentioned in the text, 'He is your Self, the Inner Ruler, the Immortal', refer, if taken literally, only to the supreme Self. And the phrase 'whom the earth does not know' affirms the existence of an Inner Ruler which the earth-deity cannot know, and thus points to an Inner Ruler who is other than any deity (conceived as presiding over some cosmic function and open to being worshipped on a subject-object basis). And the mention[109] of the characteristics 'unseen' and 'unheard' agrees with (our view that it is) the supreme Self (that is here in question), as the latter is without any form (or colour) or any other empirical quality.

Nor is it in any way a defect in our position that the Self should function as controller even if it is without a body and organs. For it may possess a body and organs in virtue of the body and organs of what it controls. Nor can there be any defect of infinite regress here, as if the Inner Ruler would presuppose another Inner Ruler to control Him and so on.[110] For in this case there is (from the standpoint of the highest truth) no distinction between the ruled and the ruler. There can only be infinite regress where there are distinctions. Therefore it is verily the supreme Self who is the Inner Ruler.[111]

❖

2. But why is it that the great deities like the earth are no more able than man is to know the Inner Ruler standing within them and controlling them from within? The text says that He is not seen, is not the object of the vision of anyone's eye, but Himself dwells within the eye as sight itself. Similarly, He is unheard. He cannot be heard by anyone's ear, but is Himself the unbroken power of hearing in every ear. Similarly, He cannot be conceived. He is not a possible object of the conception of anyone's mind. For no one conceives anything except what he has seen or heard. Because He cannot be perceived or heard, He is for that very reason not subject to

determinate conception (vijñāna). Yet He is the conceiver, for He is the unbroken power of conception dwelling in every mind. Nor is He the object of direct perception like a patch of colour or a (mental) experience like happiness, being beyond the range of direct perception also. Yet He is the perceiver, since He constitutes an unbroken power of perception and stands in immediate proximity to the mind.

The text says, 'He whom the earth does not know, whom no (finite) being knows'. This might suggest that the perceivers, who are subject to control, are different from their controller, the Inner Ruler Himself. To forestall this idea, the text says that there is no other seer but He, the Inner Ruler. Nor is there any other hearer. Nor is there any other conceiver. Nor is there any other perceiver. He, other than whom there is no other seer, no other hearer, no other conceiver, no other perceiver, who is Himself the unseen Seer, the unheard Hearer, the inconceivable Conceiver, the imperceptible Perceiver, who is immortal, void of all the attributes of the empirical world, the distributor to all those in transmigratory life of the fruits of their deeds, He is your Self, the Inner Ruler, the Immortal. Whatever is other than this Lord (īśvara), the Self, is wretched.[112]

❖

3. We now proceed to describe another feature of this same Absolute in its form as revealed in empirical experience, separated into the Lord and his creatures. It is well known to all that, within the realm of transmigration, living beings experience the fruits of their past deeds of three kinds, namely good, bad and mixed. We take up the question of whether this

experience proceeds from the acts themselves or from the Lord.

On this point the author of the Sūtras teaches that the fruit of the actions must come 'from Him', that is, from the Lord. Why? Because, as he puts it, 'This is the intelligible view'. For the Lord is the Overseer (adhyakṣa) of all. Seeing that He brings about the projection, maintenance and re-absorption of the whole universe, it is intelligible that He should be the one who distributes fruits to all active beings in accordance with their acts, especially as He is endued with knowledge of all divisions of space and time.[113] On the other hand it is quite unintelligible that future fruits belonging to a different period of time should proceed from action alone, as the latter undergoes destruction the moment it takes place, and being cannot arise from non-being.

Well, you will say, let us admit that an act undergoes destruction the moment after it takes place. But can it not first generate a fruit in the short moment of its existence and then undergo destruction afterwards, while the fruit remains in existence to be experienced by the agent after an interval of time? But this, we reply, will not help your argument, as nothing can 'exist' as a fruit until it is actually enjoyed by an experiencer. It is only in relation to pleasure or pain during the time they are actually being experienced by a living soul that we can speak of a 'fruit' according to recognized worldly usage. Ordinary people do not think of pleasure and pain divorced from all contact with a living soul as constituting a 'fruit'.

Perhaps you will reply that the fruit is not produced

immediately after the action but that it rises from an occult power (apūrva) generated by the action. But this will not do either. For the occult power, being a non-conscious entity like wood or iron, could not suddenly produce a result at a given moment unless prompted from without. And there is no evidence to show that in this case any such external prompting should exist. Nor can you say that we are necessarily driven to assume it. For we are not necessarily driven to assume it when the existence of the Lord can be proved.

Nor is it only the criterion of rational 'intelligibility' that obliges us to suppose that the Lord must be the cause of the distribution of the fruits of actions. We hold that the Lord is the distributor of fruits on the further ground that He is directly taught to be such in the Veda, as for example in such texts as 'That great unborn Self is the eater of food and the giver of wealth'.[114]

The Teacher Jaimini, it is true, holds that merit (dharma) bestows the fruit of actions (automatically). And his grounds, too, (like ours) are Vedic tradition and reason. He maintains that the Veda gives expression to his own thesis in such texts as 'Whoso desires heaven should sacrifice....'[115] We are to conclude from this text, he thinks, that the sacrificial act must be what produces (a sojourn in) heaven, for it is the content of a Vedic injunction, and, as such, must have the productive force that is attributed to it. For if there were no universal rule that the actions enjoined by the Veda had the productive force attributed to them, no one would perform them, and it would have been useless to have given instructions about sacrifices that no one was going to perform.

Nor would Jaimini allow that he must give up his view on account of the difficulty that action, being subject to destruction the moment after it has come into being, could not intelligibly produce a fruit. For his doctrine is based on the authority (not of observation of what happens in the world but) of Vedic revelation. (In an area such as that of the hidden results of sacrificial action in the next world, where the Veda is accepted as the sole authority,) one (cannot criticize the statements of the Veda from the rational standpoint but) can only (use reason to) form constructive hypotheses to explain how the connection between action and its fruit taught in the Veda (and accepted *a priori*) could intelligibly come about. And since action is subject to immediate destruction after its performance, it cannot yield any fruit after an interval of time except through the generation of an occult potency (apūrva). Hence he would say that we have to accept the existence of such an occult potency, whether we conceive it as some mysterious subtle after-state of the action or as some mysterious prior-state of the fruit. And action can intelligibly produce fruit after an interval of time on this hypothesis, whereas the notion that 'the Lord' distributed the fruit of action is unintelligible. For the Lord is conceived as a (metaphysically) simple being (pure homogeneous consciousness), and from a simple cause there cannot arise variegated effects.

Moreover, if it were supposed that there were a God dispensing to living beings the fruits of their deeds, He could not escape the charges of partiality and cruelty. And the doctrine would have the further defect of reducing the Veda to absurdity, as it would imply that there was no real need to engage in the acts it enjoined (since everything that was acquired would be acquired through grace).[116] Hence we should conclude that the fruits of action arise from merit or demerit intrinsic to the action, and not from the Lord.[117]

But, says the author of the Sūtras, the Teacher Bādarāyaṇa regards the Lord as being the cause of our experiencing the fruit of actions, in the way which has already been explained. The author of the Sūtras uses the word 'but' to show that he too, rejects the view that the fruit arises either from the action alone or from the occult potency alone. The finally accepted view is that the fruit comes from the Lord, whether depending on the mere action or on the occult potency as intermediaries.

Why? 'Because', says the author of the Sūtras 'there is the Vedic teaching that He is the cause'. And the Lord is indeed taught to be the cause, both in the sense of being the one that prompts beings to meritorious and non-meritorious acts, and also of being the one who distributes the fruits of acts. For we have the text, 'He it is who causes those whom He wishes to raise up from these worlds to perform good acts. He it is who causes those whom He wishes to lead downwards to perform evil acts'.[118] And the same doctrine is found in the authoritative teaching of the Gītā: 'Whatever form of Mine My devotees wish to worship with faith, I grant them unshakable faith in that form. Possessed of that faith, My devotee will engage in worship of that form, and from this he will attain the objects of his desire, for they are ordained by Me'.[119]

Moreover, it is everywhere taught in the Upanishads that the Lord is the sole cause of everything created. This also implies that the Lord gives the fruits of actions in that He projects the creatures (in any given world-period) in accordance with their past actions. And the various defects mentioned above, such as the (metaphysical) simplicity of the Lord, which would not permit his producing variegated effects, and his alleged partiality and cruelty, do not really apply in his case. For He grants fruits in accordance with the efforts made by those to whom they are granted.[120]

❖

4. This world could never have been fashioned even by the cleverest of human artificers. It includes gods, celestial musicians, supernatural attendants on the god Kubera, demons, departed spirits, goblins and other strange beings. It includes the heavens, the sky and the earth, the sun, the moon, the planets and the stars, abodes and materials for the experience of the widest imaginable range of living beings. It goes into manifestation and withdrawal regularly according to fixed laws of time, space and causation. It could only proceed under the control of one who knew the merit and demerit of all the experiencers in all their variety. For it has all the above-mentioned characteristics (of order, purpose and complexity), and yet is in itself a mere effect. Hence we conclude it must have some conscious artificer, just as we do in the case of houses, palaces, chariots, couches and the like (which are designed for ends and therefore must have been made by conscious, thinking beings). When things are not the work of an artificer, they are (self-existent, eternal, simple and homogeneous) like the Self.

Nor could it be (as the Pūrva Mīmāṃsakas maintain) that everything proceeds from merit and demerit *alone*. For that which (like action) depends on an agent other than itself can be no more than an instrumental cause. (The Pūrva Mīmāṃsakas, however, argue against this as follows. They say that) this world with its multiplicity of experiences for living beings, its multiple means for this, and its regular manifestation and withdrawal according to fixed laws of time, space and causation, is not the work of any omniscient Being. It proceeds from merit and demerit, which possess unfathomable powers. Everyone, indeed, accepts the law of cause and effect. As merit and demerit belong to the realm of cause and effect, why make unnecessary hypotheses about the existence of 'the Lord' to control the process? Hence causality should not be taken to proceed from any eternal and omniscient 'Lord'.

To this we reply that experience in all its variety is not explicable on the basis of merit and demerit alone. Why not? Because action depends on an agent. Action proceeds from the consciously directed efforts of a conscious being. When the effort ceases, so does the action. It can only produce future results for the agent at a different time and place if it is conditioned to do so by some definite external cause. One cannot say that it is the agent himself who prompts the act to produce its future effect at the time of the latter, as if he could say to it, 'O my former action! Did I not previously perform you? Now I charge you to produce your appropriate fruit'. For the individual soul as agent does not know the particular operation of the laws of time, space and causation in all their details. If the individual soul as agent did know all this he would perform all his actions in perfect freedom and would then never charge them to produce results unpleasant to himself (whereas in fact everyone in worldly life has to experience the unpleasant). Nor (in an attempt to explain the fact that people have to face unpleasant experiences) can you seriously claim that the action would cling to him and just undergo (unpleasant) change without his will, like his skin (which wrinkles with age), for even in the wrinkling of skin external causes are involved.[121] Nor can you say that the action, though performed by the agent himself, breaks loose from the agent and attracts its fruit at the appropriate time like a magnet (without the agent being involved), for it is agreed that action clings to its agent.

It cannot be said that action resides in the material elements, as these are but instruments. They are the instruments of the agent of the act. Their aid is experienced at the time of the action. But when it is over they are abandoned by the agent, as the ploughman abandons his plough after ploughing. They cannot then proceed to operate further in any way, any more than the plough could pick up the crops and deposit them in the barn. Moreover, both action and the elements are non-conscious and hence incapable of initiating any new action of their own. You cannot cite the wind as a contrary example (of a non-conscious thing that initiates action of its own), as there is nothing to prove that it really is a contrary example. We cannot suppose that the wind is non-conscious but capable of acting on its own, but have to reason, on the analogy of chariots and the like, that its motions are initiated by some conscious cause.

It might be urged against us that the Veda itself shows

that the distant (future) fruits of action rise from action alone. For it is implied (the Pūrva Mīmāṃsaka might say) in the maxim, 'Whoso desires heaven should sacrifice...'[122] that the fruit of one's actions arises from the actions themselves and not from 'the Lord' or any other external cause. And one cannot just dismiss traditional maxims as nonsense. Nor is there any other proof of the existence of 'the Lord'.

But all this is wrong, for one cannot ride rough-shod over rules that are seen to hold good. Action is of two kinds, that in which the fruit is perceived, and that in which it is not. That in which the fruit is perceived can be subdivided again into that in which the seen fruit is immediate and that in which it occurs in the future. Examples of action in which the fruit is both perceived and immediate are walking about from place to place and eating. Examples of action in which the fruit is perceived but occurs later on are agriculture and paid service. When the seen fruit is immediate, the act perishes with the arrival of the fruit. In the case where the fruit is perceived but occurs later, action is something produced at one moment and undergoing destruction later. For the fruits of agriculture depend on one's own action and those of paid service depend on those of one's employer. Independent action or fruit — action or fruit, that is to say, which depend neither on oneself nor on one for whose sake one acts — are a thing that simply does not exist. Hence it is not right to ignore a rule that is universally found to hold good in regard to the obtaining of fruits from action. Therefore one must reason that a Lord must exist who knows what fruit should accrue to what agent from what acts, and who, after the ritualistic actions are over, distributes their appropriate fruits like a master who has been served. As the Self of all, He is the Witness of all acts, all fruits and all cognitions, being of the very nature of pure Consciousness, untouched by any of the qualities of the realm of transmigration....

The actions of a servant leave an imprint (saṃskāra) on the mind of his master. And in an analogous way, ritualistic sacrifices, etc., leave an imprint on the mind (buddhi) of the omniscient Lord.[123] Then, when the ritualistic act itself has perished, He grants the fruit to the agent, like a master to a servant. It is wrong to suppose that entities can abandon their own essential nature at another place or at another time under the influence of even a hundred Vedic texts. Fire cannot become cool at some other place and time.

And so we have to accept that action, too, is found to yield fruit after a lapse of time only in the two following ways. Agriculture and the like will only yield their fruit if the agent devoted to them knows how to treat the seeds and the field for growing of crops and knows how to store and protect them when they are reaped. On the other hand, service and the like bear their fruit (in the form of wages) only if some impression is made on the mind of the master. Now, ritualistic action cannot belong to the first class, because there (in the first class) the fruit depends on the agent having knowledge (of the results and stages of maturation of his work). But because the fruits of ritualistic action accrue to the agent long after the performance of his act, it follows that they depend on an impression implanted into a mind that knows about the maturation and distribution of the fruit according to the laws of time, space and causation. In this respect it is analogous to service, where reception of the fruit depends on the mind of the master receiving an impression and knowing what reward would be appropriate to the service. Hence it follows that there must exist an omniscient Lord, the Witness of the minds and acts of all living beings and the one who distributes to them the fruits of their acts, and is their inmost Self.[124]

❖

5. The Vedic text has indicated the existence of an Imperishable Principle by the method of negating a number of its supposed particular characterisics. Yet it foresees that people may draw the wrong conclusion from this (namely, that it does not exist) and hence proceeds to lay down a positive line of inference in favour of its existence. 'At the command of this Imperishable Principle'. This Imperishable Principle, which has been seen to be the Absolute, present within all, directly and immediately evident — that is the Self, beyond hunger and all empirical characteristics.[125]

Just as government proceeds in a regular and orderly way at the command of a king, so, O Gārgī, proceed the sun and moon, which serve as lights for the people by day and night, and which were devised for this purpose by a ruler, a conscious being who knew what the needs and purposes of the people were and made them for the good of all living beings, just as lamps are ordinarily made in the world. Therefore some principle must exist by the command of which these two great luminaries, lordly and independent beings as they are, were devised and made so that they rise and set and wax and wane at fixed times. Therefore an Imperishable Principle must exist to devise and make them, as there must be a lamp-maker to devise and make lamps.

And, O Gārgī, it is at the command of the Imperishable Principle that the sky and the earth proceed in good order, though they are composed of parts and therefore liable to disintegrate, and though they are liable to fall on account of their weight, and liable to break asunder as they have been joined, and capable of spontaneous action of their own in that they are presided over by deities endowed with consciousness. It is this Imperishable Principle which rules all as law (maryādā), so that the earth and the sky do not transgress the bounds imposed. And the fact that they do not do so proves the existence of such a principle. The fact that the earth and sky obey regular laws is an infallible sign that a regulating power exists. It would be unintelligible without a conscious overlord not Himself subject to the conditioning of transmigratory life. And (quite apart from rational considerations) there is the Vedic verse, 'He who has made the heavens awesome and the earth firm...'[126]

O Gārgī, under the command of this Imperishable Principle, the moments and hours and other divisions of time are supported, which measure the span of everything that has birth, past, present or future. As in the world the accountant who carefully records all income and disbursements is the one who has been appointed to do so by some master, so, in the case of these divisions of time, we must assume some power analogous to the master, which has appointed them....

Further, we observe that knowledgeable people praise those who make gifts of gold and the like, even when such gifts cause them loss. We see before our eyes the coming together and parting of the donor, the recipient and the gift. But we do not see the (later) conjunction (whereby the donor receives the fruit of his act of giving). And yet knowledgeable people will praise the charitable, even though they do not see them receive the fruit of their act.[127] And this would not be the case if there were not a World-controller who knew how to distribute the fruits of action and who rendered back to the donor the fruits of his act. For the act of giving is over as soon as it is done, so that we have to assume the existence of some Being which connects the donor with the fruit of his act. We cannot say (with the Vaiśeṣikas and Pūrva Mīmāṃsakas) that it lies in the occult potency latent in the act, as there is no proof of the existence of such a potency. But you cannot retort that there is no proof of the existence of a World-controller either. For it has been shown that the Vedas teach its existence, and we have already explained[128] how (contrary to the Pūrva Mīmāṃsaka view) the purpose of the Veda is to give information about already existent things.

And there is another point. The assumption of an occult potency proves groundless because the phenomena it is invoked to explain can be otherwise accounted for. We see, in general, that the wages for service come from the one served. Now, service is an act, and sacrifices, charities and oblations are also acts, and it would be but proper to assume that the reward for these acts comes from the one served, be it the Lord or whoever else. As it is possible, in this way, to explain the reception of reward generally on the analogy of what is actually observed in some instances, it is not right to abandon what has been observed and resort to some different theory.

The theory of an occult potency is also unsound because it involves a whole set of unnecessary assumptions. The choice is between assuming the presence of the Lord (as

World-controller, which the Pūrva Mīmāṃsaka rejects) and the occult potency residing in the act (which he accepts). Now, as far as our actual experience goes, the nature of an act is that its rewards are paid to the agent by the one whom it serves, and do not proceed from any occult potency. Experience tells us nothing about any occult potency. The existence of an occult potency, being *ex hypothesi* outside experience (because *occult*), is something that can only be *assumed*. It also has to be assumed that it actually has the power to render back to the agent the rewards of his deed. And even when it has been assumed that it has the *power* to render back to the agent the reward of his deed, it still has to be further assumed that it *actually* does do so. But if it be taken that it is the Lord who is served, all that has to be assumed is his existence, not his power to render back the reward of the deed or the fact of his actually doing so. For the fact that one receives the rewards of one's acts from the one served by them is a matter (not of assumption but) of common experience. And the grounds for inferring the existence of the Lord have already been given (by the present upanishadic text) in the words 'The earth and the sky stand in their fixed positions (at the command of this Imperishable Principle)....'[129]

❖

6. Once again the author of the Sūtras raises another (hypothetical) objection against the doctrine that the Lord is the cause of the rise, maintenance and dissolution of the world, in order to strengthen the student's conviction about the doctrine in hand by hammering it in again and again, as a post is set firm in the ground by strokes of a mallet.

The Lord (says the supposed objector) cannot be the cause of the universe. Why not? Because it would involve Him in the charges of injustice and cruelty. To some, like the gods, He grants supernal joy. Some, like beasts of burden, He sentences to excruciating pain. Others, like human beings, enjoy a middle station. If the Lord were responsible for an unjust order like this, it would show He was afflicted with attachment and aversion like the cruder sort of men. And since both Veda and Smṛti declare Him to be pure, this would lead to the (absurd) consequence that He has lost His own nature. Not only this. He would be guilty of cruelty on a scale to inspire horror even in the greatest imaginable rogue, in that He would ordain suffering and ultimate destruction for all His creatures. Hence we should conclude that the Lord cannot be the cause of the universe, as this would involve Him in injustice and cruelty.

In answer to this objection we reply as follows. The Lord is not involved in injustice and cruelty (through being the cause of the universe). Why not? Because He proceeds 'with due regard'. It must be admitted that if the Lord had proceeded to create a universe associated with inequalities arbitrarily and according to his own caprice, then the two charges of injustice and cruelty would both hold. But the fact is that His creation is not arbitrary. It is with due regard (to merit and demerit) that the Lord creates a universe having inequalities.

You ask what it is that He pays due regard to? To merit and demerit, we reply. Creation contains inequalities because its particular nature depends on the merit and demerit of the living beings within it. Hence the charge of injustice cannot be laid at the Lord's door. The function of the Lord is to be viewed like that of rain.[130] Rain, indeed, is the common cause in the case of the production of rice, barley and other crops. But the seeds yielding each of these distinct crops all have their own special causal power which renders the crop different in each case. Similarly, the Lord is the common cause of the birth of gods, men and other living beings. But the seeds from which each of these different classes of living beings are born have their own special component of merit and demerit, which accounts for the different fate of the beings born, whether as god, man or beast. Hence, because the Lord acts dependently in this way, He cannot be accused of injustice and cruelty....

A further objection against our (Vedantin's) position is raised by the claim that in the text 'All this, my dear one, was Being alone in the beginning, one only, without a second'[131] we have a declaration that there were no distinctions before the creation of the world, and that this implies that there could have been no merit and demerit to account for distinctions. Merit and demerit, the objection runs, can only arise after creation. They depend on (action in) a body, so that the original (world-creating) distinction into bodies cannot be attributed to them (as part-cause) without circularity of reasoning. Hence we must accept that the Lord is dependent on merit and demerit *after* the original world-creating distinction only. Since merit and demerit, the causes of variety, are not present before the original world-creating distinction, it ought to follow that the original creation contained no distinctions (which is absurd).

But we reply that this objection does not hold, because, as the author of the Sūtras puts it, transmigration is a beginningless process. This objection would only hold if the process of transmigration had a beginning. But as it is beginningless, there is no contradiction if merit and demerit on the one hand and a creation having distinctions on the other be assumed to operate alternately as cause and effect, on the analogy of the seed and the sprout.

But how do we know that this transmigratory life is beginningless? To this the author of the Sūtras replies as follows. It follows logically that transmigratory life must be beginningless. For if the process of transmigration had a beginning, the possibility would arise that transmigratory life might at any time be rekindled even in released souls. Moreover, it would involve the individual in a fate that was not determined by his own prior deeds, as the initial unequal apportionment of pleasure and pain would have no intrinsic cause, while we have already explained how the Lord is not personally responsible for any inequality. Nor could it be said that nescience *alone* could stand as the cause of this inequality, as it is *per se* homogeneous. Nescience can be responsible for inequalities only as associated with merit and demerit proceeding from impressions derived from attachment and aversion and other passions.

And again, there cannot be a body without previous merit and demerit, and there cannot be merit and demerit without previous possession of a body, so that the opponent's doctrine that transmigratory life is not beginningless would involve circular reasoning. Whereas if it is taken that transmigratory life is beginningless, all becomes explicable on the analogy of the seed and the sprout.[132]

5. The Absolute as the Lord of Māyā

The usages to which Śaṅkara puts the term 'māyā' may be analysed briefly as follows.[133] It is found in certain non-philosophical contexts in the non-technical sense of duplicity or dishonest dealings in the world, but these passages have no relevance to our present enquiry. Its most common meaning is 'magic'. It is clear from the literature of Śaṅkara's day that there was a widespread belief that certain strolling magicians had the power to induce visions and hallucinations by hypnotism, not of mere individuals alone but also of whole congregations of spectators. In fact there is evidence that such mass-hypnotists still existed in India in recent times.[134] Two well-known literary works, probably composed about Śaṅkara's day, the romance of Daṇḍin called 'The Ten Princes' and Śrī Harṣa's play 'The Pearl Necklace', provide colourful pictures of a mass-hypnotist, armed with a peacock's feather wand, conjuring forth magic visions at the court or palace of a king. Ānandabodhendra's Commentary on Yoga Vāsiṣṭha III.65.6 makes it especially clear that mass-hypnosis was involved, in that it speaks of the juggler's power to attune the minds of many observers gathered in an assembly to one and the same false vision.[135]

Magic or hypnotism *per se* have nothing to do with philosophy. But Śaṅkara puts the word 'māyā' in the sense of hypnotist's magic to philosophical use through comparison. Invoking the Indian rope trick he can say, 'Just as the real magician is different from his unreal image climbing the rope, so is the supreme Lord different from the individual soul'.[136] Often the intention of such illustrations is not merely to bring out the illusory nature of the object that has been compared to the magic display, but also to emphasize that the Creator of it is not touched by his creation and that the latter is effortless.

That the term 'māyā' was used before Śaṅkara in orthodox Vedanta to mean a mere illusion is proved by the presence of the phrase 'māyā-mātra' applied to dream experience at Brahma Sūtra III.ii.3. And we have already seen[137] that there is evidence of other Vedanta and Vaiṣṇava writers before Śaṅkara dismissing the world as an illusion in some of their texts. It would probably not be wrong to see the influence of Mahāyāna Buddhism here, direct or indirect. In the case of Gauḍapāda, it is explicit and avowed. Śaṅkara's philosophy, however, is a philosophy of Being, in which the Absolute is permanent, stable, eternal and static. This gives his world-view a radically different complexion from that of the universal dynamism propounded by the Mahāyāna, a philosophy which resolves the world into a product of karma. Nevertheless, even Śaṅkara does not hesitate to speak of the experiences of transmigration openly in terms of images derived from the staccato Buddhist world-view, calling it momentary (kṣaṇika), like the ever-changing stream of a river or the sputtering jets of flame that underlie the apparent unity and continuity of the flame of a lamp.[138] We have seen that he uses, though very rarely, the simile of the apparent lines described in the sky by the whirling torch (alāta-cakra), a simile that is appropriate to the empty, atomic, nominalistic world of the Buddhists, where the function of imaginative construction (kalpanā) is to fill in gaps, but less so to the world of Advaita, where reality is a plenum, and the function of nescience is to produce the appearance of fissures and rifts. This was the element in Śaṅkara's texts that was later to inspire the phenomenalism (dṛṣṭi-sṛṣṭi-vāda) associated with Prakāśānanda of the sixteenth century and others, including the nineteenth century Vedantin of Delhi, Niścala Dāsa, who wrote in the vernacular.

But Śaṅkara also uses the term 'māyā' in a religious rather than a philosophical sense, under inspiration from older Brahminical and Vedic sources. We need not concern ourselves here with the various conceptions of the 'māyā' of the gods and demons to be found in the ancient hymns of the Ṛg Veda. The Brahminical conception of 'māyā' had many transformations to undergo before it fell into the hands of Śaṅkara. By the time of the Śvetāśvatara Upanishad and the Mahābhārata, the power of self-projection (māyā) of the gods of the polytheistic period had become transformed monotheistically into the power through which the one Absolute manifested itself under a plurality of finite forms in accordance with the 'seeds' left by the acts and thoughts of living beings, and this power was identified with the Sāṅkhya concept of Nature (prakṛti) composed of the three 'constituents' or guṇas. In this guise Śaṅkara regarded it as the Nature (prakṛti) or Māyā of Viṣṇu, the latter being spoken of also as Nārāyaṇa or Vāsudeva and identified with the Absolute or Brahman of the Upanishads. The identification of Vāsudeva with the highest Self (paramātman) was also a practice of the Pāñcarātra sect of the worshippers of Viṣṇu.[139]

The theistic mediaeval commentators on the Brahma Sūtras, whose doctrines resemble those of Śaṅkara's predecessors of the Bhedābheda school in varying degrees, frequently accuse him of suppressing the rich religious heritage left by the Bhedābheda Vāda tradition. This involved a realistic interpretation of the Sūtras, in which a real God helps a real soul by real compassion and real acts of grace to a real change through which it becomes really aware of its fundamental identity with, and superficial difference from, the Lord, retaining enough difference and individuality to be blissfully aware that it is part of an immeasurably great and majestic whole. But the sympathetic student of Śaṅkara will hardly accept this criticism as just. No state achieved as a result of a 'real change' can be permanent. Śaṅkara preserved the religious heritage deriving from the Upanishads, Gītā, Epics, Purāṇas and Brahma Sūtras, in a way that his Vedantic predecessors of the Bhedābheda school failed to do, by placing it in a defensible metaphysical setting that paid due attention to the element of transcendence. As will be shown in Volume IV, Chapter X, section 3, below, he found the interpretations of his Bhedābheda predecessors lacking in logical consistency and inadequate to the deepest intuitions of the upanishadic sages, intuitions which also find an echo in certain texts of the Gītā, Mahābhārata and Purāṇas. Śaṅkara saw that the specifically religious consciousness, in which the soul feels itself humbled and dwarfed before a power mightier than itself, is but a *phase* of the spiritual life, which is never complete without the attainment of absolute freedom. But the realm of the religious consciousness, though usually the forecourt through which one has to pass on the way to the realm of absolute freedom, is not itself the realm of absolute freedom. The deeper metaphysical teaching of the Upanishads is, 'Where there is duality there is fear'.[140]

Śaṅkara was able to preserve this tradition because he took the Māyā of the Lord, the great cosmic power of the Lord spoken of in the Epics, Purāṇas and earlier tradition, as that through which, though remaining one, He manifested as the universe in all its variety. Māyā so conceived was a power comparable to that of the mass-hypnotist, a power exercised without effort and involving no activity or change on his part, of hiding his true nature as infinite Consciousness and appearing under manifest finite forms that were illusory and did not, from the standpoint of the highest truth, exist.

As will become clearer in the second section of the next chapter, in which we shall be studying the 'indeterminability' of name and form, Śaṅkara identified the traditional religious conception of the Lord's 'power of Māyā' with the 'name and form' spoken of in the Upanishads. In this sense it was for him neither identical with, nor different from the Absolute. It was non-different from the Absolute and so not a second thing over against it, in that it was entirely dependent on the existence of the Absolute for its existence and never available without the latter. This also followed from the fact of its being a mere illusory appearance. But an illusory appearance is not only an 'appearance of' but an 'appearance to'. As 'appearance of', an illusory appearance cannot be anything real and different from that of which it is an appearance. But as 'appearance to', it cannot be identical with that which witnesses it as an object. The Witness of the world-appearance, by the very fact of being Witness of it, is different from it and not affected by its distinctions. The Witness of the world-appearance is not any of the psycho-physical organisms that form part of the appearance, for within every psyche there exists a changeless principle of Consciousness witnessing the rise and fall of its vicissitudes, and therefore different from it. It is impossible to point to any differentiation in the latter or to anything which could cause any differentiation in it. Hence it has to be accepted as the one Witness and knower of all experiences, the same in all bodies.[141] Śaṅkara calls it the Self (ātman) and also the Lord (īśvara). The world appears before it and is therefore not identical with it.

But there is also the other aspect of the world-appearance, its aspect as 'appearance of'. Ignoring the ambiguity in the word 'appearance' and adhering to the meaning 'false appearance', we may say that it is never available without the reality of which it is a false appearance. Hence, while a false appearance is not determinable as identical with that of which it is an appearance, it is not determinable as different from it either. Where, as in the case of the world-appearance (prapañca), the reality is Consciousness, this has important implications. Because the Absolute is pure Consciousness (cit), it is not merely the passive ground of the illusion, as the rope is the mere passive ground of the appearance of the snake. The objective, non-conscious element in the world-illusion, some phases of which are mental and are illumined by a reflection of Consciousness, has no existence independent of pure Consciousness, any more than the illusory snake has existence independent of the rope when a rope is mistaken for a snake in the dark. Thus the world is through and through penetrated by Consciousness, as the snake is by the rope. Consciousness not only witnesses the world-appearance but is reflected in it and witnesses the reflection. As reflected in certain phases of the world-appearance, the more subtle phases that constitute mind, Consciousness appears to become diffracted into separate units in line with distinctions in the external reflecting medium (upādhi). Such distinctions affect only Consciousness *qua* reflected in the medium, and not pure Consciousness, which is ever and everywhere one and the same, a mere Witness.

Units of reflected Consciousness constitute 'souls' (jīva). Belonging to the phenomenal world, souls have the powers of knowledge and activity within that realm in varying degrees, ranging from the powers of plants upwards through the animal and human kingdoms, and reaching even higher to celestial beings and deities, culminating in the world-soul, otherwise known as Prajāpati, Hiraṇyagarbha or Brahmā, at the top. They depend for these powers, which fall wholly within the world-illusion, on the Light of the Witness, which is itself not literally a power, though it is sometimes referred to as such when considered in relation to its illusory external adjuncts. In truth, however, it is not in any way characterized by motion or change, and is for that very reason eternal and real.

In all souls the reflected Consciousness assumes the powers of knowledge (jñāna-śakti) and activity (kriyā-śakti), and in the case of the world-soul there is the power to project the whole universe in the form of thoughts which exist at first in an inscrutable condition as 'seeds' which result from the actions and thoughts of the creatures in previous world-periods, and which later expand out into the whole manifest universe. Whatever power the world-soul has to effect this manifestation proceeds from, and depends on, the Lord as pure Consciousness. So this power can occasionally be spoken of as the Cosmic Power (māyā-śakti) of the Lord (Bhagavān), and this

Cosmic Power is the 'seed of the production of the world (utpatti-bīja)' and the 'repository of the impressions left by the actions of the various living creatures in their previous lives'.[142]

Speaking in the anthropomorphic language intelligible to those still under the sway of nescience, the Vedic and Smṛti texts sometimes attribute this power to the Lord and call it His 'Māyā' or 'Prakṛti'. They speak of its development and of its power to 'bind' or keep the individual enmeshed in future experiences and future lives according to the doctrine of the three 'constituents' (guṇa) evolved by the Sāṅkhya philosophers. Śaṅkara expressly says that the Sāṅkhya philosophers are authoritative in their pronouncements about the play of the 'constituents', even though they were wrong in their estimate of the metaphysical truth purveyed by the upanishadic texts.[143] From the standpoint of the highest truth, no doubt, it is incorrect to attribute any power whatever to the Self or the Lord (interchangeable terms in Śaṅkara), as He is not subject to any form of modification.[144] The ancient texts, however, do not, according to Śaṅkara, always speak the literal truth. They say what is good for the student and will help him to understand the unity at the back of all variety even when what they say is not literally true, just as we say 'This will make your hair grow' to recalcitrant children when we want to induce them to drink milk.[145]

The view that the Lord, though pure Consciousness in his true nature, is somehow at the same time an active being manipulating his power of Māyā, is appropriate and useful for the development of the religious consciousness, which is a necessary preliminary before the final stages of the spiritual path for most people. But if it is taken as the final truth, it will imply that the Lord is an agent and is subject to change and is consequently Himself phenomenal. The stricter usage, therefore,[146] is to reserve the terms Hiraṇyagarbha, Brahmā or Prajāpati for the world-soul and to use the term 'Īśvara' (the Lord) to denote pure Consciousness as Witness and that by whose Light the world-soul and all living beings carry out their powers of activity and knowledge within the phenomenal world. Within the world-appearance there are deities or powers which carry out their cosmic functions owing to the presence within them of the Light of the Lord, who is Himself a motionless, actionless Witness.[147] So Śaṅkara says, 'Thus the lordship, omniscience and omnipotence of the Lord exist relative to the limitations and distinctions of nescience only, and in reality there can be no practice of rulership or omniscience on the part of the Self, in which all distinctions remain eternally negated in knowledge'.[148] Nevertheless, precisely because He is thus pure Consciousness (cit), He is the only effective root of all activity and knowledge, for He is that which alone exists. Thus, although He is in the true sense bereft of all form, body, organs or action, He is in fact the effective controller of the world-display. For 'The cosmic powers take up and lay down their activities in a controlled way through the mere proximity of the Lord as actionless Witness'.[149] Thus the Lord, though without bodies and organs of His own, carries out activities through the bodies and organs of the deities or cosmic powers.[150] The conception of unmoving mover is illustrated[151] by the analogies of a magnet and a king, both of which cause *directed* activity in others by their mere presence.

The forms assumed by the Lord when He undergoes manifestation as the phenomenal universe are a means to the liberation as well as to the bondage of the individual soul. As the false image of the snake, though illusory, leads on to the discovery of the rope, so the world-manifestation, with the Lord at the heart of it, should be taken basically as a means to the liberation of the soul from nescience and as a kind of grace. In the system of Śaṅkara's Vedantic predecessors, the Bhedābheda Vādins, the Absolute in his form as the cause of the world stood in reciprocal relation with his manifestation as 'effect' in the form of a real world, and was consequently conditioned by it. One cannot speak of the freedom of the

Lord or his power to dispense grace if He is conceived in this fashion. But for Śaṅkara the Lord is the Absolute in its form as pure Consciousness, ever free, ever transcendent, and it is his motionless Light that *appears* as grace when viewed as associated with a certain phase of the external adjuncts set up by nescience. Thus Śaṅkara says, 'In the state of nescience, where the individual soul is blinded and does not distinguish himself from his instruments of action and knowledge (the senses and mental and physical powers), his repeated rebirths, in which he has the powers of agency and enjoyment, can proceed only by the permission (anujñā) of the highest Self, who, in the name of the Lord, dwells in all beings as their Witness, the controller of their actions and the source of their intelligence. And the liberation of the soul can only come through knowledge proceeding from his grace (anugraha)'.[152]

In any instance of false appearance, the reality is not only hidden: it is also partially revealed, and such revelations display variations of degree. The rope-snake hides all but the bare outline of the rope, while the reflection of a face in a mirror, likewise illusory and displaying features such as the specks on the mirror that do not belong to the face, reveals the nature of the reality of which it is an appearance to a greater degree. The circumstance which prevents man from realizing his own true nature as pure Consciousness is attachment to the forms set up by nescience, and the deeply rooted habit of taking them for real. The purpose of all religious practices, when viewed in the context of the path to liberation, is to weaken the hold of the illusory forms by developing a counter-awareness of deeper levels of reality hidden beneath the more superficial forms. These 'deeper levels' of reality are themselves ultimately illusory from the very fact of being accessible to the understanding and will of man. They are, according to the rather drastic formula of Śaṅkara's Commentary on Gauḍapāda's Kārikā II.4, 'false because seen'. Nevertheless, the contemplation of the Lord as manifest under illusory forms relieves the mind of its burden of attachment to the grosser and more oppressive phases of the world-appearance, in particular to the objects of crude sense-enjoyment. Thus it prepares the soul for the final rejection of all forms as illusory, consummated only through the specific Advaita discipline.

Śaṅkara says that wherever in the world there is a special emergence of glory and power, there the Lord has manifested through the world-appearance in a form suitable for worship (upāsanā). Included here are the deities and some of the entities connected with the old Vedic ritual, according to the special meditations on these subjects enjoined in the Veda.[153] In this connection, the sacred syllable OM is of special importance.[154] Other manifestations of the Lord suitable for contemplation and worship are mentioned in the Gītā, Mahābhārata, Rāmāyaṇa and Purāṇas, the most important being the 'descents' (avatāra) or Incarnations of the Lord Viṣṇu in the form of Rāma or Kṛṣṇa. But in a wider sense every phase of the world-appearance displaying special eminence or power (vibhūti) can be used as a focus for the contemplation of the Absolute.[155]

The Extracts on Māyā to follow, more numerous but mostly shorter than the Extracts of previous sections, may be brought together in three groups. Extracts 1-7 show Śaṅkara identifying Māyā with the Nature (Prakṛti) of the Gītā, which is the same conception of Māyā that is found in the Śvetāśvatara Upanishad and in many texts of the Mahābhārata and Purāṇas. Here the power of the Lord to undergo manifestation in manifold form is 'objectivized' as the world of Nature (Prakṛti) composed of, or, according to some texts,[156] 'giving birth to' the three 'constituents' (guṇa). It is the 'constituents' which make up the bodies and organs of all beings, which bind the soul to further experiences if it becomes identified with them and acts from egoistic motives. It is the guṇas alone which act and think, while the soul in its true nature as the Lord, abides as the unchanging Witness. In Extracts 4 and 5 the word 'kūṭa' means 'Māyā', but the compound 'kūṭastha' in which it occurs has been interpreted differently in the two Extracts, according to the context of the two Gītā passages under discussion. (See Note 168)

Extracts 8-18 show how the One manifests Himself in plurality without forfeiting His unity or undergoing any change or performing any activity, even like a 'māyāvin' or mass-hynotist producing unreal visions in the world. Extract 13, from the Aitareya Commentary, recalls Gauḍapāda in its emphasis on the provisional character of all speculative world-views and its relegation of causality to the sphere of appearance.

Extracts 19-21 emphasize the benevolent aspect of the Lord of Māyā. He does not *merely* accord beings the deserts of their deeds. He *also* freely assumes special forms within the world of his Māyā for the preservation of the path that leads to worldly welfare and final liberation and for the good of those of his devotees (the great majority) who cannot worship Him in abstract 'qualitiless' form.

TEXTS ON THE ABSOLUTE AS THE LORD OF MĀYĀ

1. Nature (Prakṛti) and Spirit (Puruṣa) are the two 'natures' (prakṛti) of the Lord. Know (says the Lord speaking in the Gītā) that both are beginningless. Since the 'Lordship' of the Lord is eternal, it follows that His two 'natures' must be too. For the Lord can only be a 'Lord' through the instrumentality of his two 'natures', whereby He projects, sustains and withdraws the world. These two principles, being beginningless, are the cause of transmigratory experience.

Some have taken the word 'anādi' (beginningless) in an opposite sense as 'an-ādi' and as a tat-puruṣa compound, explaining the sentence to mean 'Nature and Spirit did not constitute beginnings'. Their idea was that the doctrine that the Lord Himself alone was the sole cause of the world could only be safeguarded in this way. If, on the other hand, Nature and Spirit had both been beginningless, (they thought), then the world would have been created by them alone, and the Lord would not have been the Creator of the world.

But this view is wrong. For if it were accepted, it would imply that the Lord was not a Lord, as before the production of Nature and Spirit there would have been nothing for Him to be the Lord over. Further, transmigratory life would have no efficient cause (nimitta), so that there could be no definitive release from it.[157] This would also abolish the distinction between bondage and release, and so render the Upanishads useless.

If, on the other hand, the Lord and his two natures are all (three) taken as eternal, then all becomes explicable, as the Lord proceeds now (in the text of the Gītā under comment) to point out. For He says that one must realize that all effects from the intellect down to the senses and body, as well as the 'constituents' (guṇa) as transformed, in a way to be explained later,[158] into the form of mental ideas coloured by pleasure, pain and delusion, are all transformations of Nature (prakṛti).[159]

❖

2. Having first engaged the hearer's attention by depicting the rare benefits of the teaching to follow, the Lord proceeds further. By 'earth' He means the subtle element (tanmātra)[160] of the earth, not the gross earth that we perceive. Only thus

can we explain the term 'eightfold' where the verse speaks later of 'Nature divided eightfold'.

By 'mind' (manas) the Lord means the cause of mind, namely the cosmic principle called the Ego Sense (ahaṅkāra). By 'intellect' (buddhi) He means the cosmic principle called Mahat.[161] By the term (cosmic) Ego Sense, the Lord here means the principle of Nature itself in its (pristine) state called the Unmanifest (avyakta), which is permeated by nescience. Just as food permeated by poison is called 'poison', so is the root-cause of all, the principle called the Unmanifest, associated with the latent impressions of ego-sense, here called the (cosmic) Ego Sense, because ego-sense is what sets everything in motion.[162] Even within the world, it is seen that the ego-sense is the cause of all courses of activity.

This Nature (prakṛti), thus described, is My Divine Power of Māyā, divided eightfold.[163]

❖

3. My 'Māyā', My 'Nature' composed of the three 'constituents', is the womb, the (material) cause, of all beings. It is called the Great Principle (mahat) because, as cause, it is greater than all its effects. It is called 'Brahman'[164] because it is what nourishes its own modifications. Into this womb, the Mahat, the Brahman, I place the seed leading to the birth of Hiraṇyagarbha.[165] It is the seed (bīja) in the sense of being the cause of the birth of all creatures.

I who place the seed am the Lord, having the power (śakti) consisting in the two natures (prakṛti), known respectively as the Field (of objective experience) (kṣetra) and the Knower of the Field (the ray of Divine Light illumining the experiences of the individual experiencer) (kṣetra-jña). What this 'placing of the seed' means is that I connect the subject (kṣetra-jña) of experience, as associated with the external adjuncts of nescience, desire and action, with the field of his objective experience (the body and the world of objects in which it is situated) (kṣetra). From that impregnation, O descendant of Bharata, arises the birth of all creatures, mediately through the birth of Hiraṇyagarbha.[166]

❖

4. The people of the world, says the text, speak of the two Spirits (puruṣa), which form two separate categories. The one is perishable.[167] The other is imperishable, the Lord's 'Power of Māyā (māyā-śakti)'. It is the seed from which the 'perishable Spirit' proceeds and the repository of the latent impressions (saṃskāra) left by the desires and actions of the innumerable creatures undergoing transmigratory life.

What, then, are these two 'Spirits'? The Lord Himself replies that the perishable Spirit consists in 'all beings', that is to say, the whole mass of modifications (assumed phenomenally by the Absolute).

The imperishable Spirit is called 'Kūṭastha',[168] and is so known because it stands as a mass (kūṭa). Or else the word 'kūṭa' here stands in its meaning of deceit and crookedness, synonymous with 'māyā'.[169] The Kūṭastha (taken in this sense) is that which stands as a mass of tricks (māyā) and deceptions of various sorts. The same principle is called 'the Imperishable' (akṣara) because it is never exhausted, on account of the seed of transmigratory life being infinite. But there is another principle, the Supreme Spirit (puruṣottama), different in kind from these two, namely the perishable and the imperishable, unaffected by either of these adjuncts, ever pure, enlightened and liberated by nature.[170]

❖

5. Next the Lord further specifies the nature of this Imperishable Principle (akṣara) that has to be contemplated. It is all-pervasive like the ether. It is unthinkable. That which is inaccessible to the perceptions of the senses[171] may yet be accessible to the thought of the mind, but this Imperishable Principle is other than that and unthinkable. He (the Lord) is also 'kūṭastha'. The word 'kūṭa' is used to stand for any object that is fair to outward view but contains hidden defects within. The word is familiar in worldly dealings in the meaning of false, as in 'false coin' (kūṭa-rūpaka) and 'false witness' (kūṭa-sākṣyam). So in the present case the reference is to a well-known deception referred to by the word 'kūṭa', which contains many seeds of further transmigratory experience like nescience, which has interior defects, which is designated by a variety of different names such as 'Māyā' and 'the Unmanifest Principle' and is referred to in the texts 'One should know that Nature (prakṛti) is a magic display (māyā) and that the Great God (Rudra) is a magician'.[172] 'Kūṭastha' refers to the one who is established as present within this deception (kūṭa), that is to say, who presides over it.[173]

❖

6. What are the 'constituents'? And how do they bind? The 'constituents' are the principles called sattva, rajas and tamas. The term 'constituent' (guṇa) is here used in a special sense. The word 'guṇa' does not have its usual meaning here of a quality, like a colour inhering in a substance. Nor is there any corresponding implication that the 'constituents' inhere in any substance different from themselves. The 'constituents' are *like* qualities in point of being dependent for their existence on something else, in this case (not, as with the Vaiśeṣikas, on an objective substance in which they inhere but) on the experiencing subject, because they are of the nature of nescience. By '*bind* the embodied one', the text means 'appear to bind'. For the term 'bind' here really only means that they come into existence supported by Him (that is, by the Lord as witnessing Consciousness within the body)....

Of these three 'constituents' (sattva, rajas and tamas), the Lord now proceeds to define sattva. Clear as crystal, luminous, resistant to evil, sattva is yet (apparently) a binding force. It binds by attachment to happiness. Attachment to happiness means the false connection of the subject, with the object, happiness, in the feeling 'I am happy'. And this is the very core of nescience, for no quality of the object can really pertain to the subject....[174]

Hence it is nescience itself which appears to cause the subject to feel attachment to a happiness which is not really part of its own true nature, and this through its (nescience's) intrinsic character of non-discrimination between subject and object. That is, it makes that (the Self) which is essentially unattached to appear to be attached, and that (the non-self, including the body and mind and their states) which intrinsically has nothing to do with happiness, to appear to be happy.

And it also (apparently) binds the embodied one through attachment to knowledge. Knowledge must be understood here in some sense which places it in the same category with happiness and makes it an attribute of the 'Field',[175] that is to say of the mind, not of the Self. For if it had been meant in the sense of a characteristic of the Self, it would have been inappropriate for the text to have spoken of attachment or of this attachment as leading to bondage. Attachment to knowledge arises in the same way as attachment to happiness.[176]

Know, the Lord proceeds, that rajas has the property of colouring. Colouring proceeds from tingeing, as in the case of colouring-matter like red chalk.[177] It is of the nature of thirst (tṛṣṇā) or desire for what one does not yet have. Attachment is the pleasure the mind takes in what it already has, and rajas gives rise to both thirst and attachment. Thus rajas (apparently) binds the embodied one through attachment to action for immediate and remote ends.

The third 'constituent' is tamas (literally, darkness). Know that it is born of ignorance, and that it is what causes delusion or absence of discrimination in all living beings. It causes bondage through negligence, laziness and sleep.

Then the Lord recapitulates the function of the 'constituents' briefly. Sattva causes attachment to happiness, rajas causes attachment to action, while tamas obscures the discrimination produced by sattva. It does so through its own intrinsic veiling nature and causes attachment to a negligent way of life. Negligence is the non-performance of any duties with which one may be faced.

But one might want to know on what typical occasions the various 'constituents' assert themselves. When sattva emerges and suppresses both rajas and tamas, it gives rise to its natural effects, happiness and joy. When rajas waxes strong and overrides sattva and tamas, it starts its peculiar function of engendering thirst and action and the like. And when tamas waxes strong suppressing both sattva and rajas, it starts its special functions like veiling of wisdom.

What are the marks of the emergence of each of the various 'constituents'? When light in the form of a cognition of the mind enters any of the 'gates of the body' or sense-organs, that is knowledge and it implies a preponderance of sattva. Different are the signs revealing the emergence of rajas. Greed or the desire to secure the property of others, activity in general, being busy, distraction in active manifestations of joy, and attachment and thirst for sense-objects in general are the signs that appear when rajas is in the ascendant. When tamas is predominant, there ensues a total loss of all power to discriminate, and the result of this is failure to act. In characterizing this state as one of negligence and delusion (moha), the text equates loss of power to discriminate (aviveka) with delusion (moha).[178]

❖

7. Nature (prakṛti) consists of the 'constituents' sattva, rajas and tamas in their state of equilibrium.[179] All our acts, secular and spiritual, are performed by the 'constituents' of Nature, these being its modifications which assume the form of our

bodies and organs. He whose mind is variously deluded by ego-feeling (ahaṅkāra), by the notion that he is identical with the body and the organs, thinks he is the agent in their various actions. He assumes the attributes of the body and senses, and identifies himself with them and ascribes their actions to himself through nescience.

Different, however, is the case with the enlightened man. He knows how the 'constituents' and action are distinct (from the Self). The 'constituents' as organs of the body function amidst the 'constituents' in the form of sense-objects. Clearly aware that it is not the Self that so functions, he is not attached.[180]

❖

8. Nor should one raise the objection that there could not be any multiform creation in the one Absolute without the latter forfeiting its essential nature as One. For the texts themselves refer to the way in which multiform creations occur in the one soul of a person dreaming without his forfeiting his essential unity, as in the passage, 'There are no chariots nor teams of horses nor roads (where the dreamer lies down to dream), so he creates chariots and teams of horses and roads (in his dream)'.[181]

In ordinary worldly experience (in the waking state) too, it is accepted that we meet with multiform creations, including elephants and horses and other such illusory beings created by gods[182] and strolling magicians (māyāvin), without their creators forfeiting their own essential unity. So there is nothing wrong in supposing that multiform creations can arise in the Absolute without the latter's forfeiting its essential nature, even though it is essentially One.[183]

9. If the Self is one and one alone, how does it come to be associated with this infinite variety of forms, beginning with the Cosmic Vital Energy (prāṇa), that make up the content of transmigratory experience? Listen. This is all a magic display (māyā) of that divine Being, the Self. The magic spread forth by a magician can cover the spotless sky with blossoming trees. And it is a magic of the same kind whereby this Self is 'deluded', which means apparently deluded. There is the saying 'My Māyā is hard to cross'.[184]

❖

10. And in this connection there is another illustration. The magician himself is in no way affected in past, present or future by the magic display he has spread forth by his hypnotic power (māyā), as it is nothing real. And in just the same way, the supreme Self is unaffected by the magic display of the world of transmigratory experience (saṃsāra-māyā). Similarly, the one who sees a dream remains one only, quite untouched in his real nature by the hypnotic effect of the dream (svapna-māyā), as it does not persist with him when he is awake or when he has attained identity with all in dreamless sleep.[185] Likewise, the Witness of the three states of waking, dream and dreamless sleep is one. It never fails, and is untouched by the three states when they come and go. This appearance of the supreme Self as being characterized by the three states of waking, dream and dreamless sleep is a mere illusion (māyā-mātra), like the appearance of a rope in a snake.

In this connection, one who knows the traditional interpretation of the Upanishads (Gauḍapāda Ācārya) has said,

'When the individual soul, asleep under a beginningless hypnotic illusion, finally awakens, he awakens to a knowledge of the unborn, sleepless, dreamless, non-dual reality'.[186]

❖

11. Also in regard to the souls and other phenomena supposed to be born, the same illusory character is taught when the text says, 'Phenomena are born through illusion only, and are not born in the true sense'. Their birth 'through illusion' is like birth through magic (māyā), and such a birth should be adjudged a pure illusion.

But would it not follow that this illusion was itself a reality? Not so. 'For this illusion is itself non-existent'. The meaning is that the word 'māyā' is a term for something that does not exist.[187]

❖

12. Some theorists suppose that creation is an expansion undergone by the Lord Himself. It is believers in the doctrine that creation is real who think this, the verse under comment implies. For those who are preoccupied with the final truth do not think much about creation.

On this topic we have the Vedic text, 'Indra assumed many forms through his magic powers'. When the magician throws up a rope into the sky, takes a sword and climbs up the rope till he disappears from view, engages in a fight, falls down cloven apart bit by bit and finally gets up again whole, the spectators do not greatly puzzle their heads about this magic show and what lay behind it. This prolongation of successive experiences of the states of dreamless sleep, dream and waking and so on (including other states like swoon, concussion, trance, etc.) is comparable to the magician's prolongation of the rope.

Prājña, Taijasa and Viśva, etc.,[188] associated with these three states, correspond to the magician's double who climbs (that is, appears to be climbing) the rope. But there is also the final reality called 'the fourth' (turīya),[189] which corresponds to the real magician in the illustration. He is other than either the rope or his double appearing to climb it, and stands invisible on the ground, hidden by his own magic display.

The noble ones (ārya), the seekers of liberation, are preoccupied only with the ultimate reality, not with useless speculations about creation. Hence the various alternative theories about creation come only from believers in the doctrine that creation is real. This is what the author of the verse under comment (Gauḍapāda) means to imply when he says that creation is like the illusion of a dream.[190]

❖

13. Or else we may even better liken the process (of world-creation) to that of the magician's art. The magician (māyāvin), as a conscious personage, makes himself into another being appearing to move about in the sky, without resorting to any external materials. In the same way, the omniscient, omnipotent Lord, possessed of a cosmic magic power (mahā-māyā), makes Himself into another being in the form of the world. This avoids all speculative views (which try to explain world-causation on the analogy of causal relationships that hold good within the world), such as those which fasten onto the reality of the cause or onto that of the

effect or onto that of both or onto the unreality of both. And these views may be considered to have been very well refuted.[191]

❖

14. The Lord begins the following verse with a view to setting aside any idea that He has previously contradicted Himself by saying in one breath that He had projected all the creatures of the universe and in the next that He sat unmoving like one unconcerned.[192] It is primordial Nature (prakṛti), My Māyā, composed of the three 'constituents', of the nature of nescience, that brings forth the universe with all that moves and all that is fixed. I am in all cases no more than the Overseer. I am of the nature of Consciousness and not subject to modification.[193]

❖

15. One should know that what is perceived is (called) waking and that what is remembered in dream is that same (material). Its absence is (called) dreamless sleep. But the highest state (beyond these three) is one's own Self. When sleep, understood as darkness (tamas) and ignorance (ajñāna), the seed of waking and dream,[194] is burnt by awakening to the nature of the Self, then it becomes void of progeny,[195] like a seed that has been burnt.

That seed of illusion, though one, must be known to assume three forms successively.[196] The master of the illusion, the Self, though undergoing no change (vikāra), and though one, appears as many, like the (one) sun reflected (as many) in (different surfaces of) water. Just as the one seed, (which is beyond the three states of waking, dream and dreamless sleep) is differentiated into the Cosmic Vital Principle (prāṇa) and into dream, waking and other (swoon, etc.) states, in the same way, the Self is differentiated into dream-bodies and waking-bodies, like the moon (apparently pluralized by being reflected) in (different pots of) water. The Self appears to traverse the states of dreamless sleep, dream (and waking, etc.), but is really changeless, just as (in a display brought about through mass-hypnotism) the magician mounts (that is, appears to mount) the magic elephant and to come (and go, while in reality doing nothing at all). There is (in reality) no elephant, nor anyone riding on an elephant. Similarly, there is no dreamless sleep (dream or waking state, etc.), nor is there any empirical subject perceiving them. The one knowledge-principle, the eternal immutable Consciousness, is different (from the changing states of consciousness and their contents).

For the one who resists the hypnosis there is no illusion. And neither is there any illusion for the magician. It is only for the one hypnotized that the illusion exists. Therefore, only that (the Self) exists which does not (in truth) produce any illusion.[197]

❖

16. The meaning (of the old Ṛg Vedic verse quoted in the Upanishad) is: 'He (Indra)[198] conformed to (assumed) every form'. Every son that is born conforms to the form of the parents. A quadruped is not born from a biped nor a biped from a quadruped. The same one supreme Lord, unfolding name and form, Himself conformed to (assumed) every form.

But why did He appear in so many forms? The text says, 'He assumed forms that he might become manifest'. If He did not unfold name and form his unconditioned form called Massed Consciousness (prajñāna-ghana) would not be manifest. But his nature does become manifest when name and form are unfolded as cause and effect.

By 'Indra' is meant the supreme Lord. 'By his magic powers' means through false cognitions (prajñā),[199] or else 'through false identifications wrought through name and form and the elements' — false, be it noted, and not true. In this way the Lord is perceived as having many forms (continues the verse). That is, though He is of one form only, namely massed Consciousness, He appears to have many forms through the cognitions of nescience (avidyā-prajñā).[200]

❖

17. If creation had been a real fact, then it would be quite true that plurality would be real and there would have been no passages in the Veda expounding its non-existence. But we do in fact find such passages denying the existence of duality, such as 'There is no plurality here whatever'.[201] Hence we must conclude that creation never occurred and that the teachings about it were fictitiously introduced, just like those about the 'conversations' held between the various faculties of the Vital Energy.[202] For in a text like 'Indra by his magic powers (māyā)'[203] we find the use of the word 'māyā', which means 'something that does not exist'.

Perhaps you will say that the word 'māyā' means 'knowledge' (prajñā).[204] Granted. But this does no harm to our position, since what we take as 'māyā' is the knowledge yielded by the sense-organs and mind, where nescience predominates. The text, in speaking of 'magic powers', meant 'sense-cognitions, of the nature of nescience'. And this follows also from the text, 'Though never (in reality) undergoing birth, He is (apparently) born under various forms',[205] which shows that He is born only by way of illusion (māyā). The word 'tu' (but) in the Kārikā is for extra emphasis, i.e. 'quite definitely an illusion'. One and the same being cannot both be unborn and born under various forms, any more than fire could be cold and hot at the same time.[206]

❖

18. This Spirit is hidden beneath all beings from Brahmā down to the meanest clump of grass. He is hidden by the illusion (māyā) of nescience, even though it is He who performs seeing and hearing and other functions. It is for this reason that He is not manifest (fully in his true nature) as anyone's Self.

See how deep and unfathomable this power of illusion (māyā) is, whereby every living being, though in truth the supreme Self,[207] fails to grasp that he is the supreme Self even after he has been properly taught! On the contrary, he thinks of himself as the not-self, as the psycho-physical organism, even though it is an object experienced by the Self as something different from itself, like a man perceiving an external object such as a pot. And he regards himself as 'the son of so and so', even though this is not what the Veda tells him at all. It is indeed a fact that the whole world errs grievously, bemused by the deluding power (māyā) of the Lord. And so, also, affirms the Smṛti, 'I am not evident to any, veiled as I am by the machinations of My Māyā'.[208]

19. 'Nārāyaṇa stands supreme beyond the Unmanifest Principle. The Cosmic Egg proceeded from the Unmanifest Principle. Within the Cosmic Egg stand these worlds and the earth with its seven "continents".'[209]

This Lord Nārāyaṇa, when He had created the world, wished to ensure its stability and therefore, at the very beginning of creation, projected the Prajāpatis, Marīci and the rest, and imbued them with a knowledge of the spiritual law (dharma) as far as it concerned the active life enjoined in the Veda. Then He projected other exalted beings such as Sanaka, Sanandana and the rest, and imbued them with a knowledge of the spiritual law as far as it concerned the life of withdrawal, consisting of knowledge and renunciation. For the spiritual law taught in the Veda has two aspects, marked respectively by activity and withdrawal.

The spiritual law (dharma) is the one source of the stability of the world and the direct cause both of the material well-being and the spiritual beatitude of living beings when it is followed by Brahmins and other castes in their various stages of life (āśrama) with a view to promote their own highest spiritual good.

But in the course of a long period of time, it happened that sensuous passions rose up in the hearts of those following the spiritual law, which affected their power of discrimination. On account of this, adherence to the spiritual law declined and addiction to evil ways began to flourish. When this occurred, the primaeval Creator, Viṣṇu Himself, called Nārāyaṇa, is said to have taken birth with a part of Himself in the womb of Devakī, with Vasudeva for his father, in order to preserve the

Brahminical way of life, which is the Absolute (brahman) itself in earthly form. For if the Brahminical way of life is preserved, the spiritual law taught in the Veda is also preserved, as the members of all the different castes and stages of life depend on the Brahmins for the proper fulfilment of their functions, (as the latter keep the texts and rituals and pious ideals in being).

The Lord Nārāyaṇa is ever possessed of his supreme knowledge, lordship, might, energy and brilliance. Though unborn and indestructible and the Lord of all creatures, ever pure, enlightened and free by nature, He assumes special control over his Māyā, the Māyā of Viṣṇu composed of the three 'constituents', the primary matter (mūla-prakṛti) of the world, and takes on the illusory appearance, through this illusory power (māyā) of his, of becoming embodied, of being born, of acting to help the people of the world.[210] In this way He taught the spiritual law declared in the Veda in both its aspects to Arjuna, when the latter was submerged in the ocean of grief and delusion, and this without any thought of personal advantage, and solely with a desire to benefit his creatures. His idea here was that if the spiritual law were adopted and followed by men of outstanding spiritual merit, it would be spread abroad among the people from them. And holy Vyāsa, the omniscient composer of the Veda, set down the seven hundred verses called the Gītā to embody the spiritual law as it was taught to Arjuna by the Lord.[211]

❖

20. 'Though I am unborn, (says the Lord in the text under comment), and though I consist in inexhaustible knowledge-

power (jñāna-śakti) by My very nature, and though I am the Lord of all creatures from Brahmā to the meanest clump of grass, I assume control over My Nature (prakṛti), that is, My Māyā, the Māyā of Viṣṇu consisting of the three "constituents", under the control of which all the world-process unfolds'. The last phrase means 'stupefied by which the world does not know its own true Self, Vāsudeva'. Assuming control over this My Nature, I am 'born'. This means I appear to have a body, as apparently born, through My own magic power (māyā). It is not a real birth, like birth in the world.[212]

❖

21. The complete and sovereign dominion over the world and power to fulfil His desires that are attributed to the Spirit (puruṣa) in certain Vedic texts show that He is the highest Lord. As to the difficulty that the Vedic texts also attribute to Him (that is, to Puruṣa) a golden beard and the like,[213] and that this is not compatible with his being the highest Lord, we reply to that as follows. The golden-bearded form could very well be one of those illusory (māyā-maya) forms deliberately assumed by the Lord for the sake of His devotees. For we have such texts as, 'This, O Nārada, is a mere illusion (māyā) that I have projected whereby thou beholdest Me associated with the qualities of all the creatures. Know that it is not My true nature'.[214]

NOTES TO CHAPTER V

References to Extracts are in bold type

(List of abbreviations, pp 271-273; Bibliography, pp 274-292)

1 Sadānanda Yati, 198.

2 Chānd. VIII.vii.1.

3 B.S.Bh. II.i.13. It may be doubted whether the author of the Sūtras really intended to distinguish two standpoints here. Probably he only wished to point to analogies in the world that supported his view. Cp. Ghate, 35ff. Śaṅkara, however, absorbs the words of the Sūtra into his higher synthesis.

4 **B.S.Bh. II.i.14.**

5 B.S. II.i.22.

6 Bṛhad. II.iv.5.

7 Chānd. VI.viii.7, etc.

8 The opponent has claimed that to attribute Creatorship of the World to the Absolute is to suppose the absurdity that it would invite onto its own head a host of limitations and evils.

9 Chānd. VIII.vii.1.

10 **B.S.Bh. II.i.22-23.**

11 The use of the plural form 'names and forms', which became standard in later Advaita, is not found in the classical Upanishads and is comparatively rare in Śaṅkara.

12 **B.S.Bh. II.iv.20.**

13 Taitt. II.1.

14 Chānd. VIII.xiv.1 and Śvet. VI.12. The Extract is from **B.S.Bh. II.i.14.**

15 The present section is very heavily indebted to Hacker, *Eigentümlichkeiten*, 277ff.

16 B.S.Bh. I.ii.7, translated by Gambhīrānanda, 116. (Swāmī Gambhīrānanda's translation is henceforth abbreviated to G.)

17 I.ii.3, G. 113.

18 I.i.20 (introduction), G. 79. IV.iv.21, G. 911.

19 II.ii.39, G. 437f.

20 III.iv.8, G. 763.

21 I.ii.8, G. 118.

22 II.iii.46, G. 510.

23 I.iii.19, G. 196.

24 I.i.20 (introduction), G. 78.

25 I.ii.21, G. 139.

26 I.iii.7, G. 166.

27 I.i.17, G. 70. I.i.21, G. 81. I.ii.8, G. 117. I.ii.20, G. 137. III.ii.5, G. 595.

28 I.iii.19, G. 196.

29 I.i.5, G. 51. I.iv.6, G. 257. I.iv.22, G. 286f. III.ii.6, G. 596.

30 I.iv.22, G. 286f. II.iii.47, G. 513.

31 I.i.31, G. 105.

32 I.ii.20, G. 137.

33 I.iii.19, G. 193.

34 *Ibid.* G. 195.

35 Compare the rather similar insertion of an 'iva' (meaning 'like','as if') at Bh.G.Bh. XV.7.

36 III.iv.8, G. 764.

37 IV.i.3, G. 820.

38 I.iii.19, at the end of the 'tentative view', G. 190.

39 III.iv.8, G. 764.

40 I.iv.3, G. 249.

41 I.iv.16, last sentence, G. 279.

42 I.iii.30, G. 220f.

43 I.i.5, G. 49 and often.

44 II.ii.2, G. 372.

45 sarvajña, often.

46 II.iii.13, G. 466f.

47 II.i.14, G. 334.

48 I.iii.41, G. 239.

49 I.iv.23 *ad fin.*, G. 294.

50 Often.

51 I.i.5, G. 49.

52 I.i.2, G. 14.

53 Hacker, *Eigentümlichkeiten*, 281

54 Cp. Bṛhad. Bh. I.iv.7, Mādhavānanda, 92. 'The question of the authority or absence of authority of a text does not depend on whether it states a fact or enjoins an action, but on whether or not it generates certain and fruitful knowledge'. Cp. also B.S.Bh. I.i.4, Gambhīrānanda 39, where Śaṅkara contrasts the (useless) statement 'The earth has seven continents' with the sentence 'This is a rope, not a snake', which brings a tangible reward in the form of relief from fear.

55 B.S. I.i.2.

56 Praśna VI.3 and VI.4.

57 Śvet. VI.19.

58 Chānd. VI.i.2-3.

59 Chānd. VI.i.4.

60 Chānd. VI.ii.1

61 Taitt. II.7.

62 On the spheres of reason and revelation, see Vol.V, Ch.XIII, section 2, below.

63 Selected from B.S.Bh. I.iv.23-27.

64 Śvet. VI.8.

65 The Vedanta accepts the traditions about supernormal powers possessed by ṛṣis, while the Pūrva Mīmāṃsā, at least in its post-Śabara phase, does not. The Mīmāṃsaka, the exponent *par excellence* of the ritual, was not prepared to tolerate any power to interfere with the laws of karma even on the part of an Īśvara, let alone a ṛṣi. Cp. Biardeau, *Connaissance*, 145. See also Note 117, below.

66 A convention of the poets, cp. Mallinātha on Kālidāsa, *Meghadūta*, Part 1, verse 9.

67 We may smile at the botany. But the Indian scientist, Sir Jagadish Chandra Bose, made discoveries about the presence of life in plants under inspiration from the classical Indian conception of plants as living beings which Śaṅkara is here voicing, albeit in the person of an objector.

68 From B.S.Bh. II.i.24-25.

69 Chānd. VI.iii.2 and Chānd. III.xii.6, reproducing R.V. X.90.3.

70 Chānd. VIII.iii.3.

71 Chānd. VI.viii.1. On dreamless sleep, see Vol.III, Ch.IX,

section 2, below.

72 M.Bh. VI.5.12, G.P. Ed. Vol.II, 302.

73 P.M. Sūtra X.viii.6: Śabara, trans. Jhā, Vol.III, 2034f.

74 On this phrase, see Chap.VI, section 2, below.

75 Chānd. VI.i.4.

76 Cp. Note 54, above.

77 Bṛhad. IV.ii.4. **B.S.Bh. II.i.27.**

78 Chānd. III.xiv.4.

79 Chānd. VIII.vii.1.

80 Muṇḍ. I.i.9.

81 Bṛhad. III.viii.9.

82 Bṛhad. III.viii.8.

83 Bṛhad. III.ix.26, etc.

84 The reference is to B.S.II.i.27, the Sūtra under comment in the previous Extract.

85 Śvet. III.19. **B.S.Bh. II.i.30-31.**

86 The Gītā term 'viparivartate' is here used in the same sense that the term 'vivartate' was usually used before Śaṅkara, namely 'to unfold', cp. Śvet. V1.2. Śaṅkara only uses the term 'vivartate' three times (B.S.Bh. I.iii.39, II.ii.1 (disputed reading) and Taitt. I.6, trans. Gambhīrānanda, 261), each time in the sense of unfold or roll out. He does not use the word 'vivarta' at all. It was only by such later authors of Śaṅkara's school as Padmapāda, Prakāśātman and Vācaspati, that the latter term was gradually introduced in the meaning of 'illusory change', for which Śaṅkara was content with 'mithyā pariṇāmā'. The use of the term 'vivarta' in this sense began with the Grammarians of Bhartṛhari's school and was only

gradually adopted by the Advaitins. See Hacker, *Vivarta, passim* and *Darśanodaya*, 99-107.

87 R.V. X.129.7.

88 Bh.G. V.15. **Bh.G.Bh. IX.10.**

89 Bṛhad. II.iv.5.

90 On this point, see Chap.VII, section 1, below. **B.S.Bh. II.i.32-33.**

91 For which see below, section 5, Extracts 6 and 7 of the present Chapter.

92 Taitt. II.6.

93 Śatapatha Brāhmaṇa VI.i.iii.2-4.

94 Kauṣītaki II.14.

95 Unless there were some superiority in the material cause over the effect, there would be no basis for a distinction into cause and effect.

96 Cp. above, Vol.I, Chap.IV, section 2, Extract 5.

97 **From B.S.Bh. II.i.4-6.**

98 Obviously an important formula in Śaṅkara, but it is worth noting that the same idea occurs in Maṇḍana, B.Sid. 20, trans. Biardeau 166, 'The Absolute is not the all, but the all is the Absolute'. One cannot fix the label 'pantheist' on either writer.

99 Bṛhad. II.iv.6.

100 **B.S.Bh. II.i.8 and 9.**

101 Taitt. II.6.

102 Chānd. VI.i.4.

103 **B.S.Bh. II.i.13 and II.i.14.**

104 Cp. *Darśanodaya*, 147.

105 Bṛhad. III.vii.1-3.

106 The division of the universe into 'planes' was characteristic of the Brāhmaṇas (cp. above, Vol.I, page 3) and re-appears in some of the older upanishadic texts.

107 It occurs also at Māṇḍūkya 6. It is not certain whether Śaṅkara regarded this brief Upanishad as Śruti, though his pupil Sureśvara did (see, for example, B.B.V. III.viii.26), and it is quoted by Maṇḍana, B. Sid. 127.

108 Bṛhad. III.ix.10.

109 At Bṛhad. III.vii.23.

110 It might be said, for instance, that a Controller would require a body and organs to control anything, and so would require a further body and organs to control his body and a fresh body and organs to control the first set and so *ad infinitem*.

111 **B.S.Bh. I.ii.18.**

112 **Bṛhad. Bh. III.vii.23.**

113 Cp. Bh.G.Bh. VII.22.

114 Bṛhad. IV.iv.24.

115 *Taittirīya Saṃhitā*, Black Yajur Veda, II.v.5, trans. Keith, I.194.

116 If any line of interpretation could be shown to render any part of the Veda useless, it was regarded by the old commentators as refuted by that very fact. Only that interpretation of the Veda can be sound under which every text of the Veda can be seen to be of benefit to man.

117 This is the characteristic Pūrva Mīmāṃsā hostility to anything

that could threaten the rigid impersonal laws governing the results of ritualistic acts. Whereas the post-Śabara Mīmāṃsakas held to the dead letter of Vedic ritualism, Śaṅkara drew inspiration from the theistic texts of the Upanishads, Epics and Purāṇas. It is interesting to note that he and the author of the Sūtras could quote Bādarāyaṇa in their support in this context. Cp. Note 65, above.

118 Kauṣītaki Upanishad III.8.

119 Bh.G. VII.21 and 22.

120 The arguments for this had already been stated at B.S.Bh. II.i.34-36 and are given in the present work at Extract 5 of the present section. **B.S.Bh. III.ii.38-41.**

121 E.g. sun and rain, cp. Sureśvara, N. Sid. II.60.

122 *Taittirīya Saṃhitā*, II.v.5, trans. Keith, I.194.

123 The present extract is from the 'Vākya' (as opposed to 'Pada') Bhāṣya to the Kena Up. Sac queries the authenticity of this Bhāṣya in his edition of the Kena Bh., 8-11. S. Mayeda defends it elaborately in I.I.J., Vol.X, 1967, 33-55. Sac queries whether Śaṅkara would have ever attributed a buddhi to Īśvara, but we find the expression sarva-sattva-upādhiḥ at Muṇḍ. Bh. III.i.1, so he may have been ready to attribute a buddhi to the Lord as an external adjunct. The close agreement of the argument about the distribution of the fruits of deeds with that contained in the following Extract seems to speak for authenticity.

124 **Kena (Vākya) Bh. III.1.**

125 Bṛhad. III.v.1.

126 R.V. X.121.5.

127 Reading apaśyantaḥ.

128 I.e. at Bṛhad.Bh. I.iii.1, cited below, Vol.V, Chap.XIII, section 2, Extract 11.

129 Bṛhad. Bh. III.viii.9.

130 Malebranche uses the same simile to make a similar point, Cresson, *Courants*, Vol.2, 120.

131 Chānd. VI.ii.1.

132 B.S.Bh. II.i.34-36.

133 For an exact analysis of Śaṅkara's use of the term Māyā in the B.S.Bh., see Hacker, *Eigentümlichkeiten*, 269ff.

134 In this connection, the discussion of the Indian rope-trick in Lehmann (3rd Ger. Ed. by Dr. Petersen, 1925), 367-369, is interesting, as fresh evidence compelled the editor to reverse Lehmann's sceptical conclusions as to the possibility of mass-hypnosis being used to perform the trick. There have been controlled experiments with educated witnesses testifying that they saw the visions while the camera revealed only the faqir gesticulating on the ground. Modern descriptions agree in essentials with Śaṅkara's, the earliest substantial account extant. The late Mr. J.F.H. Spaan of Amsterdam informed the writer that he witnessed a performance of the trick shortly after the first World War and attributes it to mass-hypnotism. The writer recalls a debunking account of Indian magic written in the thirties by a French journalist, who was nevertheless constrained to admit that he met a man who induced him to see a blossoming tree where there was only an empty courtyard. Extract 9 below refers to this trick, Extract 12 to the rope-trick.

135 sāmājika-dhī-samūhānāmindrajāla-māyā-kṣubdhānām ekākāratā-bhrama-vad utthitaḥ.
For the earlier literature, cp. Daṇḍin, *Daśakumāra Carita*, Pūrva Pīṭhikā, Ucchvāsa V, trans. Kale 37f., and Śrī Harṣa,

Ratnāvalī, Act IV.

136 B.S.Bh. I.i.17, cp. below, Vol.III, Chap.VIII, section 4, Extract 6.

137 Vol.I, Chap.I, section 7, above.

138 Bṛhad. Bh. I.v.2, trans. Mādhavānanda, 146.

139 Kavirāj, 68 (footnote).

140 Bṛhad. I.iv.2.

141 Cp. U.S. (verse) XV.12, Bh.G.Bh. X.20 and XV.15.

142 Bh.G.Bh. XV.16.

143 Bh.G.Bh. XVIII.19.

144 Na cātmanaḥ śakti-pratibandhaḥ sambhavaty, avikriyatvāt. B.S.Bh. II.iii.32.

145 Bh.G.Bh. XVIII.67 introduction, trans. Śāstrī, 514.

146 As at Bṛhad. Bh. I.iv.10, trans. Mādhavānanda, 101.

147 Cp. Chap.V, section 2, above.

148 B.S.Bh. II.i.14, trans. Gambhīrānanda, 334.

149 Bṛhad.Bh. III.vii.3, trans. Mādhavānanda, 349.

150 *Ibid.*

151 U.S. (verse) XVII.80.

152 B.S.Bh. II.iii.41, cp. below, Vol.III, Chap.VIII, section 4, Extract 5, *ad init.*

153 See Vol.VI, Chap.XIV, section 1, below.

154 See Vol.VI, Chap.XV, section 5, below.

155 Bh.G. X.19ff.

156 E.g. Bh.G. XIII.21.

157 What is not brought into being by an efficient cause has no beginning and exists, if it exists at all, naturally and eternally and cannot be annihilated. It is because the Lord stands behind the transmigratory process as its efficient cause that it can be brought to an end through His grace.

158 See Extract 6 of present section.

159 Bh.G.Bh. XIII.19.

160 The term tanmātra for the elements in their subtle, imperceptible form is not found in the actual text of the Gītā, but is part of the thought-world of the M.Bh. in which it is embedded. Śaṅkara does not resort to it himself in his accounts of the elements, see Chap.VI, section 3, below.

161 'Mahat' means 'the Great', and is often identified, as here, with 'Buddhi' or 'Cosmic Intellect' which forms the first evolute from Nature in its primeval unmanifest state. Cp. M.Bh. XII.194.18, G.P. Ed. Vol.III, 527, 'This whole world, consisting of the moving and the fixed, is formed by the Cosmic Intellect, arises with it and dissolves with it'. In this sense it may be identified with Brahmā or Hiraṇyagarbha, for whom see Chap.VI, section 4.

162 Ego-sense 'sets it in motion' because it is the latent impressions left by the past egoistic actions of creatures in previous world-periods that cause the evolution of Nature from its unmanifest state at the beginning of the world-period. Śaṅkara here traces these impressions to action dictated by ego-sense: the ego-sense in each creature is what prompts it to desire and to self-interested action.

163 The eight elements are the tanmātras of earth, water, fire, wind and ether, plus Cosmic Mind, Intellect and Ego-sense. **Bh.G.Bh. VII.4.**

164 As we have seen, Vol.I, Chap.I, section 4, there is a tendency in the middle Upanishads and Gītā occasionally to exalt the

personal aspect of the divine over the impersonal. The impersonal (or supra-personal) principle, known as the Absolute (brahman) or Imperishable (akṣara) in the oldest Upanishads, is retained as the final reality in some passages in the Gītā, since it is said that one may dissolve into it through knowledge, e.g. Bh.G. II.72, V.24, V.25-28. Yet it is also identified in some places, as here, with Mahat, the passive womb (yoni) which needs the activation of the personal God (puruṣa, puruṣottama), and from which Hiraṇyagarbha or Brahmā proceeds as the first-born. It is here equated with Māyā and Prakṛti. Modern philologists often derive the term 'Brahman' from root bṛh meaning to expand, in agreement with Śaṅkara.

165 On Hiraṇyagarbha, see below, Chap.VI, section 4.

166 Bh.G.Bh. XIV.3.

167 The Gītā is here speaking about a conception of two great puruṣas, perishable and imperishable, then current. The perishable was identified with all objects, the imperishable with the seed from which they proceeded.

168 The word 'kūṭa', both here and in the following Extract, is interpreted as deceit = Māyā. But the notion of the Imperishable is different in the two passages, and the word 'kūṭastha', used to describe it, is interpreted in two different ways accordingly. Here it means 'that which stands as a mass of deceit', i.e. Māyā itself. In the following Extract, where the reference is to the true Imperishable, it is interpreted as 'He who stands *within* Māyā and guides it', i.e. the Lord or supreme Self.

169 That is, with 'māyā' in its secular sense of common trickery or deception, referred to briefly above, right at the beginning of the section.

170 Bh.G.Bh. XV.16.

171 Reading karaṇāgocaram with D.V. Gokhale.

172 Śvet. IV.10.

173 The supreme Spirit stands within the 'Imperishable Unmanifest' guiding its manifestation and evolution. **Bh.G.Bh. XII.3.**

174 Because subject and object are utterly distinct in nature, any identification of the two is necessarily a case of superimposition, of false knowledge, of nescience. Cp. above, Vol.I, Chap.II, section 3.

175 On the meaning of the term 'Field', cp. M.Bh. XII.351.6, G.P. Ed. Vol.III, 730: 'For the bodies are fields, and the seeds (sown in those fields) merit and demerit. As the one Self connected (with all) takes cognizance of them (all) it is called the Knower of the Field'.

176 I.e. through false identification with it.

177 Gairika is the colouring matter applied, for instance, to draw patterns on the body of an elephant for ceremonial purposes. Cp. Māgha, V.39. Rajas and rāga and vairāgya all come from the same root 'raj'.

178 **Bh.G.Bh. XIV.5-13.**

179 The term Nature (prakṛti) is strictly only applied to the material cause of the world. But as Nature unfolds from seed form and expands into the world of time and space, the latter may also be referred to as Nature.

180 **Bh.G.Bh. III.27-28.**

181 Bṛhad. IV.iii.10.

182 There were generally accepted traditions that gods had produced illusions of various kinds that had deluded ordinary dwellers on earth. In Kālidāsa's *Raghuvaṃśa*, II.27ff., it is described how the image of a lion was conjured up by Śiva to test the courage and devotion of King Dilīpa.

NOTES TO CHAPTER V

183 **B.S.Bh. II.i.28.**

184 Bh.G. VII.14. **G.K.Bh. II.19.**

185 Śaṅkara adhered to the upanishadic teaching that the soul attained to pure Being in dreamless sleep, see Vol.III, Chap.IX, section 2, below. He does not refer to the doctrine of some of his later followers that in dreamless sleep the soul enters a 'causal body'.

186 G.K. I.16. **B.S.Bh. II.i.9.**

187 **G.K.Bh. IV.58.**

188 On these terms, see Vol.III, Chap.IX, section 3.

189 *Ibid.*

190 **G.K.Bh. I.7.**

191 **Ait. Bh. I.i.2.**

192 Bh.G. IX.8 and 9.

193 **Bh.G.Bh. IX.10.**

194 The sleep here envisaged is that of 'not-being-awake-to-the-Self', what one might call metaphysical sleep. From it as 'seed' or prior condition proceed waking and dream. But the whole distinction of waking, dream and dreamless sleep is a relative one, peculiar to a metaphysically ignorant person in the waking state.

195 No more egotistic action is performed binding one to new worldly experiences in future births.

196 I.e. the three 'states' of waking, dream and ordinary non-metaphysical dreamless sleep.

197 **U. S. (verse) XVII.25-31.**

198 Identified by Śaṅkara with the supreme Lord or Self, in

conformity with the spirit of the Upanishad passage which he is interpreting.

199 Yāska, *Nirukti*, III.9, Bibliotheca Indica Ed., Vol.I, 324-6.

200 Bṛhad. Bh. II.v.19.

201 Kaṭha II.i.11.

202 Chānd. I.ii.1ff., Bṛhad. I.iii.1ff., Praśna II.3ff. Cp. below, Chap.VII, section 1, Extract 3.

203 Bṛhad. II.v.19.

204 On the basis of the synonyms given at Yāska, *Nirukti*, III.9.

205 Taitt. Āraṇyaka III.13, Ā.Ś.S. Ed. Vol.I, 201, apparently alluded to by Gauḍapāda in the Kārikā under comment.

206 G.K.Bh. III.24.

207 Reading, with Sac, paramātma-satattvo'pi.

208 Bh.G.VII.25. **Kaṭha Bh. I.iii.12.**

209 According to Ānandagiri, this is an obeisance to Śaṅkara's iṣṭa-deva. Cp. above, Vol.I, Chap.I, section 3.

210 Cp. V.P. I.23.76 and V.3.12.

211 Bh.G.Bh. I.1, introduction.

212 Bh.G.Bh. IV.6.

213 E.g. Chānd. I.vi.6.

214 M.Bh.XII.339.45 and 46, G.P. Ed. Vol.III, 705. This is almost the only passage where the M.Bh. unequivocally speaks of the world as an illusion, and it is typical of Śaṅkara that he is able to put his finger on it. **B.S.Bh. I.i.20.**

CHAPTER VI

THE WORLD AND ITS PRESIDING DEITIES

1. Sat-Kārya Vāda

Śaṅkara believed, as we shall see at Chapter VII, section 2, below, that all causation implies duality and that from the standpoint of the highest truth no causality exists. But the student of Advaita has not attained to the standpoint of the highest truth, or he would not be studying Advaita. It may be that on the later stages of the path a dialectical criticism of the notion of causality such as that offered by Gauḍapāda (Kārikās, Book IV) may be a useful support for the life of sustained yogic meditation. But a mere dialectical critique of causation unsupported by any corresponding intuitive vision will be of small help to him on the earlier stages of the path, while nescience still has him firmly in its grip. What he then needs is not the negation of causality but a rationally defensible theory of causality which will enable him to accept and make sense of the Vedic texts at the level of ordinary subject-object experience, while at the same time leaving the window open looking out onto the vistas of infinity in which causality is finally transcended.

The theory which Śaṅkara used for this purpose was his own adaptation of the old doctrine, apparently championed by the Brahma Sūtras and in pre-Śaṅkara Vedanta generally, called Sat-kārya Vāda. Sat-kārya Vāda originated with the Sāṅkhya philosophers, who applied it to explain the transformations undergone by the principle of Nature (pradhāna, prakṛti). It is the doctrine that the effect is already real before it is 'produced', that production of an effect is not the creation of anything new but the bringing into manifestation of something that already exists but in latent form.

Nature, or the realm of change, was conceived by the Sāṅkhyas as a unity, but as a unity capable of sustaining differences. The reality of change was admitted, but it was affirmed that the differences introduced thereby did not affect the unity and persistent identity of the whole. The coming-to-be and passing-away of finite entities should not be regarded as the production of anything new or the annihilation of anything previously existent. It is only by an act of false abstraction that we regard finite entities as totally distinct from their material cause. They should be considered, rather, as successive modifications assumed by one all-embracing substance, in the rise and fall of which nothing is gained or lost. As statues and pots are already virtually present in the stone or clay from which they are made, so the whole universe as manifest effect lies first unmanifest in the all-embracing substance as cause. Since only the effect is manifest, the existence and nature of the material cause have to be inferred from the nature of the effect. In endeavouring to account for the cause of the many we are forced to assume the existence of the one. The Sāṅkhya doctrine brings to mind the theories of Meyerson, for whom 'What superficially appear to be processes of creation and destruction are actually no more than readjustments within a substance which retains its identity through apparent changes' and 'Conservation laws are the typical outcome of scientific investigation'.[1]

The pre-Śaṅkara Vedantins generally, including the author of the Sūtras, seem to have preserved the logic of identity in difference evolved by the Sāṅkhyas to account for the mutations of non-conscious Nature or the realm of change, but to have applied it, more broadly, to the upanishadic Absolute itself. They adopted the upanishadic distinction between a higher, unmoving immortal form of the Absolute and a lower form in which it manifested itself as the world of effects.[2] The Absolute, in its unmanifest form as the cause, stood to the world, and also to the individual souls, in the same relation that the Nature of the Sāṅkhyas, as infinite cause, stood to the world as a system of finite effects (vikṛti). The Absolute in its causal form stood to the Absolute as manifest in its effects as the independent to the dependent, the cause to the caused, the one to the many, the whole to the parts, the indeterminate to the determinate, *natura naturans* to *natura naturata*. The logic is not applied, however, in a spirit of rationalism, as it had been by the dualistic Sāṅkhyas. It is not claimed that the cause either must or can be inferred by the mind of man. Rather, the logic is applied in defence of upanishadic conceptions accepted in faith as revealed doctrine. The structural pattern of the twenty-four principles (tattva) used by the Sāṅkhyas to describe the evolution of Nature is avoided, and the stages of the Absolute's self-transformation into the souls and the objects of the world are described in terminology based on the Upanishads. As rationalistic philosophers, the Sāṅkhyas had had to face up to the intractable problem of the how, why and when of the universe, and had weakly tried to solve it by an appeal to the 'needs of the soul'. One might well wonder, with Radhakrishnan,[3] what genuine need of the soul could be served by experience of a world of woe. But the pre-Śaṅkara Vedantic monists, as we saw in Extract 4 of the preceding section, abandoned the whole problem as beyond the comprehension of man. This attitude was justifiable within the limits of a philosophy based on religious faith such as their own. But Śaṅkara went beyond the standpoint of religious faith. While agreeing that the problem of God and creation could not be solved on the plane of discursive thought, he maintained that it could be, if not solved, at any rate *dis*solved in concrete mystical experience.

For the author of the Sūtras, the objects of the world existed, in potential form, in the Absolute, their material cause. They came out into manifestation for a time and then dissolved back into their material cause like waves arising and subsiding on the surface of the sea, or like a cloth or banner, first unfolded and then furled or folded up again.[4] In a doctrine of causality of this kind, the Absolute taught in the Upanishads can be retained as first cause, and the world can be represented as its self-expression or self-manifestation, and explained intelligibly as an organic unity, and not as a mere cluster of disparate atoms brought together and controlled in some inexplicable way from without. Śaṅkara noticed some metaphysical difficulties about the theory, but he accepted and defended it as providing a sensible and coherent basis for interpreting a large part of the upanishadic revelation, in the light of which the dualism of the Sāṅkhyas, the atomistic pluralism of the Vaiśeṣikas and the exaggerated '*hic et nunc*' scepticism of the main stream of Buddhist thought could be exposed for the thoroughly incomplete theories of reality they were. We see him doing so in the Extracts to follow in the present section, taken largely from his commentary on the first Quarter of the second Book of the Brahma Sūtras.

But Śaṅkara had the consistent tendency to go beyond the author of the Sūtras as well as to defend his positions. We saw in the latter half of Chapter V, section 3, how, having first defended the Sūtras' appeal to blind faith in the revealed texts even when they were contradictory, he then went on to show how the contradictions could be reconciled through appeal to the principle of nescience. And we shall see now, in the course of the Extracts presented in the present section, how he first accepts and defends the Sat-kārya Vāda doctrine of causality implicit in the Sūtras, and yet *also* goes on to interpret it in such a way as to lead the mind beyond the realm of causality altogether, thus contriving to use the doctrine of Sat-kārya Vāda, which is after all itself a theory of causality, to point beyond the realm of causality to the realm of transcendence.

Thus Śaṅkara is entirely on common ground with the Sūtras when he defends upanishadic monism by declaring not only that the effect is real before its production, but also that it is real before and during manifestation, and even that its future existence is real now and subject to apprehension by a yogin. It is real, however, not in itself, but only *as* the cause, as the pot is real not *qua* pot but *qua* clay. The doctrine of the Sūtras that the objects come forth from, and return back to, the Absolute is defended. But at times Śaṅkara goes back behind the doctrine of the Sūtras to certain texts of the old Upanishads and maintains that the effect is strictly nothing over and above the cause. As we already know, if the cause is said to be identical with the effect, this means that the effect has the nature of the cause, while the cause does not have the nature of the effect.[5]

This, however, is to reduce the effect to the cause. If the world has an intelligible structure, and curds can only be obtained from milk and not from clay, this means that a certain power or predisposition to evolve into curds must be in the milk. But Śaṅkara declares that all objects are non-different from the 'powers' (śakti) or predispositions from which they proceed, while the powers, in turn, are non-different from the substances in which they lie, and the substances themselves are traceable finally to the great elements from which they proceed and into which they will eventually dissolve back, so that the whole world, beginning with the primordial element ether, is reduced to a mere inexplicable appearance arising on the face of the Absolute, while causality, law and intelligibility still reign within the appearance.[6] Śaṅkara transforms the older doctrine of Sat-kārya Vāda, the mere doctrine of the reality of the effect before its manifestation, into an instrument for affirming, yet again, the transcendence of the Absolute, which triumphs ultimately over all predicates attributed to it by the human mind.

The content of the Extracts might be briefly summarized as follows. No.1 remarks that if a certain upanishadic text speaks of the non-existence of the world prior to creation this does not mean that anything was created from nothing. It has to be understood that name and form, hitherto unmanifest, were brought out into manifestation. This distinction between unmanifest and manifest name and form, capital for Śaṅkara but on the whole allowed to lapse by his followers, will be examined further in the following section. Here, however, Śaṅkara is only concerned to point out that the effect is never different from the cause and that the cause is in this case

Being. Extract No.2 claims that the non-difference of the effect from its material cause is actually perceived. No.3 argues that nothing can be produced *de novo*: you cannot extract oil from sand but only from seeds where it already exists.

Extract No.4 includes several new points. The source of the effect need only be a *power* inherent in the material cause, and the power may operate without the cause being active in its true nature. Again, production is an act having an object. No effect could be 'produced' unless it already existed in some sense in order to be the object of the act of production, which means that all so-called 'production' amounts to manifestation. At the very least, causation would imply that the effect to be 'produced' was in relation with its material cause before 'production', and there cannot be a relation between an existent and a non-existent term. Even assuming action is present in causation, it is only needed to hasten the transformation of the material cause into the effect, not to create the latter. But qualitative change is apparent only, and can be reduced to quantitative change in the form of accretion of similar parts. The doctrine of the persistent identity of the cause agrees with our experience of our own identity through the changing states of childhood, youth and old age.

Extract No.5 re-affirms the view that causation is the bringing to manifestation of an effect that pre-exists in its material cause. A whole debate is set up to bring out the implications of this view. For simplicity's sake, the interlocutors have been reduced to three main categories. The first, labelled Buddhists, hold that neither the effect itself nor a material cause pre-existed before the production of the effect. The second class of opponents, called Ārambha Vādins, while denying that the effect in any way exists before its production, accept the existence of a material cause from which it proceeds. They hold, however, that since the material cause consists of a particular configuration of eternal atoms, the effect cannot emerge until that particular configuration has been destroyed. If the opponents labelled 'Buddhists' are mainly, but not exclusively, Nihilists of the Śūnya Vāda school, the Ārambha Vādins are recognizable as Hindu Vaiśeṣikas. The third class of opponents, here called 'Critics of Sat-kārya Vāda', only appears towards the end of the debate. These theorists are given a nondescript title as they merely criticize and do not clearly show their own hand. They are introduced to bring out, by their criticism, how the doctrine of the pre-existence of the effect (in the material cause) before its production is *not* self-contradictory. It leaves room for creative activity to bring the hidden effect to outward manifestation.

Extract No.6 explains how, though a doctrine of the modification of the Absolute is here being propounded, it does not imply real parts or plurality in the Absolute but only imaginary ones. In this passage of the Chāndogya Upanishad Commentary, Śaṅkara employs arguments somewhat reminiscent of the subjective idealism found in places in the Commentary on Gauḍapāda's Kārikās.

TEXTS ON SAT-KĀRYA VĀDA

1. *Objection:* If you maintain that the Absolute is pure and void of all the great physical elements beginning with sound, and yet at the same time the (material) cause of the (world as) effect, which is of opposite nature, then the non-existence of the effect before its production would follow. And this is not acceptable to an exponent of the doctrine of the reality of the effect before production (sat-kārya vādin) like yourself.

Answer: There is nothing wrong in our position here. For, as the author of the Sūtras puts it, '(The opponent's position proceeds) from a bare negation'. For this is a bare negation, without anything to be negated. This negation cannot negate the pre-existence of the effect before its production. Why not? Because, just as, even at the present moment, the effect is real only as the cause, so was it also real as the cause before its production.

Well, but is not the cause of the world the Absolute 'void of sound and the other elements'? Yes. But it does not follow that the (world as) effect, which is associated with sound and the other elements, is void of its true nature as the cause, either before its production or at the present moment.[7]

❖

2. Another ground for the non-difference of the effect from the material cause is that the effect is only perceived in the presence of the material cause and not otherwise. For example, the pot is only perceived when the clay is present, cloth is only perceived when threads are present. When two things are different, we do not regularly see one whenever we see the other. For example, a horse is different from a cow and we do not see a horse only in the presence of a cow.[8] Nor do we see a pot *only* in the presence of a potter,[9] for the potter and the pot are different, even though they are respectively the efficient cause and the effect....

There is also an alternative version of this Sūtra, 'And because it is perceived'. That is, the non-difference of the effect from the material cause does not only follow from revelation. It also follows because it is *perceived* as non-different. And it is indeed a fact that the non-difference of the effect from the material cause is actually perceived. For example, in the case of a cloth, which is the product of threads, no effect called cloth is perceived over and above the threads themselves. All that is seen is the interwoven threads. And similarly, all that we really perceive in the threads is finer strands twisted together, and all that we see in the finer strands is their own component parts. From perceptions such as these we have to infer (that at the back of all objects lie) the three forms (i.e. the primordial elements fire, water and earth), the red, the white and the black,[10] and beyond these the (two more subtle elements, the) wind and the ether, and beyond them the supreme, the Absolute, one without a second. And this, as we have said, is the final reality to which all the various means of knowledge ultimately point.[11]

❖

3. And there is another reason why the effect must be non-different from the material cause. The Veda tells us, namely, that the future effect exists in the material cause before its production, with the nature of that cause. For in passages such as, 'In the beginning, my dear one, this was Being only' and 'In the beginning, verily, this was the Self alone'[12] the world, as effect, is designated by the word 'this' and placed in apposition with the world-cause. And that which does not already exist within anything with the nature of the latter cannot be produced from it, as one cannot squeeze oil from sand. Therefore, because the effect must have been, even prior to its production, non-different from the material cause, we conclude that it must be non-different from it also after it has been produced. And just as the cause, the Absolute, never deviated from Being in past, present or future, so the effect, too, the world, never deviates from reality in past, present or future. And Being is one. Hence this is another reason for the

non-difference of the effect from the material cause.[13]

❖

4. It follows from reasoning also, as well as from further Vedic passages, that even prior to its production, the effect both exists in, and is non-different from, its material cause. Let us begin by going over the reasoning.

We see in the world that those who want to make curds invariably first procure milk, those who want to make pots procure clay, and those who want to make ornaments procure gold. Those who want to make curds do not first procure clay, neither do those who want to make pots procure milk. On the theory (of the Vaiśeṣikas) that the effect does not pre-exist in the cause, however, this would be inexplicable. For if an effect were non-existent anywhere at all before its production, how could it happen that curds are regularly produced *only* from milk and not from clay, while pots are produced *only* from clay and not from milk?

Perhaps it will be claimed that while curds are non-existent anywhere before production, milk possesses a certain aptitude leading to the production of curds not possessed by clay, and clay a certain aptitude for yielding pots not possessed by milk. But to affirm that an aptitude for producing the effect pre-exists in the material cause before the production of the effect is to refute the doctrine of the non-existence of the effect in the material cause and confirm that of the pre-existence there of the effect....

And there is another point. If the effect did not (in some sense) pre-exist before coming into being, then there could be no entity capable of the act of coming into being, so that act could not take place. For coming into being is an act, and, as such, must have an acting entity, like the act of walking. To say that there was an act and no agent for it would be a contradiction in terms. On this basis, if one spoke of the coming into being of a pot, and the pot did not already in some sense pre-exist in order to form the agent of that act of coming into being, one would have to assume some other agent for that act in order to give the statement any sense at all. And if you said, 'It is the raw fragments of clay or other (component factors) that are coming into being (as the pot)', you will still have to look further afield for the agent in this act of coming into being too. Eventually you will find (on this theory) that when you are saying 'The pot is coming into being' you are saying that the whole complex of causes of the pot, including the potter, is coming into being. But when people say 'The pot is coming into being' we do not understand them to be saying that all the factors in the production of the pot, including the potter, are coming into being, as we assume they are already in existence.

Perhaps (in order to avoid any connotation of action) you will try to redefine 'coming into being' as a mere affirmation of the pot's coming into relation with its cause or with Being (sattā), signifying the attainment of concrete existence. But in that case you must explain how that which is not yet in concrete existence can enter into relation with anything. A relation can subsist between two existent things only, not between an existent thing and a non-existent one or between two non-existent ones. And since (the whole concept of) non-existence is unintelligible anyway, it is wrong to try to assign boundaries to it and to speak of 'non-existence prior to production'. In ordinary experience, boundaries pertain to existent things like houses and fields, not to non-existence. If anyone says, 'The son of a barren woman was king before the coronation of Pūrṇavarman',[14] a specification of that sort (apparently implying existence in past time) does not, in the case of an unintelligible being like the son of a barren woman, really specify either that he was a king or that he is king or that he will be. Of course, if the son of a barren woman could really come into being as a result of the operation of factors of action, then it might also make sense to think that a previously non-existent effect might come into existence after the operation of factors of action. But what we actually find is that the son of a barren woman and the previously non-existent effect are both equally non-entities, and for this reason neither the one nor the other will come into being as a result of the operation of any causal factors.

Objection: If what you say were true, the operation of the factors of action would be useless altogether. No action is required to establish the cause, as it is already established according to the terms of your position. Nor is any action required to establish the effect, as that, also, is already established according to the terms of your position, and is in any case non-different from the cause. And yet the fact is that action *is* required for the production of effects. So we adhere (to our doctrine of) the non-existence of the effect in the material cause prior to its production in order to explain the fact that the factors of action come into operation.

Answer: This in no way undermines our position. For the operation of the factors of action is needed to transform the material cause into the form of the effect. Even the effect-form has concrete existence through being of the very nature of the material cause, for, as has already been said, what does not have concrete existence already cannot enter into an action. And the mere perception of some distinction or other does not imply that a new substance has supervened. Devadatta may look different when he has drawn in his hands and feet from what he did when he stretched them out, but it does not follow from this that he is another being, for he is recognized as 'the same'. Similarly, it does not follow that, just because our close relatives undergo slight changes of appearance from day to day, they become different beings. For we still recognize them as 'my father', 'my brother', or 'my son' as the case may be.

Objection: Your theory applies only to those cases of causation where no changes are introduced through birth and destruction, but not to others.

Answer: No. It is a matter of ordinary perception that milk, for instance, merely assumes the form of curds. Or again, we speak of the 'germination' of a banyan tree when we mean that the seeds of a banyan tree, themselves invisible, have acquired a large increase of similar parts and come into the field of perception in the form of a sprout. And we speak of the 'destruction of the tree' as a name for the process whereby those same seeds sink back into imperceptibility through the loss of the additional parts. If birth and destruction here implied real difference, we should have to suppose that non-being could become being and being non-being, and this would imply the absurd conclusion that the new-born babe lying outstretched must be different from the unborn foetus in the womb. It would also imply that the child, the youth and the old man were different people and would undermine the notion, for instance, of a father.[15] And the arguments here given suffice also to refute the doctrine of universal momentariness.[16]

Anyone who holds to the non-existence of the effect prior to its production must also hold that the factors of action can operate without an object. As non-existence cannot possibly be the object of an act, the process (of bringing into being) would be like using an elaborate armoury of swords and other weapons to cut down the ether....

Therefore the conclusion is that it is milk and other such substances themselves which persist in new forms such as curds and the rest, and are then called 'effects'. The view that the effect is separate from the cause could not be established through arguments conducted for hundreds of years. Therefore it is the one root-cause which wears successively all the forms met with in empirical experience up to the last, like an actor dressed up for a succession of rôles. And thus reason also (besides Vedic authority) shows that, even prior to its 'production', the effect is real and non-different from the cause.[17]

❖

5. The text[18] says, 'Verily, there was nothing here in the beginning'. That is, here in the world, the sphere of transmigratory experience, there were no particulars, differentiated into name and form. 'In the beginning' means before the origination of mind and the rest (at the beginning of the present world-period).

Buddhist Nihilist: Was there just a void? There must have

been, as the text says, 'verily nothing here'. Nor was there a cause or an effect, as these depend on origination. (An effect like) a pot has to originate, has it not? Before its origination, therefore, it did not exist.

Ārambha Vādin: (Well, we can agree that the effect did not exist before it was produced, but) you cannot say that the cause did not exist, for it is perceived in the form of the lump of clay, etc. It is only that which is not apprehended that does not exist. The effect, then, may not exist before its origination. But the cause does exist before the origination of the effect, because it is apprehended.

Buddhist Nihilist: No, for before the creation (of the world) nothing was apprehended. And if the fact that we do not apprehend a thing is to be taken as a sign of its non-existence, then before the origination of the whole universe neither cause nor effect were perceived. So there must have been a total non-existence of everything.

Sat-kārya Vādin: No, for the text says, 'Verily, this was covered over by death'. If there had been nothing to be covered and nothing whereby anything could be covered, the text could not have said, 'Verily, this was covered over by death'. The son of a barren woman cannot be covered over with sky-flowers. And the text actually does say, 'Verily, this was covered over by death'. Therefore, it is clear on the authority both of the Veda and of inference that an effect existed before the origination (of the world), an effect which was (at that time) 'covered'. And there also existed a material cause, which was that by which the effect was covered.

Ārambha Vādin: The material cause of any effect must

be non-existent at the time of the production of that effect. There cannot be origination of a pot, for instance, without the destruction of the particular lump of clay from which it was made.

Sat-kārya Vādin: No, for it is the clay that is the cause. It is clay that is the material cause of the pot and gold that is the material cause of the ornament, not a particular lump-form of clay or gold, for the pot and the ornament exist when the lump-form does not. (When there is no clay or gold there can be no pot or ornament whereas) the origination of effects such as a pot or ornament can quite well take place directly from the substances clay and gold without the intervention of a particular lump-form. So it is not a particular lump-form that is the cause of the pot or ornament.... Every cause, in originating an effect, first withdraws an effect that it has previously originated and then proceeds to originate the new effect, for it would be contradictory to suppose that one could have several different effects at the same time.[19] And the destruction of the previous effect does not imply the destruction of the cause. Therefore the fact that origination of the effect is seen to be preceded by destruction of the lump, etc., is no argument for the non-existence of the cause prior to the effect.

Ārambha-Vādin: This is wrong because there is no clay (or the like) apart from the lump (or the like). It is a mistake to suppose that when the previous effect, say the lump, is destroyed, the cause, the clay, is not destroyed, on the mere ground that it endures in the effect, the pot. For no clay is perceived as cause apart from the succession of effects such as the lump and the pot, etc.

Sat-kārya Vādin: No, for it is seen, on the origination, for instance, of a pot, that the cause, such as the clay, endures, while the lump or the like is destroyed.

Buddhist: The notion of continuity here is due to similarity and not to any real persistence on the part of the cause.[20]

Sat-kārya Vādin: No, for since the same parts of clay that were in the lump are actually *perceived* again in the pot, there is no room for assuming similarity on the basis of mere fallacious inferences. Nor can inference possibly contradict perception, for it depends on perception, and to suppose that it could contradict it would imply total disbelief in any empirical knowledge whatever.

Buddhist: Everything is momentary (and therefore *sui generis*) and knowable as 'this is that and that alone'.

Sat-kārya Vādin: In this case, the interpretation of the notion 'that' would depend on some other notion, and this in turn on some further notion and so on in infinite regress. And then the very notion 'This is like that' would itself be false, so that one would be landed in total scepticism. Nor could the (necessarily successive) notions 'this' and 'that' be in any way related, for lack of a durable personage to entertain them concurrently.

Buddhist: They must be related from the mere fact of being similar.

Sat-kārya Vādin: No, for the two notions 'this' and 'that' cannot take cognizance of each other mutually, and where this is absent there cannot be perception of similarity.

Buddhist: Even though there was no real similarity, there might be the notion of similarity.

Sat-kārya Vādin: No. For this would imply that the objects of the notions 'this' and 'that' were themselves unreal, just as the notion of their similarity was.

Buddhist: Well, let us suppose that the objects of all notions are unreal.

Sat-kārya Vādin: No. For then the very notion of a notion would have no real object.

Buddhist: Let us suppose that it does not.

Sat-kārya Vādin: No. For if all notions were false, the notion of unreality itself would be untenable. So the claim that the notion of the persistence of the cause is due to similarity is wrong. And the real existence of the cause prior to the origination of the effect stands proved.

Moreover, the real existence of the effect prior to its origination is also proved by the fact that the effect is only of the nature of a manifestation. Manifestation means becoming an object of direct apprehension (vijñāna). Take the case in ordinary worldly experience of some object like a pot hidden in darkness. If the covering of darkness is removed by a light and it suddenly becomes an object of concrete apprehension, this does not mean that it was not existent before. And we see that the same is true in regard to this world. For a pot that is actually non-existent cannot be seen even after the sun has risen.

Critic of Sat-kārya Vāda: No, for (according to your own, absurd, theory) it would be seen. For according to you there is no such thing as non-existence. You do not admit that any effect, such as a pot, was ever non-existent. So even a non-existent pot would be seen when the sun had risen. For as soon as the lump-form of the clay is removed or the darkness or other covering comes to an end, the pot stands evident.

Sat-kārya Vādin: No, for there are two quite distinct kinds of concealment to which an effect like a pot may be subjected. When the pot has already manifested out of the clay, the concealing factor is (external) like darkness or an intervening wall, etc. But before it has manifested from the clay, it is the arrangement of the parts of the clay in the form of some other effect, such as a lump, that forms the concealment. Thus, before origination a pot or other such effect exists, but it is not perceived because it is concealed. It is said or supposed to be either destroyed or produced, existent or non-existent. But the choice between these epithets and notions depends in reality on the choice between 'manifest' and 'hidden'.

Critic of Sat-kārya Vāda: This is wrong, because the lump of clay or raw fragments from which it is formed are something different from a mere concealment. External factors which obstruct the perception of a pot, such as darkness or an intervening wall, are seen to occupy a certain portion of space different from that of the pot. But this is not the case with the lump or the raw fragments of clay. Therefore it is quite wrong to say that the reason why the pot is not perceived prior to its origination is the fact that it is concealed by other forms of the clay, such as the lump or raw fragments. For the nature of the concealment is different in the two cases.

Sat-kārya Vādin: Not so. For we see, for instance, in the

case of milk obscuring the water in which it has been diluted, that the milk, the concealing factor, occupies the same space as the water.

Critic of Sat-kārya Vāda: But still, in the case of an effect like a pot, the clay-fragments and powdered clay, etc., cannot actually conceal the pot, for they are in it.

Sat-kārya Vādin: Not so. They can very well conceal the pot. For, being *different* effects (of the clay), they are (in some sense) different from the pot.

Critic of Sat-kārya Vāda: Well, if that were true, one's efforts (in regard to producing the effect) should be limited to removing the concealment. That is to say, if the pot were really present in the lump and in the raw fragments and *only* unperceived because concealed, the one who wanted a pot would simply set about destroying the concealment. But this is not what actually happens. So the statement that the pot exists (prior to its 'production'), and is just not perceived because it is concealed, is wrong.

Sat-kārya Vādin: Not so. For there is no universal rule to show that, (if pre-existent in the material cause) the pot could be brought into manifestation only by the (negative) efforts made towards the destruction of the concealment. For example, when a pot or other such effect is concealed by darkness, we see that (positive) efforts are made to procure a lamp.

Critic of Sat-kārya Vāda: Well, but that is only to destroy the darkness. The positive effort towards procuring a lamp, we repeat, is only to destroy the darkness. When that is destroyed, the pot is perceived automatically. No positive contribution is made thereby towards the 'production' of the pot.

Sat-kārya Vādin: Not so, for the pot is perceived as possessed of light. When a lamp has been procured, the pot is perceived as invested with light, whereas before the procuring of the lamp it was not so (i.e. it was not invested with light). So the lamp is procured, not only to remove the darkness but also to confer light on the pot. For it is perceived only when it is invested with light.

There are also cases where the efforts are solely directed towards destruction of the concealment, as in the case when, in order to perceive some object, one destroys an intervening wall or the like. But all this goes to show that (according to our own principles) there is no universal rule that one who wants to bring anything into manifestation has only to engage in destruction.

Moreover, the universal rule that positive creative action is required (to bring the pre-existent effect into manifestation) is intelligible. We have already said that one effect abiding in a cause stands as a covering hiding other effects. This being so, if one's sole efforts were directed towards the destruction of the previously manifested effect, the lump or the raw fragments that formed an obstruction, one would be left with a new effect in the form of powdered clay. And as the pot would not be manifest through this, it follows that something further (apart from mere destruction) is required to manifest the pot. So the universal rule that he who wishes to bring into manifestation a pot or the like must resort to the factors of positive, creative action is intelligible. And thus it is that, even before its positive, creative action is intelligible. And thus it is that, even before its origination, the pot must exist (or otherwise it could not be the object of an act).

And there is another reason, deriving from the difference between the notions of the pot in the present and in the past. We have the ideas 'the pot in the past' and 'the pot in the future'. These ideas can no more be without a (real external) object than the notion 'The pot exists now'. The same thing follows from the fact that people act for the sake of a future pot. No-one in the world is seen to act for the sake of something non-existent. Moreover, yogins possess knowledge of the past and future. And if the future pot were unreal, the direct perception of it possessed by the Lord (īśvara)[21] would be false (which is absurd). Nor is this power of perception a mere figure of speech. For we have already given reasons for supposing that the future pot really does exist now.

And there is another argument showing the pre-existence of the effect before its production, derived from the absurdity of supposing otherwise. Potters engaging in activity for the sake of a pot do so with the conviction based on sound evidence 'There will be a pot'. To say that the pot would be non-existent at the time predicted for its existence would be a complete contradiction. It would be like saying 'This pot (existent here) does not exist'. Of course, if, when the potter and his instruments are in course of work to produce the pot, you say, 'The pot is non-existent before origination' and by using the word 'non-existent' only means that the pot is not existent in the sense that the potter and his instruments are, there is no contradiction between us. For the pot exists only in its future (i.e. potential) form. The present existence of the lump or of the raw fragments does not imply the present existence of the pot. Nor does the fact that the pot has now a (potential) future existence imply that that of the lump and of the raw fragments is of the same kind. Therefore there is no contradiction (of our position) if you say, while the activity of the potter with his materials and instruments is still in progress, that the pot is not existent before its production. If, however, you were to deny that (at that stage) the pot had *future* existence, then such a denial *would* constitute a contradiction (of our position). But you do not make this denial. Nor is there any rule that everything relating to an action should either have present existence (only) or future existence (only).

Again, of the four kinds of non-existence of a pot,[22] mutual non-existence (i.e. the mutual exclusion subsisting between it and any other object) is found to be different from the pot. A cloth, for instance, which represents the non-existence of a pot understood in this sense, is not itself non-existent, even though it represents the non-existence of the pot. On the contrary, it is something positively existent. And in the same way, the previous non-existence of the pot, the non-existence of the pot on its destruction and the absolute non-existence of the pot are also different from the pot. For they are referred to in relation to the pot, just like that which is the non-existence of the pot by mutual exclusion. This being so, to assert the previous non-existence of the pot does not amount to asserting that the pot does not exist at all before coming into manifestation, (since a *relation* with the pot has been asserted, and a relation can only subsist between two real terms).

Or, if you contend that a reference to the previous non-existence of the pot is a reference to the pot itself, you must explain in what sense you mean this. For if the phrase refers directly to the pot, it is hard to explain the meaning of the words 'of the pot' (which imply something different from the pot itself but relating to it). Perhaps you will say that it is a mere fiction, as when one says 'the body of the stone figure' (when the stone figure itself *is* the body). But in that case when you spoke of the 'non-existence of the pot prior to its production' you would not be referring to the true nature of the pot. You would be (implicitly assuming the existence of the pot because) referring *through* the pot to a purely fictional non-existence.

If, on the other hand, you say that the non-existence of the pot is something other than the pot, then the answer to this has already been given.[23]

And again, if before its origination the pot were completely non-existent like the horns of a hare, it could not come into relation with Being, its cause. For a relation requires two (real) terms. Nor will it help to invoke 'inseparable relation' (ayuta-siddhi), for this cannot subsist between the existent and the non-existent.[24] Two existents may be said to be either available separately or to stand in inseparable relation, but not either an existent and a non-existent or two non-existents. So it stands proved that the effect must be real (in the form of the cause) before its origination.[25]

❖

6. *Objection:* Even those who affirm pure Being cannot give an example of the real arising from the real. One does not see one pot arising from another pot.[26]

Answer: Quite right. No new reality springs up from another reality. What, then, does happen? The one Being persists under a different configuration. It is like a snake assuming coils. Or like clay assuming different successive forms such as powder, lump, pot or potsherds.

Perhaps you will say: If Being is only what persists under forms, what can it mean to say that there was Being before the rise of the world? To this we ask, in reply, whether you heard the specification 'only' in the text 'Being *only*, (my dear one)'?[27]

Objection: Well, in that case the effect proceeding from Being denoted by the word 'this' will have been non-existent before production, and the text will mean that what is called 'this' (i.e. the universe as effect) did not exist then and has come into existence now.

Answer: No, for it is always some determination of Being only that is referred to by the notion and term 'this', just as it is only clay in some determination that persists ultimately as the common meaning of the notions and terms 'lump' and 'pot', etc.

Objection: The lump and the pot are (separate) realities, just as much as the clay is. In the same way, the universe as effect is the object of a different notion from the notion of Being. So the whole realm of universe as effect must constitute another reality existing over and against Being, separate from it as cow is separate from horse.

Answer: No. The lump and the pot exclude one another mutually, while both constantly remaining clay. When there is pot there is no lump and when there is lump there is no pot, but neither the lump nor the pot excludes the clay. Therefore the lump and the pot are nothing but clay. There may be cow without horse or horse without cow. But the pot, etc., are but configurations of clay. Thus, on the principle that all this universe of effects is but a configuration of Being, it was but right to say that 'Being only' existed at the beginning. Modifications and configurations are mere (notions arising from the) activity of speech.

Objection: How can there be modifications and configurations of Being, when it is known to be partless from such Vedic texts as 'Partless, actionless, at rest, faultless, taintless'?[28]

Answer: There is nothing wrong. For modifications and configurations can very well arise from parts of Being that have been imagined by the mind, just as configurations like snake arise from parts mentally imagined in the rope. For the Veda says, 'A modification is the object of a name, a mere activity of speech; the truth is, "There is only clay"'.[29] From the standpoint of the final truth, there is only one without a second even at the time of (the appearance of) this universe of effects.[30]

2. Name and Form: Indeterminability

It seems worth trying to say something about the use of the term 'name and form' in earlier times as an introduction to Śaṅkara's use of it. Mention has been made of the tendency in the texts called the Brāhmaṇas to discern different planes of existence and to seek for hidden correspondences between phenomena pertaining to different planes.[31] This mode of thought helped to promote a power to make philosophic abstractions that modified and added a new depth to the mythologizing tendency of the Vedic period. What was many on the plane of ordinary physical experience could be considered as one on the divine or cosmic plane. Thus death was many in so far as it entered living beings at the time of their demise, but one as an immutable spirit abiding in the sun.[32] Later it would be said that just as there must be a transcendent Self behind the various powers of the individual's mind and body, holding them together, so there must be a unitary Self behind the cosmos holding *it* together. And as each individual has a mind and an ego-sense, so the one all-embracing cosmos has its all-embracing Cosmic Mind and Cosmic Ego-sense. And just as every individual object consists basically in name and form, so the cosmos as a whole consists basically of the modifications of one cosmic principle, Name and Form.

Many students of Advaita first meet with the concept of 'name and form' as it appears in the texts of Śaṅkara's later followers, where the perishable and pluralistic 'names and forms' (plural) of the objects of the world are contrasted with the non-duality and permanence of the Absolute. This is, indeed, a fair representation of the meaning of the term in some places in Śaṅkara's texts. But it is worth noting that he much more commonly uses the term in the singular in the same way as it is used in the older texts, where it implies a kind of unitary entity that unfolds into the many names and forms of the pluralistic universe. Śaṅkara distinguishes between the unmanifest or seed condition of name and form before the beginning of a new world-period (kalpa) and their manifest form as the totality of the phenomena of the world. In their unmanifest form, where they stand as the material cause of the world, Śaṅkara identifies them with certain other concepts. Some of these, such as akṣara, avyakta, avyākṛta, ākāśa, derive from the Upanishads; others, such as mahā-supti, māyā, avidyā, śakti, māyā-śakti, daivī-śakti, tamas and nidrā suggest, in the present context, Epic or Purāṇa sources.

It is remarkable that in this context Śaṅkara identifies avidyā and māyā, and both terms appear among the synonyms standing for the material cause of the world. But except where they appear among lists of synonyms for name and form in their unmanifest state, the terms avidyā and māyā have their separate functions in Śaṅkara's system, and are not usually interchangeable. The meanings of avidyā have already been shown above in Volume I, Chapter II, and those of māyā in the present volume, Chapter V, section 5, above.

Where the term 'māyā', used on its own, refers to the creative power of the Lord, it has a material aspect and may be regarded as the material cause of the world. But this is less true of nescience. The latter is the fateful condition (avasthā) of ignorance of the true nature of the Self, followed by false superimposition, that gives rise to a world and worldly experience. It is the precondition for the possibility of *any* appearance, including that of a material cause. The unmanifest name and form are called 'a seed-power of the nature of nescience',[34] which suggests material causality. But they are also 'imagined through nescience'.[35] It is not possible to explain the causality of nescience on the exact analogy of any form of causality found within the world-appearance.

As for the formula 'name and form', Śaṅkara took it over from the Upanishads. Certain pre-upanishadic texts describe how the first self-projection of the creator-god was chaotic, but how he then entered into his chaotic projection to unfold name and form, that is, to organize it into a world of distinct, durable and nameable objects.[36] This idea re-appears in the older texts of the upanishadic period in modified form.[37] Commenting on Chāndogya VIII.xiv.1, Śaṅkara says that name and form are the seed of the world (jagad-bīja) and exist hidden and latent in the Absolute, like foam lying latent in water. Commenting on Chāndogya VI.iii.2, he enquires into the meaning of the phrase 'Let Me bring into manifestation name and form'. It cannot mean that He creates them *ex nihilo*, as that would contradict the Sat-kārya Vāda theory of causality that, as we have just seen in the previous section, can alone relate the phenomena of the world to their transcendent source. So to bring name and form into manifestation means to allow them to emerge from their seed-condition and to separate out into the world of distinct objects with their different names. In Saṅkara's own words, manifesting name and form means bringing them 'into manifestation as "this has such and such a name and has such and such a form".' Name is what is heard and form is what is seen, but Śaṅkara says that the phrase 'name and form' includes the objects of the other senses also by extension.[38]

The distinction between unmanifest and manifest name and form, all but lost in Śaṅkara's successors, is fundamental for Śaṅkara himself. If Śaṅkara's later successors were primarily metaphysicians and theorists of illusion, he was primarily a commentator on the ancient texts. In this capacity his task was to harmonize texts that had arisen at widely separated intervals of time in response to different needs. The conception of unmanifest name and form enabled him to preserve the doctrine of world-periods which he accepted from the Epics, Purāṇas and Brahma Sūtras, and the doctrine of the reality of the effect in or as the cause (Sat-kārya Vāda) which he had also inherited from the Brahma Sūtras, and to ally these doctrines with the creation-texts of a less sophisticated period, when the sages still sought for an origin or beginning of the world and had not yet come to the conclusion that it was a beginningless process.

The ancient texts could say, without inhibition, 'In truth, all this, at the beginning, was ether about to assume manifestation.... This "all" was... without distinctions. He made name and form and thereby introduced distinctions'.[39] But this conception would not do for Śaṅkara exactly as it stands. As we have already seen,[40] the Self could not be the eternal Lord unless the unmanifest seed of name and form were already present *before* the projection of the world for Him to be Lord over. Through this distinction between the unmanifest seed state of name and form and their subsequent deployment into the objects of the world, Śaṅkara is able to accommodate the theory of world-periods and the doctrine of the pre-existence of the effect in the material cause (Sat-kārya Vāda) to the old upanishadic teaching. Extract 11 below epitomizes Śaṅkara's teaching on this point.

Nevertheless, Śaṅkara does somewhat modify the old upanishadic teaching. In the upanishadic form of the doctrine, what are initially projected are the primordial elements in the form of deities, and Being enters into *them* to organize them and *introduce* name and form. In Śaṅkara's form of the doctrine, name and form in their unmanifest state are the truly primordial factor, since they are somehow objects of the Lord's omniscient knowledge before the manifestation of anything at all at the beginning of the world-period. Nevertheless, the distinction between unmanifest and manifest name and form enables Śaṅkara to preserve the upanishadic doctrine that Being enters the creation that it has projected and manifests name and form. He explains 'entering' as a metaphorical expression for 'being already present in',[41] and the unmanifest name and form are developed, through the 'entry' of Being, into manifest name and form, which latter, as an ancient Vedic text has said, are co-extensive with the universe. In fact, for Śaṅkara, name and form *constitute* the objects of the world.[42] He says, 'Apart from the

Absolute, nothing else differs from name and form, since all modifications are but manifestations of name and form'.[43] As constituting the objects of the world, name and form may sometimes be given a plural inflection as 'names and forms'.[44]

At the time of the earlier Vedic texts, the name was not yet separated in thought from the object it denoted and conceived as a mere conventional sign used to denote it. The name of the object was still regarded as a constituent element of the object itself, just as the form was.[45] Chāndogya VI.iii.2, the upanishadic passage on which Śaṅkara bases his own conception of name and form, still follows this archaic mode of thought. But the upanishadic text just referred to comes down embedded in a much more sophisticated body of teaching, according to which all forms are in some sense the mere creation of name. In the pre-upanishadic traditions about name and form, texts can be found in which the form is glorified above the name.[46] And the two stages of teaching imply a different evaluation of name and form. In the older texts, name and form lend stability, order and duration to objects, draw a cosmos out of chaos. When Being enters the 'deities (elements) with name and form', He confers a favour, so to speak, on living beings, by assuring them the use and enjoyment of durable objects. But this high valuation of name and form implied by the old creation myth preserved in the Chāndogya Upanishad is modified by the more rationalist tone of the doctrines of Uddālaka Āruṇi in which it is found embedded. Name and form are here the fleeting insubstantial appearances that hide the true face and immortality of Being, the illusion that has to be overcome if one's true nature as immortal infinite Consciousness is to be known. And it is this later conception of name and form that is typical of the upanishadic period.[47]

Where 'a modification is a mere activity of speech', a form is clearly dependent on a name, and Śaṅkara seems in some places to uphold this doctrine explicitly.[48] But Śaṅkara did not want the idea to be taken too literally. For instance, he does not seem to have upheld the idea that the objects of the world have the words of the Veda for their material cause, as if the whole world-process consisted in the vibrations and reverberations set up by the utterances of the primaeval creative principle sound. In one text (Extract 16 below) he reduces all objects to names and all names to the holy syllable OM. But here he is concerned not with the attribution of creative power to the physical vibrations of the syllable OM, but with the reduction of objects to illusion. The explanation follows the line not of the ancient texts that proclaimed that the objects of the world came forth from the texts of the Veda, but the sceptical line of the teachings of Uddālaka. Objects are illusions, entirely dependent on their names. They are the mere illusory appearance of a plurality of isolated units in the Absolute that results from the arbitrary activity of naming. In this sense, the object is entirely dependent for its existence on, and therefore identical with, its name. And the name, too, is an illusion. For all modifications of sound are reducible to the one basic sound, OM. And, as will become clear in Volume VI, Chapter XV, section 5, below, the syllable OM itself is ultimately reduced to the Absolute, which has no empirical features and certainly does not consist of a plurality of four component elements like the vocalized syllable OM. So what we have here is not a theory of the creative power of sound in which words are regarded as the subtle vibrations from which gross objects come forth, but a resolute reduction of all plurality to illusion on the lines of Uddālaka. A similar view is also found at Extract 17, where Śaṅkara reduces all words to the principle speech (Vāc), and reduces Vāc to the Absolute. In this case, what was originally a doctrine describing creation is reduced to a doctrine of illusion.

Śaṅkara's cosmological teaching, as we know, was provisional. While still under the influence of nescience and working for liberation, the student must be made to see that all the traditional texts are helpful and significant at their own particular level, even though destined to be superseded by 'Not thus, not thus' in the end. Thus Uddālaka was right to maintain that an object can only come into being at all as a result of an arbitrary (and illusory) piece of isolation effected in the massed identity of the Absolute by the application of a name. On the other hand, the Mīmāṃsakas were also right to hold that a name could only function as a name if it had an eternal, innate connection with its meaning. At the beginning of the world-period, Prajāpati, the deity presiding over creation, proceeds to bring unmanifest name and form into manifestation. The eternal texts of the Veda are in his 'mind', but the ultimate conditioning force in the bringing to manifestation of unmanifest name and form is the deeds and thoughts of living beings in previous world-periods.[49] Name, form and action are all said to condition one another mutually,[50] while the fact that they do so is said, at Extract 15, to prove their mutual relativity and consequent unreality. Thus the shell of the ancient myths about creation is retained, but they are deprived of their original content and meaning in the light of the illusionistic teachings of a later epoch.

But quite apart from theological considerations, speculation about name and form was important to Śaṅkara from the purely philosophical point of view, as it involved a key point in his system. The basic factors of that system were the Absolute and nescience, the latter accounting for the empirical fact that the true nature of the Absolute is hidden, plus the results of that occlusion in the form of the various false imaginations that go to make up worldly experience. But worldly experience involves a world, and a world is composed of matter, and neither the Absolute nor nescience can be taken as the material cause of the world. The Absolute cannot be the material cause of the world on the exact analogy of material causes found within the world-appearance, for it undergoes no modification or change. Neither can nescience fulfil this function, because Śaṅkara did not conceive it as a thing or substance on the analogy of material causes in the world. His way of putting it is to say that the

Absolute appears in worldly experience to undergo modification on account of external adjuncts consisting of name and form which are imagined through nescience and have an unmanifest and a manifest state.[51] Elaborate expressions of this kind are not uncommon in Śaṅkara,[52] and they tend to state that the external adjuncts that make worldly experience possible have their material cause in name and form which in turn are conditioned by nescience. Thus the external adjuncts through which the Absolute appears to undergo modification and stand as the material cause of the world themselves have a material cause in name and form. And it is of importance to Śaṅkara to establish with care the exact nature of the relation between the Absolute and the material cause of these adjuncts, because he has to do justice to the plurality of our world of empirical experience, while at the same time steering a safe course between the Scylla of imputing activity or change to the Absolute and the Charybdis of admitting a second (dualistic) principle over against it. He answers this problem through appeal to the principle of the indeterminable (anirvacanīya).

Professor Hacker has drawn attention to the four occasions where the term anirvacanīya occurs in Śaṅkara's Brahma Sūtra Commentary,[53] to which must be added the appearance of the same term at Upadeśa Sāhasrī (prose) section 18 and at Bṛhadāraṇyaka Bhāṣya II.iv.10.[54] These are the only six places where the term anirvacaniya occurs in Śaṅkara's probably authentic works. Unfortunately, commentators and translators have disagreed with one another over its meaning, and several of them have given different interpretations of it at different places.

Of the three usual interpretations, the commonest is really only a reading back into Śaṅkara's phrase 'tattvānyatvābhyām anirvacanīya' (literally, indeterminable as a 'that' or an 'other') of the phrase 'sadasadbhyām anirvacanīya' (indeterminable as existent or non-existent) which he himself never used, but which is found in the Brahma Siddhi of his contemporary Maṇḍana Miśra, and which became the standard doctrine of the 'indeterminable' (anirvacanīya) in Śaṅkara's school from the time of Vimuktātman on. As Maṇḍana Miśra states and attacks the doctrine in its application to the theory of error in his Mimāṃsaka work called the Vibhrama Viveka,[55] known to have been composed before the Brahma Siddhi, it is clear that it was current amongst Advaitins before Śaṅkara's day, so that the fact that it does not appear in the latter's pages is perhaps a sign that he wished to avoid it deliberately. 'Neither real nor unreal' was, after all, a term that for him applied to the Absolute, so that he may not have wanted to extend it to nescience as well.[56]

It will be enough to sketch in an account of Maṇḍana's use of the phrase 'sadasadbhyām anirvacanīya' in the Brahma Siddhi[57] to show that the conception of the indeterminable embodied there is not quite the same as the 'indeterminable' that was of interest to Śaṅkara as evidenced by the Extracts below. Maṇḍana begins by referring to an opinion according to which, if the Absolute were something that had to be 'realized', it must be something that has to be brought into being. For if it already existed, the argument runs, this would render the Veda's teaching about realizing it useless. The Advaitin naturally replies that the Absolute is eternally existent but that ignorance (avidyā) of the Absolute is the enemy that has to be destroyed with the aid of the upanishadic texts. The opponent then replies that, in that case, ignorance of the Absolute must itself either be part of the nature of the Absolute or else something different. If it is neither part of the Absolute's nature nor anything different from the Absolute, then what could it be to need destruction? Nor will it do to say that ignorance of the Absolute is the mere negation, 'non-knowledge', and hence existent and yet not a second positive reality over against the Absolute. For if ignorance were conceived as mere 'non-knowledge' it would always be automatically annulled by knowledge, and the Absolute is omniscient.

To all this and more the Advaitin finally gives his reply. Ignorance is not of the nature of the Absolute, nor is it a second *real* principle. It is not absolutely existent or absolutely non-existent. That is why it is labelled 'an illusion' (māyā) and a 'false appearance'. If it were the true nature of anything, then, whether the true nature of the thing were taken as identical with the thing or as something over and above it, ignorance would be a truth and therefore not ignorance. If, on the other hand, it were *absolutely* non-existent, it would be like a sky-flower, something that never impinged on us in experience. In this case it would not *need* to be got rid of, and the whole doctrine would render the Upanishads useless. And so we have to say that nescience is indeterminable either as totally existent or as totally non-existent. Thus the 'indeterminability' of nescience not only explains how nescience is not a second real thing over against the Absolute but also how it can be brought to an end and why it needs to be. Had ignorance been real, it would not only have been a second thing over against the Absolute but also impossible to be got rid of. Had it been absolutely unreal, it would not have impinged on us in experience and so would have caused no 'headache'. The empirical fact of suffering would have been left unexplained, and the theory would have implied that the Veda, or at least the upanishadic part of it, was useless.

Here, surely, are the main features of the standard post-Śaṅkara theory of the indeterminable, which modern translators of the Brahma Sūtra Commentary have often been ready to read back into Śaṅkara's words. But if the six places in which Śaṅkara actually uses the word 'indeterminable'[58] be examined, it will be found that Śaṅkara's concern is really with a slightly different problem. In all six places where he uses the phrase 'tattvānyatvābhyām anirvacanīya' he applies it not directly to nescience but to name and form. In four of them he applies it to name and form in their unmanifest state, and in the other two[59] he is concerned with their transition from the unmanifest to the manifest state. In the case of Maṇḍana and of Śaṅkara's followers from the time of Vimuktātman on, the term 'indeterminable' occurs in the context of trying to reconcile the pain inflicted by nescience, and hence the utility of the Upanishads in providing the knowledge that will abolish it, with the omniscience and non-duality of the Absolute. Empirical errors were explained on the basis of their 'indeterminability' and the world-illusion was explained on the analogy of empirical errors. But in the case of Śaṅkara the term is used in a slightly different context, the context of cosmogony, of explaining how a world could *arise*, of *what the world could be made from* if we are not to admit the existence of a second reality over against the Absolute or that the Absolute can undergo change or that the world can come into being from nothing. In short, Śaṅkara's concern in his use of the term 'indeterminable' is to show how the world-appearance could have assumed phenomenal existence; Maṇḍana uses it in the course of showing how it can and must be brought to an end.

It is Professor Hacker who has drawn the attention of modern scholars to the fact that Śaṅkara uses the term 'indeterminable' in the context of problems of cosmogony, and not of defining the reality-grade of nescience, in such a way as to preserve both the non-duality of the Absolute and the significance and utility of the upanishadic teachings on liberation. The fact that there was a difference between Śaṅkara's use of the term and that of Maṇḍana and of the main stream of teaching in Śaṅkara's own school has not, however, passed entirely unnoticed in India itself,[60] even though the general tendency there (as elsewhere) has been to read back the conception of the indeterminable found amongst Śaṅkara's followers into his own texts.

Even when it is realized that the term occurs in Śaṅkara in the context of problems of cosmogony, however, difficulties about its exact interpretation remain. The classical sub-commentators on the Brahma Sūtra Commentary interpret it, where they notice it, as 'neither identical with the Absolute nor different'. Professor Hacker, however, fixes attention on the term where it appears at Brahma

Sūtra Commentary I.iv.3 *ad init.* (see Extract 10 below), where the sub-commentators are silent, and claims that the term here stands too far removed in the text from any words meaning the Absolute or the Lord to justify us *on purely grammatical grounds* in interpreting it as meaning 'neither identical with the Absolute nor different' — although, for a reason to be explained later, that has in fact been the interpretation adopted in the present book. Śaṅkara in this passage ostensibly applies the term 'indeterminable' to Māyā, but if the Extract be considered as a whole and compared with the other previous Extracts containing the word 'indeterminable', it will be seen that the reference is really to name and form in their unmanifest state. These form the power (śakti) through which the Lord creates the world, and they are sometimes spoken of in the ancient texts as Māyā and as Prakṛti or referred to by other such names.

Professor Hacker makes the interesting claim that Śaṅkara is saying at the end of Extract 10 (here translated a little differently) that Māyā is unmanifest because it cannot be described as a definite reality (tat) or as anything else. Even in the earlier passage at Brahma Sūtra I.i.5,[61] though Gambhīrānanda and Thibaut (presumably following Ānandagiri) interpret the phrase as meaning 'neither identical with the Absolute nor different', Professor Hacker is able to point to the fact that Śaṅkara speaks of name and form as unmanifest but tending towards manifestation, 'about to manifest'. He thinks that the term 'indeterminable' in Śaṅkara expresses the instability of the primary matter of the world in its unmanifest state. You cannot say that it has reality (tattva), as it is not yet anything definite. Yet you cannot say that it is anything other than a reality, because if nothing existed there would be nothing for the world to evolve from, and this view is unacceptable to an adherent of Sat-kārya Vāda. Professor Hacker thinks the term 'probably' has this meaning at all four of its appearances in the Brahma Sūtra Commentary. Where, as at Brahma Sūtra Commentary II.i.27, a reference to the manifest state of name and form is included, this is to be explained on the basis of the law of the pre-existence of the effect in the cause (Sat-kārya Vāda), where the manifest state would be in some sense identifiable with the unmanifest state. The passage from Śaṅkara's Commentary to Chāndogya Upanishad VI.ii.1 to be quoted below as Extract 9 could be seen as supporting an interpretation of this kind. Professor Hacker has drawn attention to the parallel between Śaṅkara's conception of the indeterminable, as he interprets it, and the opening phrase of the Creation Hymn of the Ṛg Veda, 'There was not the existent or the non-existent then'.[62] There are references to this parallel in the later Advaita literature. Thus Prakāśātman says that Māyā is not real from the standpoint of the highest truth 'because the Vedic text "There was not the existent or the non-existent then, there was darkness", proclaims that in its primordial (seed) condition the world was neither existent nor non-existent and inexplicable'.[63]

However, while Professor Hacker was undoubtedly right in pointing out a certain difference between Śaṅkara's use of the term indeterminable and that of his followers from the time of Vimuktātman on (the term is variously used by Maṇḍana), his own explanation of it is not entirely satisfactory. It was based on an examination of its four appearances in the Brahma Sūtra Commentary only. It seems, however, that the references to foam and water at Upadeśa Sāhasrī (prose) section 19 (Extract 1 below), especially when taken together with several other references to foam and water occurring in various other Extracts, force us to interpret the term 'indeterminable' as 'indeterminable as either different from or identical with the Absolute' in those cases where it occurs in association with foam and water, for example in both of the cases that fall outside the Brahma Sūtra Commentary. This once admitted, it is arguable that one should interpret the term the same way throughout. This has been the line followed in the present book.

The Extracts to follow illustrate points raised in the preceding paragraphs. Like all other doctrines, the doctrine of name and form as constituting the world-seed is provisional only, and the last four Extracts (14-17) concentrate on the illusory character of the world, dependent for its existence on name as a mere 'activity of speech'.

TEXTS ON NAME AND FORM AND INDETERMINABILITY

1. When the pupil has recalled the characteristics of the supreme Self, the Teacher should proceed: 'He it is whose name is ether, who is other than name and form, who is bodiless... who, by the unthinkable power inherent in His mere existence, is the Bringer into Manifestation of unmani-fest name and form, which have characteristics different from the Absolute, their true Self, which are the seed of the universe (jagad-bīja), which rest in Him as their Self, which are not determinable (anirvacanīya) either as the real principle itself (tattva) or as anything different (anyatva), and which are known as objects by Him.

This name and form, being originally unmanifest, manifested out of this Self in the name and form of the 'ether' (ākāśa). And, in this way, the element (bhūta) called 'the ether' was born from the supreme Self, like the impure (cloudy) foam from clear water, and yet it is not completely different from water, for it is never found apart from water. But water is clear and different from foam, which is of the nature of impurity. In the same way, the supreme Self is different from name and form, which answer to foam in the example. For it is pure and clear and of a different nature. Those two, name and form, being first unmanifest, are afterwards brought out into manifestation as the name and form of the ether. They correspond to foam in the illustration.

Becoming progressively grosser and grosser in nature, name and form assume the form first of air, then from air they become fire, from fire water, from water earth. In this way, with each previous state of name and form entering into the next one in a definite order, the great elements (mahābhūta) are produced, ending with earth.[64]

❖

2. *Objection:* Is it not a fact that builders and so on require material and so on before they can construct a house or the like? How can the Self construct the worlds if He has no material with which to do so?

Answer: This does not detract from our position. For unmanifest name and form, which *are* the Self in the sense that foam lying latent and potential in the water *is* the water, and which (in their unmanifest state) cannot be called anything but the Self, can well stand as the material cause of the universe, which would correspond (in the illustration) to the foam as brought out from latency into manifestation. So there is nothing contradictory in saying that the Omniscient One created the universe. For He Himself is the material cause as name and form, which are (nothing but) Himself.[65]

❖

3. Name and form, imagined through nescience as if they were the very nature of the Omniscient Lord, indeterminable either as the real principle or as anything (independent and) different from it, the seed of transmigratory experience and the

differentiated world, are spoken of in the Veda and the traditional literature as 'The Power of Māyā (māyā-śakti) belonging to the omniscient Lord' and as 'Nature' (prakṛti).[66]

❖

4. The context shows that the reference in verse IV.5 of the Śvetāśvatara Upanishad is to that same divine power (śakti) in which name and form are not yet manifest, that is to say, to name and form in their primaeval form before manifestation.[67]

❖

5. The modification and distribution of form is dependent on the light (prakāśa) of name. Name and form, indeed, constitute, in their various conditions, the whole world of transmigratory experience. They are the (most immediate) adjuncts (upādhi) of the supreme Self. When brought into manifestation, they are indeterminable either as the real principle itself (tattva) or as anything different (anyatva), just as foam is indeterminable either as water or as anything different. That is why it is said (in the text) 'Name was breathed forth (in the form of a manifestation of the Vedic texts)'. And it follows from that statement that the other (i.e. form) was also breathed forth.[68]

❖

6. (The upanishadic text under comment begins: 'OM! In the beginning, verily, all this was the Self, one only'.) The Self is called 'Ātman' either because it is all-pervading (deriving the word ātman from the verb āp, āpnoti), or because it destroys (deriving it from at, atti, meaning 'eats') or because it is infinite (deriving it from aṭ, aṭati, meaning 'wanders').[69]

It is supreme, omniscient, free from all empirical defects like hunger and thirst, pure, enlightened and liberated, unborn, immortal, fearless, without a second. Before the initial projection of the world at the beginning of the world-period, this world, already referred to (i.e. in the preceding portion of the Aitareya Āraṇyaka in which the Aitareya Upanishad is embedded), which is differentiated into diverse names and forms and acts, was none other than the Self.

You will ask, 'Is it not one with the Self even now?' We reply that it is. You will ask, 'How, then, can you say it *was* one with the Self?' We reply that, even though it is still one with the Self, there is nevertheless a difference. Before the projection of the world it had no manifest distinction into name and form. It *was* the Self. It could only be thought of and spoken of as the Self. *Now* it is characterized by manifest distinctions of name and form. It can now *either* be thought of and spoken of in a variety of ways, *or else* thought of and spoken of as the Self alone. That is the difference.

The matter may be illustrated by a simile. Before the name and form of foam manifests as something different from the water, the foam can only be thought of and spoken of as water. But when the foam has manifested as separate from the water through a distinct name and form, then the foam may be thought of and spoken of variously as water or as foam, or else it can be thought of and spoken of just as water alone. This is the meaning (i.e. this is the nature of the distinction between the world of name and form now and that same world before the initial world-projection).

There was (then) nothing else but the Self, either active

or inactive. For example, there was nothing like the independent Nature of the Sāṅkhyas, which falls within the domain of the not-self. There were no atoms, such as the Vaiśeṣikas believe in. Nor was anything whatever of that kind (i.e. eternal and beginningless and real like the Nature of the Sāṅkhyas or atoms of the Vaiśeṣikas) to be found co-present with the Self. That is to say, the Self alone existed.[70]

❖

7. 'Let Me be many'. How can one thing become many without entering into another? To this it is replied, 'Let Me procreate Myself, let Me be born'. For His 'becoming many' does not refer to anything other than Himself, as it would in the case of the birth of a son.

How, then, does He become many? Through bringing to manifestation the name and form that rest in Himself. When the unmanifest name and form that rest in Him are brought into manifestation, then that name and form, without losing their nature as the Self, and never really distinct from the Absolute (brahman) in time or space, are brought out into manifestation in all the various conditions (in which they are found in the world). This manifestation (or unfolding of name and form) is what constitutes 'becoming many'. The partless Absolute (brahman) could not become many or become limited in any other way, just as the partless ether can only become limited or many through the instrumentality of something else.[71] So it is only through them (manifest name and form) that the Self 'becomes many'. For no (second) real principle is found to exist in past, present or future which could be other than the Self and could constitute a not-self, occupying a space and time different from the Self, and conceivable as subtle, separate and remote.

Thus in all their conditions (including their unmanifest condition) name and form have the Absolute (brahman) for their own real nature (ātman), but the Absolute does not have them for its real nature. They are spoken of as having the Absolute for their own real nature because, if it were negated, they would no longer exist. And it is through them as external adjuncts that the Absolute (brahman) enters into all empirical experience as knower, known, knowledge, word and meaning, etc.[72]

❖

8. The whole world was unmanifest name and form before creation. But we should not say that it was totally non-existent. For the text of the Chāndogya Upanishad will later deny the non-existence of the effect before its production when answering the question 'How can the existent come forth from the non-existent?'[73] Nor can you say that, because it is affirmed that there was non-existence here at the beginning, the two views (i.e. that the world did or did not exist prior to its projection at the beginning of the world-period) are meant to be two optional alternatives. For there can be optional alternatives in regard to courses of action but not in regard to matters of fact.

What, then, does the text mean by saying 'There was non-existence, verily, at the beginning'? Well, but have we not already said that 'non-existence' here means 'apparent non-existence'? You did, but does not the word in the text 'verily' (eva) have a specifying and emphatic force? True, it does. But it does not have the force of specifying total absence of *all* existence. What it specifies is the absence of all manifest name and form, for we see that the word 'existent' is applied (in common parlance) to the realm of manifest name and form (only)....[74]

'That became "existence" (sat)' means that a slight impulse occurred, bearing on the already pre-existent effect as it lay (unmanifest) before creation, fixed, motionless, as if non-existent and therefore open to designation (as in the upanishadic text at present under comment) as non-existence. Then that seed vibrated, and appeared, as it were, to sprout a little through fractional manifestation of name and form. Then there gradually arose an egg from the waters, growing denser by stages.[75]

❖

9. Is not this (which we experience now) Being? And, if so, why is there the distinction made, 'It existed formerly'? We reply, 'No. (this which we experience now is not in every respect identical with the Being that existed then)'. What, then, is the difference? Even now (says the Advaitin) this is verily Being. But because it is associated with distinctions of name and form and is the object of the idea 'this', it is also 'this'.

Formerly, however, before the projection of the world, Being was expressed through the word and idea 'Being'. For before the rise of the world nothing could be perceived or conceived as a definite something having this or that name and form. The case is like that of dreamless sleep. One who has just awoken from dreamless sleep is aware of Being only and thinks 'In dreamless sleep it was pure Being only that was present'. And the meaning of the present text is that it was the same before the beginning of the world.

It is also like what we hear in the world. A potter will take a look at the lump of (damp) clay that he has moulded in the morning into the shape of pots and will go off to another village and then return in the afternoon (after the clay is dry) and will see his work lying clearly and distinctly divided up into pots and dishes, and might very well have the idea 'In the morning all these pots and dishes were nothing but clay'. In the same way it is said here, 'In the beginning, (all) this was just pure Being'.[76]

❖

10. And the Vedic text 'For this was then unmanifest'[77] reveals this state (avasthā) of name and form when they were a seed (bīja) and power (śakti), when they were different from manifest name and form and lay in the primordial (pre-manifestation) condition of the world, void of all manifest name and form and worthy indeed to be called 'the Unmanifest'.

Here a (Sāṅkhya) objector might interpose: If you admit this primordial condition of the world as name and form, of the nature of a seed and worthy to be called 'the Unmanifest'...you would be but restating our own (Sāṅkhya) doctrine that non-conscious Nature is the material cause of the world (a doctrine you are elsewhere particular to disclaim). For it is just the primordial condition of the world before us that we (Sāṅkhyas) accept as Nature (pradhāna).

To this objection we reply as follows. We might fairly be accused of adopting the doctrine that the Nature of the Sāṅkhyas is the material cause of the world if we accepted any *independently existing* primordial condition of the world as the material cause (of its present manifest condition as effect). But we look upon the primordial (seed) condition of the world as something existing in dependence on the Lord, and not independently. And this primordial condition of the world is certainly something that must be accepted, because it is a doctrine that has point and significance. Without it, one could not establish the Creatorship of the Lord, for He could not act without a power (śakti). Moreover, (the presence of a power is the only possible explanation of the fact that) the liberated ones do not return (for further worldly experience). For (in their case) the seed-power is burnt by knowledge.[78] For the seed-power is of the nature of nescience, referred to by the term 'the Unmanifest', having its foundation (āśraya) in the supreme Lord, illusory through and through, the great sleep in which the transmigrating souls lie,[79] unable to awaken to their true nature. This 'Unmanifest' is sometimes referred to by the name 'Ether', as in such Vedic texts as 'O Gārgī, in this indestructible one, the Ether is woven warp and woof'.[80] Sometimes it is itself referred to as 'the indestructible', as in the text 'The Supreme, beyond the Indestructible'.[81] Sometimes it is called 'Māyā' (or the delusive power of cosmic projection), as in the text, 'Know that (this) Māyā is Nature, and that the one who owns this delusive power is the Great Lord'.[82]

That delusive power is unmanifest, as it cannot be determined either as being the real principle itself (tattva) or as being anything else.[83]

❖

11. The teaching (at Chāndogya Upanishad III.xix.1) does not imply that there was *total* non-existence before the rise of the world (into manifestation) or that the effect (the world) was then non-existent. The attributes of the world are different when name and form are unmanifest from what they are when name and form are manifest. It was on account of having these different attributes before its rise into manifestation that the world was said at Chāndogya Upanishad III.xix.1 to be then 'non-existent', though in fact it was existent, as the effect is never anything different from the cause.[84]

❖

12. The word 'this' refers to the universe as made up of manifest name and form, of the nature of means and ends, as already described. The words 'that' and 'this', denoting the universe in its unmanifest and manifest state respectively, are placed in apposition. And from this we infer the identity of the universe in its unmanifest and manifest states. That (unmanifest) was verily (none other than) this (manifest universe) and this (manifest universe) was then that (unmanifest). From all of which it is clear that there was no production of any hitherto non-existent effect or destruction of any already existent effect (when the world came into manifestation at the beginning of the world-period).

This universe, being of the nature just described, came into manifestation from non-manifestation through name and form. The expression 'brought itself into manifestation' is reflexive. It means the Unmanifest itself manifested itself.[85] The prefixes 'vi' and 'ā' which make up the opening 'vyā' of the word 'vyākriyata' imply that the Unmanifest came into *clear* manifestation. Manifestation is here conceived as clear determination into particular names and forms. We have to presume a resort to action here, analysable into such factors as controller, agent, means and instruments.

The phrase (in the text) 'that name' just means a name in general, expressed through a pronoun ('that') which introduces a distinction. The (whole) phrase (in the text) 'This person has that (i.e. such and such a) name' refers to the case where one says either 'This person's name is Devadatta' or 'This person's name is Yajñadatta' as the case might be.

Similarly, (in the next phrase) the word 'this' in 'this form' means 'any', i.e. any form, white or black or any other. 'Has this form' means 'has this white form' or 'has this black form' as the case might be. Even today, the real, which is the Unmanifest here spoken of, comes to manifestation only through name and form, through the idea 'This has this name and this form'.

He for the sake of attaining whom the whole discipline of Advaita is undertaken; He to whom agency, action and its results are falsely attributed through natural ignorance; He who is the cause of the whole universe; He who is the real nature of that unmanifest name and form which come to manifestation like cloudy foam from clear water; He who is different from that (manifest) name and form, by His very nature eternal, pure, illumined and free; He, bringing into manifestation unmanifest name and form, which were really none other than Himself, entered into all these bodies from Brahmā to the nearest clump of grass.[86]

❖

13. What is the nature of the Infinite (bhūman)? 'Where one sees nothing else, hears nothing else...' On that plane (bhūmi) or in that metaphysical principle (tattva) there is nothing else to be seen. There is no situation in which a seer, distinct and different from what he sees, sees something else through an organ of knowledge that is different again. In the same way, 'One hears nothing else'. Because all kinds of objects fall within name and form, the mention here of the two sense-faculties that perceive them, hearing and seeing, includes the other senses figuratively.[87]

❖

14. And in the same way knowledge (vidyā) and lack of discrimination (aviveka) are experienced, and people actually communicate knowledge of the Self to others (through words), while others effectively receive it. Thus knowledge and ignorance both fall within name and form, and name and form are not attributes (dharma) of the Self. For there is another text which says, 'He who unfolds name and form into manifestation and He within whom they rest is the Absolute'.[88] But these two, name and form, are just imagined, as night and day are imagined in reference to the one (unchanging) sun. In truth, they do not exist at all.[89]

❖

15. The fact that the Self alone exists has to be learned from a correct apprehension of the meaning of the Vedic texts. Distinctions in the Self are imagined on account of distinctions in the objects denoted by words. But the objects themselves are imagined through hearing words. This has been called the triad of form, name and action.[90] These three (form,

name and action) are thus unreal, being imagined relatively to one another. A word, after being heard in speech, is acted on by the mind (and projected) externally elsewhere (as an image). And when it has been seen according to its mental form (as an image), it is ready to be converted (once more) into a word. This whole universe is imagined in just this way on the basis of erroneous ideas.[91]

❖

16. But how do we know that a determination of the meaning of the holy syllable OM will be of any help towards knowledge of the Self as the principle of Reality? We know this from such Vedic texts as 'That (word which all the Vedas declare... desiring which people observe celibacy) is OM'....[92] The non-dual Self, the supreme reality, is the substratum on which the various illusions beginning with the Cosmic Vital Energy (prāṇa) that go to make up the world-appearance rest, just as the rope is the substratum on which various illusions such as the snake (trickle of water, crack in the ground), etc., rest. Similarly, we have an appearance of plurality in speech, consisting in the words which refer to the various objects of the world-appearance, beginning with the Cosmic Vital Energy, themselves mere imaginations in the Self. But this whole appearance of plurality in speech is in reality nothing but the (one) syllable OM. And the syllable OM is the true nature of the Self, as it expresses the Self. And all objects, beginning with the Cosmic Vital Energy, which are mere imaginations superimposed on the Self, are the meanings expressed by words, and have no existence apart from the words which express them, while the words themselves are but modifications of the syllable OM. For we have such Vedic

texts on the point as 'A modification is a mere activity of speech, a name' and '(Speech is his rope, names the knots.) By his speech as rope and by names as knots is all this bound. For all this is names, (and by his speech He names everything.)'[93]

The text begins 'All this (world) is the sound OM'.[94] This is because all the objects that go to form the world are subject to designation by a name and hence have no existence apart from that name. And because the names have no existence apart from the syllable OM, it follows that 'All this (world) is nothing but the syllable OM'. Even the Absolute in its highest form is the syllable OM. For it can only be known through the artifice of word and meaning.... Whatever has been or is or will be... all that is nothing but the syllable OM, according to the reasoning already given. And all that, such as the Unmanifest principle and the like, which is beyond past, present and future, and not limited by time, and whose existence (cannot be perceived but) has to be inferred from its effects, that, too, is nothing but the syllable OM.

Though the name and the named are one, this unity has so far been treated of from the standpoint of the name. It has been said, for instance, that all this (world) is but the syllable OM. Now (in the next passage of the text) the same subject is taught from the standpoint of the named, to show that the name and the named are one. Otherwise people will think that the named is equivalent to the name only in some metaphorical sense, if they are led to suppose that the named can only be known in dependence on the name (concluding hence that it must in some sense be different from it). And the purpose of knowing the identity of the name and the named is to enable oneself to dismiss name and named altogether and realize the Absolute, which is quite different from either.[95]

❖

17. But you might raise the question of how it could be shown that this whole world of transmigratory experience, manifest and unmanifest, consisting of action, its factors and results, could be of the nature of name, form and action only, and not of the Self. The Upanishad begins the reply to this question by considering the problem of name. Speech (vāc) is the sound-universal including all names, as explained in the previous section. And the statement 'Whatever sound exists it is verily (an aspect of) Vāc'[96] has already been heard. Hence it follows that the meaning of the word 'Vāc' is simply sound in general. This sound-universal is the 'uktha' or material cause of the various names, as a salt-mound is the material cause of the individual particles of salt which come from it.... All particular names such as Yajñadatta and Devadatta proceed from this sound-universal, in the sense of being separated off from it like salt particles from the parent mound. And an effect is non-different from its material cause, while the particulars fall within the universal they belong to.

But in what sense is Vāc spoken of as the universal, and names as its particular instances? 'It is their common element', says the Upanishad. A universal is what is common to a number of things. The element 'sama' implicit in the meanings of the word 'sāmānya' (meaning 'universal') expresses the idea 'samattva' or 'being universally present'. For Vāc is common to all names, which are its particular forms, and particular names cannot come into being without it. That which cannot come into being without a certain thing is non-different from that thing, as clay-pots are non-different from clay.

The Upanishad now proceeds to explain in what sense all particular names receive their being from Vāc. Vāc is their supporting principle (literally their 'brahman', their 'nourisher'), their true nature (ātman). All names receive their being from it, as names cannot be anything other than the principle of sound.... It is thus demonstrated that names are nothing but (aspects of) sound because they are effects of which it is the material cause and particulars of which it is the universal, while sound stands as their essence (svarūpa). Similarly, all forms (should be reduced to the universal principle 'sight') and all acts (should be reduced to the universal principle called 'action').[97]

3. World-Periods and Theory of the Elements

As Rudolf Otto pointed out,[98] the relation of the one to the many is conceived metaphysically by Śaṅkara, whereas in the Upanishads the relation is often expressed mythologically as a process occurring in time. From the standpoint of nescience, however, Śaṅkara is often content to retain the mythological mode of expression. Chapter VII, section 1, below, will show how he regarded the creation-texts of the Upanishads not so much as statements of historical fact as a device (upāya) to prepare the spiritually ignorant mind to receive the doctrine that behind all apparent plurality there lay real identity. Nevertheless, as an upanishadic commentator, he had to reduce them to some sort of order and give them provisional significance for those still under the sway of nescience, or there was danger that the latter would abandon not only their belief in the infallibility of the Veda but also its ritualistic, ethical and spiritual instruction, under the influence of rationalistic teachers of whom India never seems to have had any lack.

Of the Extracts to follow, the first states the famous theory of world-periods (kalpa). This doctrine of the eternal cycle of projection and re-absorption of the universe is typical of the Gītā, Mahābhārata and Purāṇas, but not of the classical Upanishads, where faint suggestions of it are to be heard only in the Śvetāśvatara Upanishad.[99] It was embraced by Śaṅkara, who had to make the older Upanishad creation-texts fit into it as best he could. By his time it had of course become standard belief amongst Hindus, and even today it has seemed to at least one modern Western physicist to offer, in its sovereign immensity, the most suitable framework for the formation of hypotheses about the ultimate nature of the universe.[100]

The first Extract, then, states the doctrine of world-periods on the basis of the Gītā teaching. Extracts 2 and 3 expound the doctrine of the 'three-folding' (trivṛtkaraṇa) of the elements found in the Chāndogya Upanishad, which is somewhat like the doctrine of five-folding (pañcīkarana) found amongst Śaṅkara's later followers,[101] though less developed. The work attributed to Śaṅkara entitled the Pañcīkaraṇa, which, together with its Vārttika attributed to Sureśvara, appears to be couched in the dry scholastic idiom of a later epoch, would not affect the issue even if it were genuine, as the 'five-folding' there envisaged is not, as in the version adopted by Śaṅkara's later followers, an intertwining-doctrine, but an evolution-doctrine, where evolution occurs in five stages.[102]

However, the doctrine that the world was composed not of three but of five basic elements had appeared as early as the Taittirīya Upanishad, and Extracts 4-9 below show that this was the doctrine of the elements to which Śaṅkara basically adhered. It is not a doctrine of three-folding or five-folding but a kind of emanation doctrine, according to which the first element to emanate from the Absolute at the beginning of the world-period is the ether, while wind emanates from ether, fire from wind, water from fire and earth from water. Each new element as one descends the hierarchy has an extra determining quality which renders it more gross and less pervasive than its predecessors, so that the universe comes into being, as it were, by the progressive solidification and diminution of the ether, itself a subtle emanation from the Absolute, and we have seen in the previous section how the ether is itself the first manifestation of unmanifest name and form. No distinction between five separate subtle elements (tanmātra) and five gross elements (mahābhūta) is involved here. That was a conception of the Sāṅkhya philosophers that was adopted in the Epics and Purāṇas but is not found in the classical Upanishads.

Extracts 8 and 9 depict the absorption of the elements at the end of the world-period, thus further establishing the connection between the doctrine of world-periods and the theory of the elements. The last Extract, No.10, attempts to reconcile the three-element doctrine of the Chāndogya with the five-element doctrine of the Taittirīya Upanishad on lines laid down in the Brahma Sūtras.

TEXTS ON WORLD-PERIODS AND THEORY OF THE ELEMENTS

1. Why is it said (in the previous verse) that all the worlds, including the world of Brahmā, 'return'? Because they are of limited duration. In what way? It is held that a day of Brahmā, who is known also as Prajāpati and Virāṭ, lasts a thousand ages (yuga), while his night is of the same length. Who hold

this? The experts on time. Hence, because the worlds are thus of limited duration, they 'return'.

Next the text states what takes place in the 'day' of Brahmā and what in the 'night'.[103] All creatures come into manifestation from the Unmanifest Principle, which is the sleep-state of Prajāpati. This refers to all individuals, both the moving and the fixed. They emerge at the onset of 'day', that is, on the awakening of Brahmā. And they all dissolve back into the Unmanifest Principle mentioned above at the onset of 'night', that is, at the sleeping-time of Brahmā.

The next verse has three purposes. The Lord wants to show that His teachings do not involve the fault of implying that people reap the rewards of deeds they have not done and do not reap the rewards of deeds they have done. He also wants to show that action taken in pursuit of the teachings on liberation bears tangible fruit. And He wants to inculcate indifference to the world based on the conviction that all creatures necessarily undergo repeated births and deaths under the force of their stock of merit and demerit derived from action based on nescience and other passions.

'O Son of Pṛthā! These creatures, moving and fixed, are the very same that existed in the world-period that went before. Again and again they are reborn at the onset of the "day" of Brahmā and again and again they dissolve back at the onset of the "night" of Brahmā. Helplessly, they are reborn again and again at the onset of the "day".'[104]

❖

2. Entering thus into the three deities, He thought 'Let Me unfold name and form, which are now in their seed state and unmanifest and identical with their own Self. And let Me make each of these deities threefold (by combining each of them with a subordinate measure of the other two).'

When the text says that each of the three is made threefold, it implies that where any one of them is being made threefold it is predominant and the other two are subordinate partners in the combination, otherwise it would only have spoken of one 'making threefold', and all three would have been equal partners throughout, as in the case of three twisted strands of a rope.... This is how it is that 'fire', 'water' and 'food' acquired their separate names and forms, so that one can say, 'This is fire, this is water, this is food'.[105] The purpose of these deities' acquiring separate names and forms was that they could become objects of experience (in the form of the three basic elements of fire, water and food).

With this thought, this (supreme) Deity entered within these three deities (fire, water and food or earth that He projected) as a living soul, in the manner previously described,[106] like the sun entering as a reflection into water. First He entered into the body of Virāṭ, and then into the bodies of the gods and other created beings, and unfolded name and form according to His will, so that everything had such and such a name and such and such a form.[107]

❖

3. Moreover, it is the settled conclusion of the Upanishads as a whole that it is the supreme Lord alone who evolves name and form into manifestation, as is clear from such texts

as 'The "ether" (i.e. the supreme Lord) draws out name and form'.[108] Therefore it is the work of the supreme Lord alone to evolve name and form, and this He does to the accompaniment of 'threefolding'.[109] For the unfolding of name and form is represented in one of the texts[110] as taking place in connection with the original threefolding, as the evolution of the three deities into name and form is explained in the very text which explains how fire, water and food (as the material elements from which the world is composed) come into being (through the inter-combination or threefolding of the three original deities).

And the Vedic text itself refers to that threefolding in the case of the fire, the sun, moon and lightning in the passage beginning 'The red form in (gross or material) fire is the form of the fire-deity, the white form in (material) fire is the form of the water-deity and the black form in (material) fire is the form of the food-deity'.[111] Here the form called fire (in the gross or material sense) is evolved into manifestation. And when the form has been evolved, then, from perception of the object, the name 'fire' is evolved.[112] And this should be understood to hold good not only in the case of the (material) element fire but also in the case of its modifications such as the sun, the moon and lightning. And this example of (material) fire and its modifications is used to assert that threefolding is present in the constitution of the (material) earth,[113] water and fire, all three....

According to the Vedic doctrine, when this principle of earth (bhūmi) has undergone threefolding and is subsequently eaten by man (in the form of rice, barley and other crops it brings forth), the result is the formation of flesh and other parts of the body. For the Vedic text says, 'Food, when eaten, becomes divided into three. The coarsest part becomes faeces, the middling part flesh and the finest part mind'.[114] The idea implied is that it is the earth-principle already threefolded (and therefore gross and material) that is being eaten as food in the form of rice and barley and the like. Its coarsest form is expelled in the form of faeces. The middling form swells the flesh of the body and the finest form nourishes the mind. And the functions (in regard to the human individual) of the other two elements, water and fire, have to be understood analogously, according to the Vedic teaching. Urine, blood and vital energies proceed from the (coarsest, middling and finest parts respectively of the) water element, while bones, fat and speech proceed from the (corresponding parts of the) fire element.[115]

❖

4. This Spirit (puruṣa) 'took thought' in the way above described[116] and projected the Cosmic Vital Principle known as Hiraṇyagarbha, the inner self and the energy of the organs of all living creatures. Next the Spirit brought forth from the Cosmic Vital Principle 'Faith' (śraddhā), that which prompts all beings to their good acts. The Spirit created the great material elements, which are the *locus* and means for performing actions and the enjoyment of their fruits and which are hence the cause of this action and enjoyment.

He brought forth ether, which has sound for its quality. He brought forth wind (from the ether) which is distinguished by its two qualities, its own peculiar quality of touch and also the peculiar quality (*viz.* sound) of its (material) cause (ether).

In like manner, He brought forth fire, which is distinguished by three qualities, its own peculiar quality of colour and the two previous ones of sound and touch. In the same way He brought forth water, which has four qualities, its own peculiar quality of taste, with the previous qualities (sound, touch and colour) also entering in. And likewise there was the earth, which has five qualities, through its own peculiar quality of odour allied to the entering in of the (four) previous qualities. And the Spirit further created organs of two kinds from these great elements, organs of knowledge and organs of action. And to stand within these ten organs and functions as their overlord, the Spirit brought forth mind, of the nature of doubt and intention.[117]

❖

5. From this Absolute, the Self in its true nature, arose the ether (ākāśa). The ether is the principle which has sound for its property (guṇa) and has the function of creating space for solid bodies. From the ether arose wind (vāyu), which has two properties, its own special property touch, and the property of its cause, namely the property sound. From wind arose fire, which has three properties, its own peculiar property of colour and the two previous properties. From fire arose water, having four properties, its own peculiar property taste plus the three previous properties. From water arose earth with five properties, its own peculiar property of odour plus the four preceding ones. From the earth arose plants, from plants food. From food converted into seed arose man with head, hands and other organs.[118]

❖

6. The instruments of cognition consisting of mind and the senses arise from this same principle, the Imperishable. And so also do ether, the external (extra-corporeal) wind with its various properties of carrying things in different directions,[119] fire, water and lastly earth, support of all.[120] These form the material cause of the body and of sense-objects. And these elements arise from the supreme Spirit successively, ether having sound for its attribute, wind having sound and touch for its attributes, fire having sound, touch and colour, water having sound, touch, colour and taste, and earth having sound, touch, colour, taste and odour.[121]

❖

7. In the causal chain constituted by the elements, which begins with the earth (as the final and densest effect) and passes through water, fire, wind and ether up to the inmost Self standing beyond the elements as their ultimate cause, each successive member of the chain is recognizable as the cause of that which has gone before because it lacks the distinguishing properties of its effects and is hence more subtle and pervasive than they.[122]

❖

8. And there is another point. It is not only at the time of its maintenance and projection that the universe is one with the Absolute on account of being non-existent apart from Consciousness. It is so in dissolution as well. Just as there are no bubbles and foam, etc., apart from the water from which they come, so none of the effects of the supreme principle of Consciousness, to wit name, form and action, exist apart from the supreme principle of Consciousness when they have been

dissolved back into it. Hence one should realize, says the text, that only the one sole Absolute exists, a perfectly homogeneous mass of Consciousness.

A comparison is given to illustrate the nature of the cosmic dissolution (pralaya). Just as the ocean is the one receptacle for the water of all the rivers, wells and tanks, the one goal and the one place of dissolution, where they lose all distinctions and amalgamate as one, just so is the skin, meaning the sense of touch in general, the one receptacle for all particular instances of touch, whether soft or hard or rough or slippery, all of which are qualities of the one great element wind. When all particular instances of touch have entered into the realm of touch-in-general, like all particular instances of water entering into the sea, then they are nothing over and above that. Even before, they were only its modifications.

In the same way, that principle of touch-in-general, in its turn, enters into the ideas of the mind, that is, into the realm of mind-in-general, just as particular instances of touch entered into the realm of touch-in-general. And when it has entered into it, it is nothing over and above it.

And in the same way, the realm of mind enters into the realm of consciousness-in-general, and is then nothing over and above it. And then, having become pure knowledge, it dissolves into the Absolute as massed Consciousness, like water into the ocean. When the whole universe, beginning with sound,[123] has dissolved stage by stage into massed Consciousness, together with the organs that perceive it, then, because there is no longer any external adjunct, the Absolute remains as massed Consciousness, perfectly homogeneous like a lump of salt, with nothing interior to it, nothing exterior to it and nothing else pervading it. Therefore one should know that all this is the Self, one without a second.

In the same way, all odours as particular instances of the special quality of the earth-element, enter into the realm of odour-in-general. And all flavours, as particular instances of the special quality of the water-element, enter into the realm of taste-in-general. And all colours, as particular instances of light, the special quality of fire, enter into the realm of sight-in-general. Particular sounds enter into the realm of hearing-in-general in the same way. Then all these universals from the realm of hearing-in-general onwards dissolve in thought, into the realm of mind-in-general. The realm of mind-in-general dissolves into knowledge or the realm of consciousness -in-general. Having become pure knowledge, it dissolves into massed Consciousness, the supreme.

In the same way, the realm of the organs in action, comprising all particular instances of receiving (hands), moving about (feet), excretion and procreation, enter each into its own principle of activity in its universal form, and having once done so are in no way separable from it, as particular volumes of water, having once flowed into the sea, are no longer separable from it. And these universals are themselves but the Cosmic Vital Energy (prāṇa), and the Vital Energy is nothing other than Consciousness (prajñāna). 'Whatever is Vital Energy is Consciousness and whatever is Consciousness is Vital Energy', says the Kauṣītaki Upanishad.[124]

❖

9. We have considered the order in which the great elements emerge at the beginning of the world-period, so now we are ready to consider the order in which they dissolve back at the end of it. Does this dissolution occur without any fixed order or in the same order that they emerged or in the reverse order?

We learn from the Vedic texts that the production, maintenance and dissolution of the great elements takes place in the Absolute. For the Veda speaks of the Absolute as 'that from which these elements (or beings) are born, that through which, once born, they live, and that into which they are dissolved when they (finally) depart'.[125] And one might initially suppose that this final re-absorption took place in no special order, as none is specified. Or else one might suppose that, because the texts teach that the emergence of the elements occurs in a particular order, their dissolution, too, must occur in a special order, and that it would be the same order as that in which they emerged.

In face of these false suggestions we reply that, on the contrary, the order of dissolution must be the exact reverse of the order of emergence. For example, we see that when a person ascends a flight of steps one by one he has to descend them in exactly the reverse order. Again, we see that everything produced from clay, whether it be pots or dishes, returns to clay, as everything produced from water, whether it be ice or hailstones, returns to water. Hence it is but reasonable that earth, which emerged from water, should dissolve back into water when its time was past; and that water, which emerged from fire, should return to fire; and in this way one must reckon that each successive cause in the hierarchy of causes among the elements dissolves back into its own cause, the next and more subtle principle in the series, until the whole mass of effects dissolves finally into the Absolute, the highest and most subtle cause of all. For it does not make sense to suppose that any cause in the series should arbitrarily skip its own cause and dissolve into the cause of its cause.

And there are passages here and there in the Smṛti which describe the order of dissolution of the elements as being the exact reverse of the order of their emergence, as for example, 'O Nārada, earth, the support of all creatures, dissolves in water, water in fire, fire in wind'.[126]

And the order of the emergence of the elements taught in the Veda is specifically said to be their order of emergence only, not that of their dissolution. And one would not expect this to be the order of their dissolution in the natural course. For it is not reasonable to suppose that an effect should remain in being after its material cause had dissolved. On the other hand, it is perfectly intelligible that the material cause should remain in being after the effect had dissolved back into it, as this is what we find in the case of clay and other material causes in the world.[127]

❖

10. Taittirīya Upanishad II.1 declares that fire was projected third in order in the words 'From this same Self, verily, was born the ether. From the ether was born the wind. From the wind was born fire'. This text cannot be interpreted differently to mean anything other than the direct meaning of the words. On the other hand Chāndogya VI.ii.3 can well be interpreted to mean, 'Having first created ether and the wind, He *then* created fire'. For the main purpose of this text is to affirm that

Being created (or projected) the deity 'Fire'. It cannot, therefore, have the additional purpose of negating the (prior) creation of ether, known from another Vedic text. For one and the same text cannot be supposed to be performing two different functions at the same time (such as affirming one thing and negating another, unless it is otherwise unintelligible).[128] And there is no reason why the Creator, Himself unitary, should not project several principles successively. On such a basis it is clear that the texts can be taken as constituting a harmonious whole, and no text need be discarded as contradictory. Nor do we mean to imply that the Creator is taught in one and the same passage (*viz.* Chāndogya Upanishad VI.ii.3) to be concerned with two different creations; for it is from a completely different passage (at Taittirīya Upanishad II.1) that we learn of the other creation (namely of ether and wind preceding fire). Further, consider the text, 'Verily, all this is the Absolute, that in which all is born, dissolves and breathes'.[129] Here it is taught that the Absolute is itself the original cause of all the objects of the world. But this text does not annul the teaching at another place in the Veda that the principles from which the world is composed came out from one another successively, beginning with fire. And in just the same way, the teaching in one text that it was fire that arose directly from the Absolute does not annul the teaching of another text that the series of productions began with ether...[130]

4. The Presiding Deities

We are not here concerned with the intricacies of the early history of the conceptions associated with the names Brahmā, Hiraṇyagarbha, Sūtra, Antaryāmin, Mahat, Buddhi, Satya, Prajāpati, Vāc, Virāṭ, Ka, Prāṇa, Vāyu and other names used by Śaṅkara in connection with the chief deity presiding over the evolution and withdrawal of the universe. Name and form, imagined through nescience, unmanifest before the beginning of the world-period and gradually brought into manifestation in accordance with the deeds of living beings as the world-process unfolds, are what constitute the stuff of the world for Śaṅkara. They and their transformations form the external adjuncts of the supreme unchanging principle of Consciousness, and when the latter is viewed in association with the universe it assumes the appearance of a deity. Various names were used for this deity in the ancient texts, of which the most important, for Śaṅkara, have been listed above. The deity can be conceived either as the universe (Virāṭ), or as the Cosmic Intellect (Buddhi, Mahat, Hiraṇyagarbha) in which all individual intellects are contained and in which the impressions of the previous thoughts and deeds of all creatures lie, or as the Vital Energy (Prāṇa, Vāyu) by which the whole process is sustained. All lesser deities that preside over natural phenomena governed by law (e.g. Āditya, the sun-god) can be represented as modifications of the one great deity called variously Brahmā, Hiraṇyagarbha, Prajāpati or by other names. The exception is Viṣṇu (alternatively called Vāsudeva, Kṛṣṇa, Nārāyaṇa and Bhagavān), who is often identified with the Absolute.[131] As for the creator-deity, he is but the instrument of the Absolute, non-conscious in himself and requiring to be sustained and illumined by the light of the Absolute before he can unfold its powers of knowledge and action.

Extracts on this topic are arranged in three groups. Group A gives texts affirming that the Absolute stands supreme, untouched by any of its adjuncts, and yet that, from the standpoint of nescience, we have to accept the traditions of the Veda and Smṛti which represent the Absolute as if it were unfolding the universe through the knowledge and activity of a great creator-deity, the first-born to emerge at the beginning of the world-period, called by any of the names listed above and functioning as the 'body' and all-vivifying 'soul' of the universe.

Group B concentrates on texts where this deity is specifically revered under the name Hiraṇyagarbha. The name 'Hiraṇyagarbha' means 'Golden Germ' or 'Golden Embryo', and referred, at an early stage of its history, to the first nucleus of manifest being that formed in the infinite waters of unmanifest being before creation, and from which all manifest being was to unfold. In Śaṅkara's texts, the term Hiraṇyagarbha tends to stand for the mental aspect of the world-soul. He speaks of it as the collective mind embracing all individual minds, as the repository of all mental impressions and as the material for the 'seventeen-fold subtle body'.[132] The texts here gathered show that the term Hiraṇyagarbha could be used by Śaṅkara to stand for the universe in its 'mental' aspect, that is, in its subtle (i.e. imperceptible) aspect of impressions awaiting future manifestation. In this sense it could be contrasted with 'Virāṭ', the 'gross' or perceptible body of the universe, consisting of perceptible physical objects. But the meanings of the two terms are not so rigidly fixed in Śaṅkara as they became amongst his later followers. In some places they are identified,[133] and we have already caught a hint[134] of the survival of a much earlier meaning of the term Virāṭ, as standing for what subsisted before the entry of the creator-deity with the organizing power of name and form into the chaos that had resulted from his own dismemberment.

Texts in Group C discuss the minor deities exercising lesser power into which the Cosmic Vital Energy (prāṇa) breaks up. Such gods have certain supernormal powers, especially that of being present at many different sacrifices at different places at the same time, while themselves remaining only one. But they are mortal and powerless on their own, receiving all their strength from the Lord. Moreover, considered as individuals, even their existence and authority is temporary: they are office-bearers, and only the office is important. In some cases names of gods refer to natural phenomena like the sun, but in such cases the reference is *also* to the presiding deity, a modification of the Cosmic Vital Energy. A final point made (Extract 14) is that, with the exception of the special case of the path to deferred release through attainment of the 'World of Brahmā', to be treated of in Volume VI, Chapter XIV, below, practice of rituals and meditation with a view to attain union with, or the status of, one of the gods is *not* part of the Vedantic discipline aiming at liberation. The subject of the power of the gods to place obstacles in the way of man striving for spiritual advance, and their motives for using such power, is not mentioned in the present Extracts, but is dealt with at Volume V, Chapter XII, section 1. Reference to the support from the deities received by the individual in the normal functioning of his sense-organs will be found in Volume III, Chapter VIII, section 2.

TEXTS ON THE PRESIDING DEITIES: GROUP A

1. In the case of those who see distinctions wherever there are external adjuncts and bodies, the Self alone appears, through nescience, to be associated with the Vital Energy (prāṇa), mind (manas), senses and sense-objects. But this is a mere illusion, like the attribution of impurities and a concave surface to the ether of the sky, and for those who have penetrated to the final truth, the Self is not in its own true nature associated with the Vital Energy or the other characteristics mentioned. It is 'without Vital Energy' in the sense that it is not naturally invested with Vital Energy, and is not by nature a cosmic force having the power of motion and a variety of

other powers of action. It is 'without mind' in the sense that it is not invested with a faculty of proposing, etc., associated with various powers of knowledge. The negation of Vital Energy and mind includes the negation of the five vital breaths of the body,[135] the physical organs of action and their objects, both the higher (buddhi) and lower (manas) aspects of the mind,[136] as also the sense-organs and their objects.[137]

❖

2. This principle, the Absolute (brahman), when considered in abstraction from all adjuncts, is stainless, actionless, peaceful, one without a second, knowable through abstraction (apoha) from all particulars through the formula 'Not thus, not thus', beyond the range of all words and notions. This same principle, through association with the adjunct of perfectly pure consciousness (prajñā) becomes the omniscient Lord, who roused to life the all-comprehensive unmanifest seed of the universe, and who is known as the Inner Ruler (antaryāmin) because He controls it. And this very same principle is called the Golden Embryo (hiraṇya-garbha) in so far as He identifies Himself with the (cosmic) Intellect (buddhi), the seed of the manifest world. The same principle is known as Virāṭ or Prajāpati when associated with the adjunct of the first body born within the cosmic Egg.[138] When associated with such adjuncts as fire, which proceed from Virāṭ, it is known as 'a deity' (devatā).[139] And then this same principle, the Absolute (brahman), when associated with all particular bodies as its adjuncts, from those of Brahmā down to the meanest clump of grass, receives the name and form proper to those bodies. And it is the same one principle, differentiated

into all its distinctions through external adjuncts (though not in its true essence), that is variously apprehended by all living creatures and interpreted differently by different speculative philosophers. Witness such a text from the Smṛti as, 'Some call this one principle the eternal Absolute (brahman), some 'Agni', some 'Manu', some 'Prajāpati'. Some call Him 'Indra', others the Cosmic Vital Energy (prāṇa).[140]

❖

3. It has been said that the Imperishable (akṣara) is the womb of all creatures. And this raises the question, 'In what sense is it the womb of all creatures?' To answer this question, the text proceeds by citing familiar examples.

It is well-known in the world how a spider projects forth its web outside itself without depending on any other source, the web being nothing but a projection from its own body. It then later withdraws the web back into itself, that is, reduces it back into its own being. Crops, too, in the soil, like rice and the rest, spring forth spontaneously from their own seeds. And hair grows forth on the head and body of a living man, and yet is different from him in nature. And on the cosmic plane, this whole variegated universe comes forth from the Imperishable as defined above in just the way these examples illustrate, without recourse being needed to any external auxiliaries, the universe being partly of the same nature as its source and partly different.[141]

When the universe arises from the Absolute it does so in a particular order which will be explained later on, and not (haphazardly) like (the landing of) a handful of plums thrown on the ground. The next verse was composed to explain this order. The Imperishable, the womb of all beings, that is to say the Absolute (brahman) when about to bring forth this world, expands (bṛh) in his preliminary brooding (tapas),[142] conversant as He is with the right procedure for creation, as a seed expands before giving birth to a sprout or a father swells with elation in the act of begetting a son.[143]

The Absolute expands through his omniscience, through the knowledge and power He possesses of projecting, sustaining and withdrawing the universe. From Him in this condition arises 'food'. Food, what is eaten, here means the Unmanifest Principle, the collective form of all beings in transmigration in their state just before manifestation (at the beginning of the world-period). From the Unmanifest, when just about to go into manifestation, arises the Cosmic Vital Energy (prāṇa) or Hiraṇyagarbha, invested with the powers of knowledge and action proceeding from the Absolute,[144] the collective form of the universe, the sprout springing forth from the seed consisting of the totality of ignorance, desire and action, the soul of the universe (jagad-ātman). From the Cosmic Vital Energy so constituted arises Mind, the principle of deliberation, doubt and decision.[145] From the principle of Mind, of the nature of deliberation, arises the principle of empirical existence (satya), (consisting of) the five elements beginning with ether (in their manifest form). And from the five elements there arise the seven worlds beginning with Bhū (the lowest of the seven 'upper' worlds), which at first lay in the form of an egg.[146] In them lie the past activities of human and other living beings, disposed according to caste and stage of life. As acts do not perish even in millions of world-periods, so their fruits remain in being also. In this sense the text here says that the fruit of acts is deathless (amṛta).[147]

❖

4. And this realm of nescience which has been treated of (in the earlier part of the Bṛhadāraṇyaka Upanishad) is of two kinds. One part is luminous and immortal. It is the Cosmic Vital Energy (prāṇa) that is within, like a pillar supporting a house. And there is an external part, of the nature of an effect, non-luminous, subject to coming-into-being and passing-away. It is mortal and like the straw, grasses and clay of a house,[148] and is known as empirical existence (satya) (composed of the five elements).... The Cosmic Vital Energy called 'the Immortal' is covered over and hidden by the 'empirically manifest' element in the realm of nescience....

This one Cosmic Vital Energy (prāṇa) is distributed manifold through various different external media. It is said that the Cosmic Vital Energy constitutes one single deity. It is the external body of this one deity, cosmic in form and having the sun and other beings as its organs,[149] that is referred to by various names suggesting bodies, such as Virāṭ, Vaiśvānara-Ātman, He with form like a Man, Prajāpati, Ka, Hiraṇyagarbha (the Golden Embryo) and others. It is typical of one in the realm of nescience to think that the Absolute is one and many at the same time in this way, that it is this and nothing more, that it is limited to its individual forms in each of its various bodies, that it is the agent and experiencer endowed with empirical consciousness and with other similar characteristics (symptomatic of limitation).[150]

TEXTS ON THE PRESIDING DEITIES: GROUP B

5. Four characteristics of both the gross and subtle forms of the Absolute have been mentioned,[151] and it is now being explained what characteristics apply to the gross form and what to the subtle form. The gross form has solid parts, interpenetrating, thick, composite. It is said in the text to be different from the two elements called the wind and the ether. From this we conclude that the gross form of the Absolute must consist of the three remaining elements, namely, earth (pṛthivī), water and fire. What is composed of these elements is mortal, subject to passing away.

Why is it thus perishable? Because, says the Upanishad, 'It is determinate'. Whatever is limited is resisted by that with which it is placed in contact, as a pot by a pillar or wall. The gross (object), which is the determinate and the limited, stands in relation with other objects, is resisted by them, and is in this sense 'perishable'. This is 'the manifest' (sat), and whatever belongs to this realm has peculiar characteristics of its own. Because of this it is limited. Because of this it is perishable (martya). And because it is perishable (martya) it is called 'gross' (mūrta). Or we may say that because it has form (mūrta) it is perishable (martya), and because it is perishable it is determinate, and because it is determinate it is manifest.

These four characteristics invariably stand together. There will therefore be some latitude in explaining their mutual relations: any one of them may be taken as subject with any of the others as predicate, and one may be taken as cause with another as effect. But however they are taken, the gross form of the Absolute consisting in the three (gross) elements (earth, water and fire) has these four characteristics. To affirm any one of these four characteristics is to affirm all four of them....

The sun is the essence of these three elements. Their various forms and distinctions arise from it. The sun, as a visible disc, is that element in the cosmic body of the Lord which shines. Hence it is called in the Upanishad the essence (rasa) of the manifest, that is, of the three elements, fire, water and earth. For this sun which shines is manifest and is the essence of the manifest. As for the organ of the cosmic body of the Lord which resides within the disc of the sun, of that we shall be speaking later on.

Next the text speaks of the subtle form of the Absolute. This consists in the remaining two elements, namely wind and ether. This is immortal because it is without (limited) form. It is not determinate and is therefore not resisted by anything. Immortal and imperishable, it is the opposite of the determinate, namely all-pervasive and unlimited. As it has no distinct characteristics that would separate it from others, it is called 'tyat'. The word 'tyat' means that which can only be described indirectly, as before.[152]

Next the Upanishad speaks of the essence of this subtle, immortal form of the Absolute, called 'tyat' because it is of that nature and has the fourfold characteristics (of being non-composite,[153] immortal, unlimited and unmanifest). What is that essence? It is the Spirit (puruṣa) present in the disc of the sun, of the nature of an organ (of the supreme Spirit), called Hiraṇyagarbha and also called the Cosmic Vital Energy (prāṇa). It is the essence of the two (subtle) elements, wind and ether.

But why is it that the two elements which make up the subtle form of the Absolute have this Spirit (Hiraṇyagarbha) as their essence? Because these two elements proceeded from the Unmanifest principle (avyakta) with a view to form the subtle body of Hiraṇyagarbha.[154]

❖

6. And we have the Vedic passage, 'To Him who first projects Brahmā and commits the Vedas to him'.[155] This is the Being which is here referred to as 'the Great Self'. As Hiraṇyagarbha was first called 'Intellect' (buddhi), it is but right that he should now be referred to under a different term to show that it is the cosmic Intellect that is in question, superior to our little intellects.[156]

❖

7. Now we shall describe the nature of the 'subtle body' (liṅga)[157] of this Spirit, which forms the latter's instrument. It is composed of impressions, and arises from the union of the organ of knowledge (vijñāna-maya)[158] with the impressions of the gross and subtle worlds. It deludes everyone like the delusions conjured up by the mass-hypnotist, or like a mirage seen in the desert. The nihilistic Buddhists of the Vijñāna Vāda school fall into the error of supposing that there is no real Self beyond these insubstantial visions. The Vaiśeṣikas think that the Self is a substance and that these illusory phantasms are solid qualities belonging to the Self as substance (and really qualifying it). The Sāṅkhyas believe that these visions are rooted in (the real principle that they call) Nature and that they are composed of the three 'constituents'

and that they constitute an independent reality and proceed to unfold themselves for the benefit of the soul....[159]

If the intention is to explain the 'Being of Being', the supreme Self in its true nature, then the whole of Being must be explained. The subtle impressions (vāsanā) form a particular aspect of Being. Here some of their forms are being described. In the case of the subtle body of Hiraṇyagarbha, the impressions assume the following forms.

We are familiar in the world with the case of a large cloth dyed in turmeric. In just the same way as the cloth, the mind (citta) assumes a dyed form, the form of an impression (vāsanā), through association with objects of pleasure such as women and the like, whereby the person in question is said to be 'attached' (stained)[160] like a dyed cloth. Another worldly example the Upanishad takes is that of pale grey wool. As wool is pale in colour, so are other impressions (not red, or, by a play on the meanings of the word 'rakta', not 'impassioned' but) pale grey. On the other hand, the cochineal insect is a vivid red (rakta) in colour, and the mind sometimes has deeply impassioned (rakta) impressions of this kind. Sometimes the element of passion is generated by the nature of the object, sometimes by qualities inherent in the mind of the person in question. And as we see that a flame will sometimes burn up briskly, so do impressions flare up, now in one person's mind, now in another's. And as the white lotus is pure, so do some people's minds assume impressions of purity. Again, as in the world a whole landscape is sometimes lit up by a flash of lightning, so a mind will sometimes assume an impression brought on by a marked increase in the light of knowledge. No one can determine the beginning or the end or the middle or the number or the place, time or immediate occasion of the rise of these impressions. Impressions are innumerable and innumerable their causes....

Hence the purpose (of the upanishadic text) in citing these particular examples was not to evaluate the number of impressions but rather to illustrate their typical nature, as much as to say that these are the *sort* of forms these impressions assume. But the impression mentioned last, the one like a flash of lightning, is said by some to refer to the sudden manifestation of Hiraṇyagarbha with a single lightning flash when he comes forth from the Unmanifest principle (at the beginning of the world-period).[161]

❖

8. And Death,[162] which is to be identified with hunger, is in fact the Cosmic Intellect, and is the collective unity of all (samaṣṭi), the First-born, the principle of Cosmic Vital Energy (vāyu = prāṇa), the Supporting Thread (sūtra), empirical being (satya), Hiraṇyagarbha. As regards its range when manifest, it is the inner nature of all. It is the unity latent in duality. It is the inner self of all creatures. It is the subtle body (liṅga) (of all creatures). It is the essence of the subtle elements (amūrta).[163] It is the repository of the merits and demerits of all creatures (and therefore the seed of their future experiences). It is the highest goal of, and supreme reward for, rituals and the symbolic meditations connected with them. One might wonder how far it stretched and what it embraced, seeing that it encompasses us on every side. To answer this question would involve all the world, the whole realm of bondage....

The principle of Cosmic Vital Energy is the inner self of all fixed and moving creatures. It alone exists outside them, too. Therefore, says the text, 'All beings are the principle of Cosmic Vital Energy'. That is to say, the latter is present everywhere on the individual plane, the plane of the cosmic elements and the plane of divine cosmic forces. And the Cosmic Vital Energy is also the totality of created being, in this aspect known as 'Sūtra', (literally, a thread). Whoso knows it thus, acquires identity with it in its individual and collective manifestations, and defeats recurring death. Having died once, he dies no more.[164]

❖

9. That in which the world of Brahmā is at the present time woven warp and woof, like the earth-principle lying in the water-principle, is the Supporting Thread (sūtra), which can only be known through properly communicated tradition (āgama)...

O Gautama, says Yājñavalkya, that Supporting Thread is the Cosmic Vital Energy (vāyu). The Cosmic Vital Energy (vāyu, the wind-element) is that which, along with the ether, supports the grosser elements. It constitutes the material for the seventeenfold subtle body (liṅga)[165] in which the impressions of the deeds of living beings inhere. It has a collective (samaṣṭi) and an individualized (vyaṣṭi) form. It is externally subdivided into the forty-nine presiding deities called Maruts, which stand to it as waves to the sea. This principle called the Cosmic Vital Energy is also called the Supporting Thread (sūtra).

For this world, O Gautama, and the next, along with all

creatures, are threaded on the 'string' (sūtra) of the Cosmic Vital Energy, as is well known. It is well-known in the world that the wind-element is a kind of thread and that all is supported on it. That is why they say of a man who has died, 'His bones are scattered'. When the thread of a necklace is removed, the gems are seen to be scattered. The Cosmic Vital Energy is the thread. If a man's bones are strung on it, it is but natural that they should be scattered when it is removed.[166]

TEXTS ON THE PRESIDING DEITIES: GROUP C

10. Very well, says our opponent. Let us grant that the gods are eligible for acquiring spiritual knowledge on account of their being embodied.[167] But if they are to be conceived as embodied, then it must be accepted that Indra and the various other gods are physically present at the sacrifice just as much as the ritual priests. But this would imply a practical contradiction. For Indra and the other gods are not seen to be physically present at the sacrifice, nor is it logically possible that they should be present. For it would be quite impossible for the one god Indra to be physically present at a great number of different sacrifices at the same time.

To this we reply that there is no contradiction here, because 'of the assumption of many forms', as the author of the Sūtras puts it. He means to say that it is possible for one deity to assume many forms at the same time. How do we know this? Because it is plainly implied by the texts. We hear, 'How many gods are there?' And this is answered 'Three hundred and three plus three thousand and three'. Then it is asked, 'What is their real number?' And the reply given is, 'These are their mysterious powers (mahiman), the gods are actually only thirty-three in number'.[168] In this passage the Veda shows that one deity can simultaneously assume many forms.

But the text goes even further. It reduces the number thirty-three to six[169] and less and finally to one. 'What is that one deity?' it asks, and gives the answer 'The Cosmic Vital Energy (prāṇa)'.[170] Hence, in showing that the gods all consist of the Cosmic Vital Energy, the text shows that the Cosmic Vital Energy is capable of assuming many different forms at the same time.

Similar points are made in the Smṛti. Consider a passage like the following:[171] 'O Bull of Bharata's line, when the yogin acquires spiritual strength (bala) he can create many bodies for himself and wander about the earth in them. He can enjoy sense-delights in one and perform awe-inspiring austerity in another. And finally he can withdraw them again, as the sun withdraws its rays'. Such passages show that (not only the gods but even) yogins who have attained the powers of a master, such as that of reducing the body to a minute size,[172] are found associated with a number of different bodies at the same time. How much more, then, will the gods have such a power, since they are equipped with all manner of perfections from birth! And because the gods are able to assume a multiplicity of forms at the same time, each individual god splits himself up into many forms and makes himself physically present at many sacrifices at the same time. The fact that he is not visible is explained by his power of rendering himself invisible.[173]

11. Nor can immortality and other cognate qualities be truly ascribed to the gods, for the Vedic texts speak of them as coming into being and passing away. Even the texts that do speak of the immortality and similar qualities of the gods only do so figuratively to express the idea of longevity. Their 'lordship', too, is not their own natural property, but is dispensed to them by the supreme Lord (parameśvara). For we have the text, 'From fear of Him the wind blows, from fear of Him Sūrya (the sun) rises; it is from fear of Him, too, that Agni (fire), Candra (the moon) and Mṛtyu (death), as the fifth, hasten to their tasks'.[174]

❖

12. Well, says a Mīmāṃsaka opponent, let us grant that no *practical* contradiction arises from your view that the gods are embodied. But the fact remains that it will involve insoluble *verbal* contradictions in the various texts. For the Veda has been established as an authoritative means of knowledge on the ground of its 'depending on no external factor'[175] and on the assumption (shared by the Mīmāṃsaka and the Vedantin) that the connection of a word with its meaning is innate. If it be taken that the gods are embodied, it may well be that one could explain how they could consume the offerings at a large number of sacrifices at the same time by claiming that they had super-normal powers. But it would nevertheless follow that if they were embodied they would be subject to birth and death like ourselves. And this would constitute a contradiction to the authority of the Veda as an impeccable means of knowledge. For the authoritativeness of the words of the Veda flows from the fact of their being found eternally connected with *eternal* realities as their meaning.

But there is in fact no contradiction here either, replies the Advaitin. Why not? Because of 'origination from this', as the author of the Sūtras puts it. Because, that is, the whole universe, beginning with the gods, originates from the word of the Veda.

Here you will perhaps object and say that it has already been laid down in the Sūtra which runs 'That from which proceeds the birth (maintenance and dissolution) of this (universe)'[176] that the universe proceeds from the Absolute (brahman). How, then, can it be said that it proceeds from the words of the Veda? Further, if it were admitted that it proceeded from the words of the Veda, it would be impossible to defend the words of the Veda from the charge of self-contradiction. For (certain groups of minor deities such as) the Vasus and the Rudras and the Ādityas and the Viśvadevas and the Maruts are evidently non-eternal beings, since they are spoken of as having an origin. But if they are non-eternal, the words such as 'Vasu' used in the Veda to denote them must be non-eternal too. For the rule in the world is that only when a son is born to Devadatta does the name of the son, say Yajñadatta, come into being. So it follows that the view that the gods are embodied implies verbal contradiction in the texts.

But all this is (from the Vedanta standpoint) wrong. For we find that the relation between the word and its meaning in the case of such words as 'cow', etc., is eternal. Although the individual cows and the individual members of other such classes come into being (and are hence not eternal) it does not follow from this that the generic forms (ākṛti)[177] they embody also come into being. For whether the discussion be of substances, qualities or actions, it is invariably individual examples only that come into being, and not generic forms. And words relate to generic forms, not to individuals, because, since individuals are infinite in number, the relation of any single word with them is unintelligible.[178] But, while the individuals come into being, the generic forms are eternal, so that there is nothing to prevent the words 'cow', etc., from referring to these. And it is in this way that there is no contradiction in the use by the Veda of names such as Vasu.

We may admit that all individuals, including gods, come into being. As the gods and other invisible beings treated of in the Veda are known to have had bodies, the distinguishing features of their generic forms must be learned from the Vedic hymns and Brāhmaṇa texts themselves.[179] And names like 'Indra' refer to an office, like a word such as 'commander-in-chief'. So that whoever occupies that office at a given moment is the one referred to by words like 'Indra', and hence there is no contradiction (between the fact that the meaning of such words is something that is eternal and the fact that the individual beings they denote come into being).[180]

❖

13. It was also affirmed that a further argument against the gods' being eligible for knowledge was that what we refer to as gods are no more than material phenomena such as light. But it is clear that we *also* refer to deities endowed with consciousness and supernormal powers, as the names are found with this meaning in the hymns and eulogistic passages and other such sections of the Veda. For the gods are able, through their supernormal powers, to invest themselves with

the nature of light and other elements and to assume this or that body at will.[181] For example, in explaining the eulogistic passage on Subrahmaṇya that begins 'O ram of Medhāthiti' the Veda says, 'Indra, assuming the form of a ram, carried away Medhāthiti, the descendant of Kaṇva'.[182] And in the Smṛti we find, 'Āditya, the sun-god, assumed the form of a man and enjoyed intimacy with Kuntī'.[183] The Veda also implies that conscious beings preside over earth and other elements, as we hear in the Veda 'Earth spoke' and 'Water spoke', etc.[184] It is accepted that light and other material substances are non-conscious. But we have already explained how it is clear from the hymns and eulogistic passages and other sections of the Veda that there are conscious beings presiding over these, in the form of deities.[185]

❖

14. These deities such as Agni and the rest, who have been created by the Lord as Guardians of the Worlds, fell into this great ocean of transmigratory life. Here the 'water' is the suffering arising from nescience, desire and action. The great sea-monsters are the dire diseases, old age and death. This ocean is beginningless, endless, supportless, shoreless. The moments of calmness are the little periods of joy occasioned by the sense-objects. Its hundreds of great waves are the evils stirred up by the winds of thirst for the objects of the five senses. Its great roar consists in the wailing and lamentation arising from its countless hells. The rafts which bear one across it consist in the perfection of knowledge, and the provender aboard consists in truth-speaking, uprightness, charity, compassion, harmlessness, inner and outer control,

firmness of purpose and other virtues. Liberation is the haven. Into this great ocean the deities fell.

The point the Upanishad wishes to emphasize is that the attainment of unity with the various gods such as Agni through the discipline of ritual conjoined with meditation that was described earlier in the Aitareya Āraṇyaka (of which larger body of texts the Aitareya Upanishad now under comment is a part) is not enough to eradicate the sufferings of transmigratory life. This being so, one should realize through direct knowledge that the Absolute (brahman) in its supreme form is one's own Self and the Self of all creatures, if one wishes to eradicate all those sufferings.[186]

NOTES TO CHAPTER VI

References to Extracts are in bold type

1 Passmore, 329.

2 Bṛhad. II.iii.1.

3 Radhakrishnan, *Indian Philosophy*, II.290.

4 B.S. II.i.19.

5 Cp. above Chap.V, section 3, Extract 8.

6 Cp. Sac, *Clarification*, 45f., who quotes B.S.Bh. II.i.18.

7 B.S. Bh. II.i.7.

8 Vācaspati's *Bhāmatī* calls this an argument from negation (vyatireka). It could be set out in the *modus tollens* form thus: If anything is different from anything, it is available separately. The effect is not available separately from the material cause. Therefore the effect is not different from the material cause.

9 This shows that, if it be accepted that when two things are invariably found together because one of them is the cause of the other, then the former must be the material cause, for efficient causes are found separately from their effects.

10 Chānd. VI.iv.1ff.

11 B.S.Bh. II.i.15.

12 Chānd. VI.ii.1, Ait. I.i.1.

13 B.S.Bh. II.i.16.

14 A king called Pūrṇavarman was ruling in Magadha (Bihar) *circa* 600 AD. (Belvalkar, Notes to his ed. of B.S., Chap.II, Quarter I, 30.) The name also crops up at Chānd. Bh. II.xxiii.1, trans. Gambhīrānanda, 146, but the reference there is not to an individual king called Pūrṇavarman but to

Pūrṇavarman as a typical name for a king. The same may be true here.

15 Inasmuch as to become a father would (absurdly) imply becoming a completely different person.

16 The Buddhists, in general, held that the object springs up and dies away again momentarily, a rapid succession of such events sufficing to convey the illusion of a stable object. Naturally the arguments against the Vaiśeṣika doctrine of causation apply with even more force against the Buddhist.

17 B.S.Bh. II.i.18.

18 Viz. Bṛhad. I.ii.1, the text under comment.

19 The clay which forms the pot cannot form the potsherds at the same time. Gold which is in the form of a pig cannot be in the form of an elephant at the same time. So the pot-form has to be destroyed before the clay can become potsherds and the pig-form has to be destroyed before the gold can become an elephant.

20 Cp. Note 16, above. Buddhist arguments are dealt with in more detail at Vol.IV, Chap.XI, section 5, below.

21 On the powers of the Lord in this regard, cp. the reference at Note 113 to Chap.V, above.

22 Svāmī Mādhavānanda explains the four as: i. Mutual exclusion, occurring between things of different classes as in 'A pot is not a cloth' (anyonyābhāva); ii. Previous non-existence, as of a pot before it is made (prāg-abhāva); iii. Non-existence on destruction, as of a pot when it is broken (dhvaṃsābhāva); iv. Absolute negation, as 'There is no pot' (atyantābhāva).

23 I.e. it would be a positive something, like the cloth, which is non-existence of the pot by mutual exclusion.

24 Inseparable relation being timeless, the opponent might suppose that he could avoid the absurdity of saying that a non-existent effect entered into relation with Being by saying that the relation was 'inseparable'.

25 Bṛhad. Bh. I.ii.1.

26 No new pot can arise from an old pot. Both the old pot and the new pot are modifications arising in clay, and in a deeper sense nothing new comes into being. The argument is not directed to denying causality but merely to denying the existence of any other material cause apart from Being. (Ānandagiri)

27 Chānd. VI.ii.1.

28 Śvet. VI.19.

29 Chānd. VI.i.4.

30 Chānd. Bh. VI.ii.2.

31 Above, Vol.I, Chap.I, section 2.

32 Śatapatha Brāhmaṇa X.v.2.3, quoted von Glasenapp, *Entwicklungsstufen*, 19.

33 Hacker, *Eigentümlichkeiten*, 272ff., cites examples from B.S.Bh. I.ii.22, I.iv.2-3, I.iv.9 and II.i.14 (towards the end).

34 avidyātmikā bījaśaktir, B.S.Bh. I.iv.3.

35 avidyā-kalpite, B.S.Bh.II.i.14.

36 Silburn, 53, quoting Taittirīya Brāhmaṇa, II.ii.7.1 (Bibliotheca Indica, II, 444) and other texts.

37 E.g. Chānd. VI.iii.2 and VIII.xiv.1, Śaṅkara's two main sources.

38 Chānd. Bh. VII.xxiv.1.

39 J.U.B. IV.22.8, Rāma Deva, 148, quoted Silburn, 53, footnote.

40 Above, Chap.V, section 1, Extract 4.

41 Bṛhad. Bh. I.iv.7, trans. Mādhavānanda, 121f.

42 Amongst his followers, it is nescience itself which does so.

43 B.S.Bh. I.iii.41, Gambhīrānanda, 239.

44 E.g. B.S.Bh. I.iii.30, Gambhīrānanda, 220: *ibid.* IV.ii.20, quoted above Chap.V, section 1, Extract 3.

45 Oldenberg, *Weltanschauung*, 103.

46 Śatapatha Brāhmaṇa XI.ii.3.6, quoted Silburn, 58.

47 Cp. Bṛhad. I.vi.3, Muṇḍ. III.ii.8, Praśna V1.5.

48 E.g. at Extract 5 of the present section.

49 Cp. above, Chap.V, section 4, Extracts 3-5.

50 Bṛhad. Bh. I.vi.3, trans. Mādhavānanda, 174.

51 Cp. below, Vol.III, Chap.VIII, section 4, Extract 1 *ad fin.*

52 Hacker, *Eigentümlichkeiten*, 265.

53 *Eigentümlichkeiten,* 261ff. They are: B.S.Bh.I.i.5, Gambhīrānanda, 50; I.iv.3 *ad init.* (Extract 10 of present section); II.i.14 (Extract 3, present section); II.i.27, see above, Chap.V, section 3, Extract 3.

54 Extracts 1 and 5 of present section.

55 *Vibhrama Viveka*, verse 29. Detailed references to L. Schmithausen's edition and translation of the Vibhrama Viveka are given at Vetter, Maṇḍana Miśra's B. Sid. 60, footnote 72.

56 Cp. Sac, M.V. 186; Hacker, 'Realitätsgraden', 282.

57 B. Sid. 8ff., trans. Biardeau, 151-153.

58 See references given at Notes 53 and 54.

59 B.S.Bh. II.i.27 and Bṛhad. Bh. II.iv.10.

60 See Darśanodaya, 122f. and 131f.; Sac, *Clarification*, 22f., and several passages in Sac, M.V., listed under 'Indeterminable' in the Index at the back of that work.

61 Trans. Gambhīrānanda, 50, and Thibaut, Vol.I, 50.

62 R.V. X.129.1, cp. Hacker, 'Realitätsgraden', 282.

63 V. 650, cp. Vidyāraṇya, P.D. VI.128.

64 U.S. (prose) 18 and 19.

65 Ait. Bh. I.i.2.

66 B.S.Bh, II.i.14.

67 B.S.Bh. I.iv.9.

68 Bṛhad. Bh. II.iv.10.

69 These traditional etymologies preserved by Śaṅkara have their suggestive value. Western philologists sometimes link the earliest use of the term 'ātman' with breath or spirit. Curtius Vol.I, 80, connects it with Greek 'atmos' = vapour (cp. atmosphere), German Odem and Atem = breath.

70 Ait. Bh. I.i.1.

71 Name and form are not a second independent reality existing over against the Absolute any more than foam exists independently of water. Yet the Absolute is not identical with them, any more than opaque foam is identical with transparent water. Hence it can remain unchanged while name and form undergo transformation.

72 Taitt. Bh. II.6.

73 Chānd. VI.ii.2.

74 Cp. Bṛhad. I.vi.3, nāma-rūpe satyam.

75 **Chānd. Bh. III.xix.1.**

76 **Chānd. Bh. VI.ii.1.**

77 Bṛhad. I.iv.7.

78 A seed will not fructify after being burnt or roasted.

79 Cp. G.K. I.16, to be commented on below, Vol.III, Chap.IX, section 3, Extract 4.

80 Bṛhad. III.viii.11.

81 Muṇḍ. II.i.2.

82 Śvet. IV.10. The context suggests that it is Māyā that is called Prakṛti and not, as appears in Deussen, Hume and Radhakrishnan, Prakṛti that is called Māyā. Cp. Oldenberg, *Upanishaden*, 241, Hauer, 136 and Johnston, 27. Śaṅkara's own interpretation seems uncertain, as the Śvet. Bh. attributed to him is probably spurious at IV.10.

83 **B.S.Bh. I.iv.2 and 3.**

84 **B.S.Bh. II.i.17.**

85 It is in fact the Self, with the adjunct of name and form, that manifests itself. See below.

86 **Bṛhad. Bh. I.iv.7, *ad. init.***

87 **Chānd. Bh. VII.xxiv.1.**

88 Chānd.VIII.xiv.1. For the interpretation, cp. Śaṅkara's Chānd. Bh., *ad loc.*

89 **Taitt. Bh. II.8.5.**

90 Bṛhad. I.vi.1, on which see Extract 17 below.

91 **U.S. (verse) XVII.9-12.** In this difficult passage I have jettisoned Rāma Tīrtha's Commentary entirely.

92 Kaṭha I.ii.15. Other such texts are also quoted.

93 Chānd. VI.i.4 and Aitareya Āraṇyaka II.i.6, trans. Keith, 207.

94 Māṇḍ. 1, opening phrase.

95 Māṇḍ. Bh. 1.

96 Bṛhad. I.v.3.

97 Bṛhad. Bh. I.vi.1.

98 Otto, 5.

99 Śvet. III.2, V.3. Cp. Hiriyanna, *Outlines*, 65.

100 Cp. Öpik, 122f., on the 'day and night of Brahmā'.

101 E.g. Vidyāraṇya, P.D. I.27, Sadānanda, *Vedānta Sāra*, trans. Nikhilānanda, 61.

102 From Brahman arises avyakta, from avyakta mahat, from mahat ahaṅkāra, from ahaṅkāra pañca-tanmātra, from pañca-tanmātra pañca-mahābhūta. Pañcīkaraṇa in the later works is more explicit. Each of the five gross elements is composed of half its own subtle element, with the other half consisting of one-eighth parts of each of the other four subtle elements. Mayeda (*A Thousand Teachings*, 60) has shown that this doctrine already existed before Śaṅkara's day in such texts as M.Bh. XII.244.2 (Poona Critical Ed.). But Śaṅkara never refers to it.

103 A Mahāyuga or Manvantara is probably the unit meant, comprising four thousand three hundred and twenty million years each for the Day and Night of Brahmā. Cp. Dowson, 382 and Öpik, 122f.

104 Bh.G.Bh. VIII.17-19.

105 I.e. once the hidden 'deities' are combined in certain proportions, this combination produces the three manifest elements, fire, water and food, of which the manifest world

is here said to be composed. For the equation 'food = earth', see Note 113, below.

106 Śaṅkara's conception of this process will be found at Vol.III, Chap.VIII, section 1, Extract 10, below.

107 Chānd. Bh. VI.iii.3.

108 Chānd. VIII.xiv.1.

109 Fire, water and food are separate principles in themselves, and in this form are called the three 'deities'. But when the world of manifest name and form, or perceptible objects, is evolved, the three basic elements of which it is composed, fire, water and food, are no longer in their pure separate form, but everywhere intermixed.

110 Chānd. VI.iii.2ff.

111 Chānd. VI.iv.1.

112 Here form conditions name, as is sometimes the case in Śaṅkara, though more frequently name conditions form. Extract 15 of the previous section (VI.2) explained how, because they both condition each other, both are 'relative' and false.

113 Here Śaṅkara equates the food-deity with the earth-element, bhaumāmbhasa-taijaseṣu triṣvapi dravyeṣu.

114 Chānd. VI.v.1.

115 B.S.Bh. II.iv.20-21.

116 At Praśna VI.3.

117 Praśna Bh. VI.4.

118 Taitt. Bh. II.1.

119 The 'various properties of carrying things' are mentioned at M.Bh. XII.328.36-52, G.P. Ed. Vol.III, 690f.(Sac).

120 I.e. the support of all earthly creatures, not least as their source of food, but not the 'support of all' in the metaphysical sense.

121 Muṇḍ. Bh. II.i.3.

122 U.S. (verse) IX.1.

123 The peculiar quality of ether.

124 Kauṣītaki III.3, embodying a play on words between prāṇa and prājñā. **Bṛhad. Bh. II.iv.11.**

125 Taitt. III.1.

126 M.Bh. XII.339.30, G.P. Ed. Vol.III, 705. Śaṅkara cannot quote an example from Śruti, as the doctrine of world-periods is hardly found in the Upanishads. Cp. 165, above, and Note 99.

127 B.S.Bh. II.iii.14.

128 The appeal, according to the Commentators, is to the rule of 'eka-vākyatā', summarized by Kumārila in the form, 'Whenever words can be taken together as forming one sentence, they should not be taken to form several different sentences'. (Quoted Devasthali, *Mīmāṃsā*, I, 215). By extension the principle was also appealed to in order to show that a sentence was completely authoritative only in its main function and not in its secondary functions. Thus the main function of the text 'He projected fire' (Chānd. VI.ii.3) is to state that fire is not a self-existent principle but depends for its existence on the Absolute. If the text also appears to imply that fire was the first element that Being projected, that is secondary, and the text as a whole cannot be supposed to have the additional purpose of negating the text Taitt. II.1, which says that ether was created first, fire later.

129 Chānd. III.xiv.1.

130 **B.S.Bh. II.iii.6.**

131 E.g. Bh.G.Bh. I.1 (intro.) and VII.19, U.S. (verse) XV.11, Muṇḍ. Bh. II.i.4, etc.

132 For which see Vol.III, Chap.VIII, section 2.

133 E.g. Extract 4, present section. Cp. Otto, 117, footnote 7. Nevertheless, it is fair to say that Śaṅkara basically separated Virāṭ and Hiraṇyagarbha, taking the former as born from the latter. Cp. Extract 2, present section, also Taitt. Bh. II.8.4 (Gambhīrānanda, 368f.), Bṛhad. Bh. V.v.1 (Mādhavānanda, 573), Muṇḍ. Bh. II.i.4 (intro.) (Gambhīr-ānanda, 119).

134 Section 3 of the present chapter, Extract 2, *ad fin.*

135 See Vol.III, Chap.VIII, section 2, Extracts 7-10.

136 See below, Vol.III, Chap.VIII, section 2, Extract 4.

137 **Muṇḍ. Bh. II.i.2.**

138 Perhaps to be connected with Chānd. III.xix.1.

139 Cp. section 3, Extracts 2 and 3, above.

140 Manu Smṛti XII.123. **Ait. Bh. III.i.3.**

141 It was argued above, Chap.V, section 3, Extract 7, *ad fin.*, that the effect could not be absolutely identical with the cause, and the example of hair growing from the body was cited.

142 The term 'tapas' involves thought or knowing here, cp. Taitt. Bh. II.6, Gambhīrānanda 347, where Śaṅkara quotes Muṇḍ. I.i.9, 'He whose tapas consists of knowledge'.

143 The Imperishable is both the material and the efficient cause of the world. The seed-example illustrates His material causality, the father-example His efficient causality. Sac, ṭīkā on Muṇḍ. Bh. I.i.8.

144 Reading, with Sac, jñāna-kriyā-śakty-adhiṣṭhitaḥ.

145 On the conception of a cosmic Mind, cp. the remarks at section 2 above, introduction *ad init.*

146 Cp. Chānd. III.xix.1.

147 Muṇḍ. Bh. I.i.7-8.

148 Which to this day get washed away in the rains in rustic houses in India, and have to be renewed.

149 The sun and moon are regarded as the eyes of the deity who is the Cosmic Vital Energy. They are also the media through which it distributes light.

150 Bṛhad. Bh.II.i.1 (introduction).

151 Bṛhad. II.iii.1.

152 As at Bṛhad. II.iii.1, where 'tyat' (transcendent) is contrasted with 'sat' (manifest).

153 Taking asthitam to mean asaṃsthitam. The context suggests that the term might here mean 'unmanifest'.

154 Bṛhad. Bh. II.iii.2-3.

155 Śvet. VI.18.

156 B.S.Bh. I.iv.1.

157 This is the cosmic subtle body, described on the analogy of the subtle body of the individual, for which see Vol.III, Chap. VIII, section 2, Extract 12, below.

158 Ānandagiri explains vijñāna-maya as 'buddhi' or the instrument of knowledge.

159 The bulk of the intervening passage will be given in Vol.IV, Chap.X, section 3, below.

160 Rakta means stained or impassioned, but also red. Cp.

virakta, dispassionate, vairāgya, dispassion.

161 **Bṛhad. Bh. II.iii.6.**

162 In the pre-upanishadic teaching of the Brāhmaṇas and A.V., some of which survives in the older upanishadic texts, when Prajāpati or Hiraṇyagarbha sacrificed himself to form the universe, the beings he created were 'the food of time' and 'the pasture of death'. In this sense, he was himself time (the year) and also death. A.V. XI.iii.37, cp. Bṛhad. I.ii.1-5. But as deity presiding over the ritual, Prajāpati made it possible for his creatures to create a new world and a new body for themselves through their ritualistic acts, whereby to escape death. See Silburn, 54. The remnants of the old doctrine of the creation of a new body through ritualistic acts in which to survive after death are still found in the B.S., adapted to the later doctrine of rebirth. Śaṅkara's treatment of the B.S. teaching on this point will be found below in Vol.V, Chap. XII, section 2, Extract 22.

163 Cp. Extract 5, present section. The subtle elements are the ether and the wind.

164 Meditation on and identification with Hiraṇyagarbha is part of the discipline of 'deferred release' (krama-mukti) through attainment of the 'world of Brahmā'. Cp. Vol.VI, Chap. XIV, section 2, below. **Bṛhad. Bh. III.iii.1 and 2.**

165 For which see Vol.III, Chap.VIII, section 2, below.

166 **Bṛhad. Bh. III.vii.2.**

167 B.S.Bh, I.iii.26, has just established that the gods can feel a hankering for liberation and are embodied beings eligible to attempt to gain it. The example of Indra receiving teaching from Prajāpati (Chānd. VIII.vii.2ff.) has been cited.

168 Bṛhad. III.ix.1-2.

169 Bṛhad. III.ix.7.

170 Bṛhad. III.ix.9.

171 M.Bh. XII.300.26 and 27, G.P. Ed. Vol.III, 652.

172 On the miraculous powers that come to yogins, see Patañjali, Yoga Sūtra III.16ff.

173 **B.S.Bh. I.iii.27.**

174 Taitt. II.8. **B.S.Bh. I.ii.17.**

175 An appeal to Jaimini's P.M. Sūtra I.i.5: 'The innate connection of a word with its meaning is (alone) the cause of knowledge arising about any matter lying beyond the range of empirical experience. For here we have teaching, and teaching that is never contradicted. And it is an authoritative means of knowledge, as Bādarāyaṇa says, because it depends on no external factor'. Śabara explains the last phrase to mean that it does not depend on any other knowledge (as inference depends on perception) or on any other (fallible) human being (as does knowledge derived from the speech of a merely human speaker).

176 B.S. I.i.2.

177 In India, the Grammarians were the first philosophers to raise the question of what a word referred to. One school thought that one word must, in order to be intelligible at all, have one meaning only; the one word 'cow' must mean one thing only, not the millions of different things, the different cows, or its meanings, being infinite in number, could never be learned, and the word could never be intelligible. So it was said that the word referred to the one generic form (ākṛti) that was present in all the individual cows. The notion of 'universal' (sāmānya, jāti, e.g. 'cowhood') was developed later by the Vaiśeṣikas, and was sometimes identified with and sometimes differentiated from the ākṛti. The generic form (ākṛti) is an eternal entity, and has been compared by Deussen with Plato's 'Idea' as expounded at

Sophist, 247Dff. It should not be confused with the external form (rūpa) of the individual object, which is transient and fugitive, though it is noteworthy that the ākṛti, too, as the next Note but one will show, is subject to perception. In Śaṅkara's texts, it is no longer the Grammarians who are the exponents of the ākṛti doctrine, but the Mīmāṃsakas, while the Grammarians oppose it with a different theory of meaning, based on the sphoṭa. See below Vol.IV, Chap.X, section 5.

178 Śaṅkara himself subscribed to the view that nouns considered in isolation referred to universals and that their meaning could only be narrowed down to particular individuals through qualification by other words in a sentence. Cp. below, Vol.VI, Chap.XV, section 3.

179 The generic form, on the classical Indian view, was something perceived and concrete, and not an abstraction. Śaṅkara seems to have accepted this doctrine as true (from the standpoint of nescience) and to have had in mind Śabara's Comm. on P.M. Sūtra I.i.5 where the latter writes: 'What is the meaning of the word "cow" when it is uttered? The generic form, we say, along with its distinguishing features, such as the dewlap. Does the existence of an entity such as the generic form have to be proved by inference? No, it does not, as it is subject to direct perception. For in such cognitions as "This is a bracelet, this is a swastika, this is a bowl" we have direct perception of the generic form. Nor can this be dismissed as an illusion. For one cannot speak of an illusion unless a cognition loses its form and assumes a contradictory one'.

180 B.S.Bh. I.iii.27 and 28.

181 Cp. St. Augustine, *De Trinitate*, III.xi.27, which attributes similar powers to the angels, through which they appeared to the prophets, as recorded in the Old Testament. The pillar

of cloud by day and the pillar of fire by night that appeared before the Israelites when they were escaping from Egypt (Exodus III.21) are classified as God appearing to man not 'in his own substance' but through the subjection of a material substance to a special act of his will. *Ibid.* II.xiv.24.

182 *Ṣaḍviṃśa Brāhmaṇa*, I.1.

183 Deussen traced this text to M.Bh. I.4397 from the old Bombay Ed. of 1854-5. The verse has been dropped from modern editions, but would have appeared in M.Bh. Chapter I.110 of G.P. Ed. or I.104 of the Poona Critical Ed.

184 *Śatapatha Brāhmaṇa*, VI.i.3.2 and 4.

185 B.S.Bh. I.iii.33.

186 Ait. Bh. I.ii.1.

CHAPTER VII

THE ACOSMIC VIEW

1. The Creation-Texts as a Device to teach Non-Duality

The texts assembled in the last section of the previous chapter constitute a sort of holding operation designed to put up a provisional defence of the literal meaning of the creation-texts for the benefit of those firmly gripped by the belief that they are embodied beings. Such persons need to be shown that the ritualistic and ethical teachings of the Veda are based on a logically defensible world-view, capable of resisting the attacks of atomists like the Vaiśeṣikas or phenomenalists like the Buddhists. But the mere fact that some people need to be told that the world is real, lest they fall away from the Vedic path altogether, does not mean that it *is* real. If creation were real, it would imply that bondage was real, and that in turn would imply that liberation was impossible,[1] and this would make a mockery of the Upanishads. It is, moreover, pointless to enquire into the unreal for its own sake, as it does not exist. One enquires into the nature of the unreal only for the sake of establishing the true nature of the real.[2] Accordingly, if we want to find out the true meaning of the creation-texts, we have to apply the rules of exegesis and dig below the surface meaning. Ultimately they will have to be interpreted as instances of the law that the Absolute, being transcendent, can only be communicated through false attribution followed by subsequent denial.

It is a principle of Vedic exegesis that every text in the Veda must be assumed to contribute in some definite way to the welfare of man. There are no texts in the Veda declaring that any particular 'fruits' result from a knowledge of the creation-texts, and knowledge of such distant matters is of no direct benefit to man. Hence we have to assume that such texts are of benefit to man *indirectly* through the help they give him in understanding the texts that *are* of direct benefit to him.

The texts of the Upanishads that are most obviously of benefit to man are those which teach him that he is identical with the Absolute, for the knowledge accruing from them is said to result in the 'fruit' of 'immediate intuition of truth' and 'immortality' and 'eternal freedom from fear'. Such knowledge is not only 'fruitful' but final and uncontradictable. Once it is gained, it is inconceivable that there either should or could be any further knowledge to add to it, further it, modify it or correct it. This cannot be said of the knowledge accruing from the creation-texts, which consequently carry less authority when they conflict with the great metaphysical teachings about the true nature of man as one with homogeneous Consciousness, the sole existent reality. Further, if the creation-texts had been relating anything true, they would not have disagreed amongst themselves as to the details of creation. The texts that teach that the creation of the world took place on the analogy of some worldly kind of creation, such as the production of pots from clay or the issuing of sparks from fire have ultimately only the *negative* force of showing that effects are non-different from their material cause. And there is the further principle of exegesis that all the texts can be reconciled and combined into a single view. According to this principle, the supreme texts of the Upanishads like 'That thou art', which affirm the identity of the individual soul with the Absolute, may be taken as fundamental, while all the rest of the texts of the Veda can be taken as auxiliaries to understanding these.

Some parts of the accounts of creation are plainly mythological, as when 'speech' is spoken of as 'desiring food' or 'food' is spoken of as 'running away'. These again should not be taken as statements of fact but as indirect aids to certain phases of the process of coming to understand the great truth that the individual soul is none other than the supreme Self. One can, says Śaṅkara, in Extract 2 below, resort to the notion of an omniscient and omnipotent deity who can work all the marvels described in these texts. But it is better to regard them as mere fanciful tales told in the course of making the ultimate message of the Upanishads easier to assimilate, as one coaxes a child to drink milk, with conscious mendacity, by telling him that it will make his hair grow.

In the same way, the doctrine that, having created the world, the Absolute 'entered' it as the principle of life and consciousness is not to be taken as a statement of historical fact, but as a pictorial representation of the truth that the Absolute is already manifest in the world-appearance, in the sense that it is the only reality in it. Both the doctrine of creation and the doctrine of the 'entry' of the Absolute into its own creation have to be viewed in a wider context and seen as part of the process of gradually conveying to the pupil a notion of his own true nature by the method of false attribution and subsequent denial.

These are the main points made by Śaṅkara in the group of Extracts that now follows.

TEXTS ON THE CREATION-TEXTS AS A DEVICE TO TEACH NON-DUALITY

1. It does not matter if the different accounts of the effect differ in the different creation-texts, as the aim of these texts is not to teach the existence of the effect (the world-appearance). To teach anything about this creation or world-appearance is not what the Veda has in view. For such knowledge would not be connected with any human end,

either evident or revealed. Nor would it be possible to assume that there was such a connection, for the passages marking the opening and closing of topics[3] found, at intervals, in the Upanishads, show that all the material in the Upanishads has to be taken as forming a unity with (and as being a subordinate annexe to) the texts proclaiming the (sole reality and) existence of the Absolute.[4]

There are texts in the Veda itself which show how the projection, maintenance and withdrawal of the world-appearance are given solely as a means to teach the existence of the Absolute (brahman). 'Taking food for the sprout, my dear one, search for water as the root. With water as the sprout, my dear one, search for fire as the root. With fire as the sprout, my dear one, search for Being as the root'.[5] And from the giving of such examples as clay, sparks and the like we see that the purpose of teaching the creation of the world-appearance was really (not to relate historical facts but) to expound the non-difference of the effect from the cause.

And thus a great one who knew the true tradition (Gauḍapāda) says: 'The doctrine of creation, (taught differently in different Vedic texts) through different examples such as clay, iron, sparks and others, is just a means (to bring the Absolute down into the universe of discourse). (In truth) there is no differentiation (and hence no creation) of any kind'.[6]

Knowledge of the Absolute, on the other hand,[7] is taught as connected with a human end. 'The knower of the Absolute reaches the Supreme'.[8] 'The knower of the Self goes beyond grief'.[9] 'Having known that, verily he goes beyond death'.[10] And this end is subject to direct perception. For when one comes to know through the text 'That thou art' that the Self is not subject to transmigration, then the feeling that the Self is subject to transmigration comes to an end.[11]

❖

2. The author of the production, maintenance and withdrawal of the universe, who is not subject to transmigration, who is omniscient and omnipotent, brought forth all this universe from Himself in due order, beginning with the ether, without having recourse to any external principle (i.e. other than Himself). Then, in order to realize his own true nature, He Himself entered into all the bodies, associated as they are with Vital Energy (prāṇa) and intelligence and organs of knowledge and action. And having entered them, He had direct experience of his own Self as 'I am in truth this Absolute'. And therefore it is He and no other who is the one Self in all bodies....

But here a difficulty presents itself. There is not so much as a tip of a hair anywhere that is not *already* pervaded by Him who is the Self of all and omnipresent. How then could it be supposed that He penetrates into bodies by opening the suture in the skull[12] and then entering in like an ant crawling into a crack in the ground?

Well, if we were going to argue like this we would have to go a lot further. What was the Self doing 'taking thought'[13] when (creation had not yet begun and) it was not supposed to have any organs of cognition? What was it doing 'creating the worlds' when it was supposed to do so without anything to create them from? What sense does it make to say, 'The Self (ātman) drew out the Cosmic Man (puruṣa) from the waters and gave it solidity and form'?[14] Further, it is said that the various limbs and organs of the Cosmic Man were separated out through the meditations of the Self on his form, and that Agni (the god of fire) and the other 'Guardians of the World' (loka-pāla) were separated from his limbs. There was also mention of their affliction with hunger and thirst,[15] of their asking for a place to live,[16] of a cow being brought to them, of their entering into several abodes, of food 'running away', of speech and other functions desiring food.[17] All this is on a par with the all-pervading Absolute entering into bodies through slitting open the suture of the skull.

Are we, then, to dismiss all these teachings as useless nonsense? No, because they form part of a passage which is concerned with realization of the Self. Nothing is wrong, as they are just parts of an eulogistic passage (artha-vāda).[18]

Alternatively, one might say that the whole process is like the work of a magician (conceived as a mass-hypnotist). Some great magician, as an omniscient, omnipotent deity, performed all these (astonishing) works. But the best explanation is to say that they are all merely stories invented to make some other point easier to understand (and accept),[19] according to a practice frequently met with in ordinary worldly experience.[20] For there is no intrinsic advantage to be derived from a knowledge of accounts of creation and the like. On the other hand it is clear from the upanishadic teaching taken in its entirety that the advantage to be derived from knowledge of one's identity with the Self of all is nothing less than immortality.[21]

❖

3. Perhaps one might agree that before creation all was one only, without a second, while at the same time maintaining that after creation all this world and the various distinct souls came into being.

But this would be incorrect. For the Vedic texts ostensibly teaching creation have a different end in view. The Teacher (Gauḍapāda) has already met this objection earlier,[22] by saying that living organisms are projected by the Self through illusion (māyā), 'like a dream' (svapna-vat), and that the notion of the 'bringing-into-being' or 'mutual-distinction-between' living creatures was comparable to the 'bringing-into-being-of' and 'mutual-distinction-between' the separate portions of the ether.[23] Hence the Teacher now refers to those Vedic texts which appear to teach the creation of distinct things in order to draw attention to their real (hidden) import.

Creation, it is true, is apparently affirmed in the Vedic texts, through the use of various analogies such as clay, iron, sparks and the like. But it is to be noted that the process of creation is explained differently at each place. According to us, the creation-texts are no more than a device for suggesting the idea that the individual Self and the highest Self are (in their true nature) identical. It is like the invention of the myth in the section on 'The Quarrel among the Senses'[24] in which it is related how the demons 'pierced' the various senses with evil, the only purpose of which is to convey some truths about the nature of the Cosmic Vital Energy (prāṇa) (especially the truth that its functioning in the human sense-organs is associated with pain).

Perhaps you will ask for grounds for this assertion. One

ground is that the myth of the 'Quarrel among the Senses' is presented differently in different Vedic texts. If the 'Quarrel among the Senses' had been a historical fact, the account of it would have been the same in all texts and there would have been no contradictions. But as we in fact find contradiction between the various accounts, we have to assume that their purpose was to teach something else. Exactly the same holds good for the accounts of creation.

But might not the various accounts of creation in the Vedic texts be explicable as referring to different creations in different world-periods? No, this is not acceptable. For unlike our own view that the texts are myths designed to introduce and impress the idea of the identity of the individual soul with the highest Self, your view that they recount historical facts would make them useless. For one cannot conceive any possible utility of the texts recounting the 'Quarrel among the Senses' or the creation-texts apart from the one we have ourselves suggested. You cannot say that they are representations of historical facts given so that they may be dwelt upon in meditation, for no one could wish to unite himself in meditation with a mere quarrel or with the creation and dissolution of the world.[25] Hence we conclude that the creation-texts and others like them serve to introduce the notion of one's identity with the Self, and have no other conceivable purpose. And from this it follows that there are no distinctions introduced into the Self through creation or any other cosmic process.[26]

❖

4. Now, you might suppose that because the Veda uses examples of clay, etc., which are used to illustrate real transformation, that the Vedic view is that the Absolute undergoes real transformation, for it is admitted in the world that objects like clay undergo real transformation. But such is not the case. For we know that the Absolute must be beyond all change from texts which deny all modification.... One cannot predicate both transformation and absence of transformation of one and the same Absolute (at one and the same time). Nor can you say that they apply (successively) like rest and motion, for the Absolute is specifically said to be raised above all change (kūṭastha).[27] The Absolute, being raised above all change, cannot harbour a succession of such contradictory qualities as state and motion. And we have already said that the Absolute must be eternal and beyond all change, because all modification is denied of it. Moreover, knowledge of the identity of the Absolute with one's own real Self is a means to liberation. But a knowledge that the Absolute assumed the form of the world would not, of its own accord, bring any fruit,[28] for there is nothing to show that it could. For the Veda mentions specifically that it is only knowledge that the Absolute, raised above all change, is the ultimate Self of man that brings fruit, in such passages as that which begins 'This Self is (described as) "not thus, not thus",' and concludes (by mentioning the supreme fruit) in the words 'O Janaka, verily thou hast reached the state beyond fear'.[29]

❖

5. And it is but right to say that the texts ostensibly proclaiming the projection, maintenance and withdrawal of the universe are really concerned with promoting vision of the

sole reality of the Self, since there are other texts in which all vision of duality is decried. Therefore the doctrine (also) of the 'entry' of the Self into the manifest world is but a figurative way of declaring that the Self is perceptible in the midst of its effects.[30]

❖

6. We cannot accept the theory that the Vedic texts teaching that the Absolute is the cause of the rise, maintenance and withdrawal of the world show that it possesses a plurality of 'powers' (śakti), as the texts denying all particularity of the Absolute cannot be explained away. Nor can you maintain that the texts speaking of the production, maintenance and dissolution of the world cannot be explained away either; for the real purpose of the latter texts is only to teach that the Absolute alone exists. When the Veda teaches by the examples of clay and the rest that the Absolute is one and that it is the sole reality and that all modifications are unreal, it cannot at the same time teach the production, maintenance and dissolution of the world as the final truth.

Well, you might ask, why is it that the texts teaching the production, maintenance and withdrawal of the world have to be taken as subordinate to the texts denying all particularity of the Absolute, and not the other way about (which would be equally reasonable from the purely logical angle)? We reply that the reason is that the texts denying all particularity of the Absolute leave nothing further to be said. For when it is once intuitively known that the Self is eternal and pure and the sole reality, then it is clear that one will have the feeling that every possible human end has been gained, and no further questions will be asked. The texts themselves hint at this, in such passages as, 'What pain or what delusion could he experience who sees only identity everywhere?...'[31] Moreover, we noticed in the case of enlightened souls that they experience extreme contentment (tuṣṭi) and have other characteristics of blessedness. On the other hand, all compromise with the illusory modifications is denounced in the text, 'He goes from death to death who sees the appearance of plurality here'.[32] So the texts which deny all particularity of the Absolute cannot be taken as subordinate to any others.

Of the texts teaching that the Absolute creates, maintains and withdraws the universe, on the other hand, it cannot be said that the knowledge they produce is such that nothing further remains to be said later by way of correction after it has been known. It is in fact obvious that they only exist to help convey some other meaning. For at one point the Veda says, 'This shoot (the body), my dear one, has grown up. Know that it cannot be without a root!'[33] And then it goes on to explain how Being alone is the one root of the universe.... Thus the passages in the Veda teaching that the Absolute produces, maintains and withdraws the world are concerned with promoting the knowledge that all is the one Self alone, and it follows that the Absolute is not possessed of a plurality of creative powers.[34]

❖

7. In this connection, one of the authorities on the true tradition (*viz.* Draviḍācārya) relates the following story.[35] A certain prince of the royal house was cast out of his home at birth by his parents and brought up in the home of a hunter.

The boy had no knowledge of his real descent, and supposed himself to be a hunter, and followed the hunter's way of life. He did not think of himself as a king and behave like a king in the midst of his courtiers. At length, however, a certain person of deep compassion, thinking that the prince was worthy of the dignity of kingship, acquainted him with his descent and said, 'You are not a hunter but the son of such and such a king and have entered the family of a hunter'. After he had received enlightenment in this way, he discarded the belief that he was a hunter, along with the habits of a hunter's way of life, and proceeded to adopt the ways of his forefathers in the conviction 'I am a king'.

Similar is the case, according to this Teacher, with the individual soul. Not knowing his true nature as the supreme Self, he proceeds, even though he is one with the latter and separate from it only as a spark is separate from fire, to enter the wild jungle of the body and sense-organs and conform to their way of life, even though he suffers no real transmigration, and to think 'I am the body and its organs, I am stout, lean, happy, sorrowful' as the case may be. But when he has been enlightened by the Teacher with the words 'Thou art not of this nature: verily, thou art the Absolute in its supreme form' he abandons his subjection to the three desires[36] and acquires the conviction 'Verily, I am the Absolute (brahman)'.

In this connection it must be observed that the words 'Thou hast come out from the Absolute like a spark from fire'[37] serve to strengthen the soul's conviction that it is the Absolute just as (the parallel phrases such as 'You were cast forth at birth from the palace' served to strengthen) the conviction of the prince that he was a king. For a spark is one with the fire from which it comes out until it actually does come out. Hence the reference (in texts about the creation of the world) to examples like gold, jewels, iron, fire and sparks are not concerned with teaching that the soul is in any way different from the Absolute, but rather with strengthening its conviction of its fundamental identity with the Absolute. For it is laid down that the Absolute is an unbroken, homogeneous mass of Consciousness, like a lump of salt...[38]

If (as Bhartṛprapañca supposed) the purpose (of the Bṛhadāraṇyaka Upanishad) had been to teach that the Absolute had a variety of different real characteristics and was the producer, maintainer and destroyer of the world in a real sense, with a relationship to the world which could be illustrated by the variously painted cloth or the tree and its branches or the sea and its waves, then it would not have stated, at the conclusion of the whole topic, that the Absolute was like an unbroken mass of salt without an inside or an outside, nor would it have remarked in passing that the Absolute 'must be viewed as homogeneous only'. Nor should we forget such words of warning as 'He goes from death to death who sees the appearance of plurality here'.[39] Hence it follows that throughout the Upanishads the notion that the Absolute performs such activities as the production, maintenance and dissolution of the universe is brought forward only to strengthen the enquiring soul's conviction of his identity with the Absolute, and not to proclaim the reality of the cosmic process.[40]

❖

8. Whoso knows the Self thus described as the fearless Absolute (brahman) becomes the fearless Absolute. This is a brief statement of the meaning of the entire Upanishad. And in order to convey this meaning rightly, the fanciful alternatives of production, maintenance and withdrawal, and the false notions of action, its factors and results have been attributed falsely to the Self. And then later the final metaphysical truth has been inculcated by negating these characteristics through a comprehensive denial of all the particular superimpositions on the Absolute, expressed in the phrase 'Not thus, not thus'.[41]

Just as a man wishing to explain numbers from one to a hundred thousand billion says (of the digits) 'This (written) figure is 1, this figure is 10, this figure is 100, this figure is 1,000', and all the time his only purpose is to explain the numbers and not to affirm that the figures themselves *are* numbers; or just as one wishing to explain the sounds of speech as represented by the letters of the alphabet resorts to an indirect means (upāya) in the form of a palm-leaf in which he makes incisions which he later fills in with ink to form letters, and all the while (even though he point to a letter and say 'This is the sound so-and-so') his only purpose is to explain the nature of the sounds and not to affirm that sounds *are* leaf, incisions and ink; even in just the same way, the one real metaphysical principle, the Absolute, is taught by resort to many indirect means (upāya), such as (falsely) attributing to it creation and other powers. And then afterwards the nature of the Absolute is restated so as to purify it of all particular notions accruing to it from the fanciful means used to explain (and affirm) its nature in the first place.[42]

❖

9. It is true that the enlightened ones, that is to say the Non-Dualists, spoke of 'birth' (jāti), because birth is perceived in the world and because people observe rules of caste and station of life (āśrama) (which depend on the belief that they have been born in a particular body). But it was only taught as a means ultimately to teach something else, and only to those persons who, while possessed of faith in the Veda, were not endowed with deep discrimination, and who consequently believed in the existence and substantial nature of the world. For them it is appropriate enough. But this is not taught as the final truth. For it is considered that those (more advanced pupils) who practise cogitation over, and sustained meditation on, the texts of the Upanishads, will one day find that they have acquired discriminative insight into the existence and nature of the unborn, non-dual Self.

As for the others, who remain attached to the letter of the (ritualistic part of the) Veda, the verse implies that on account of the crude condition of their minds they will always feel afraid of the unborn principle of Reality, thinking it means their own destruction. For they do not practise discrimination (and see that their real Self is other than the empirical personality). The Teacher said earlier,[43] '(Creation taught with examples such as clay, iron and sparks is but) a device to introduce (the notion of one's identity with the Self)'.[44]

❖

2. Nothing can come into being

In several passages in Śaṅkara's Commentary on Gauḍapāda's Kārikās and in the Nineteenth Chapter of the verse section of the Upadeśa Sāhasrī we find 'acosmic' doctrines buttressed by theoretical arguments as well as by upanishadic quotation. They are associated with a world-view in which the external world is reduced to the 'oscillation' of the mind (citta-spandana). In some places the Self is represented as imagining the individual soul, who then proceeds to imagine his own private worlds, a waking-world which recurs, and dream-worlds which differ from the waking-world and from each other. From the waking standpoint, it is clear that dreams are illusory. But for their part, the dream-worlds exhibit all the characteristics of the waking-world, including a kind of Alice-in-Wonderland time-space-causation framework of their own. More important still, from Śaṅkara's point of view, is the fact that they contain a distinction between physical and mental (external and internal) and between real and unreal. This parallel between the (admittedly) false dreaming-worlds and the waking-world is used to bring home to the mind the falsity of the latter. Both worlds are the mere play of false ideas consequent upon ignorance of the true nature of the Self. And a critique of the whole conception of causality is developed, aimed partly at refuting the natural and common conviction that dream-experience is an illusory 'effect' arising from waking-experience conceived as a real cause. In these passages there is a tendency to emphasize the irrational and spontaneous character of the experiences of *both* the dream and the waking states.

Outside the above-mentioned two works, Śaṅkara rarely if ever attacks the notion of causality, or establishes the irreality of waking-experience from the parallel with dream. He inherited this line of teaching from Gauḍapāda, who was himself largely indebted for it to Mahāyāna Buddhist teaching. If Śaṅkara made little use of it outside his commentary on Gauḍapāda's Kārikās, it may be that he considered it suitable only for a particular kind of pupil. It has been argued that he was initiated into Advaita as a pupil of a Teacher of Gauḍapāda's line and that he later gradually emancipated himself from the acosmic and subjectivist views of Gauḍapāda under the influence of other traditional Vedanta teaching.[45] Whatever be the truth here, he and his great pupil Sureśvara express a reverence for Gauḍapāda which they nowhere retract, so that the texts in which he expresses the kind of views we more specifically associate with Gauḍapāda deserve to be represented in the present volume, and find their place in this and the following section. Much of the teaching on 'Turya' to follow in Volume III at section 3 of Chapter IX likewise has the characteristic stamp of Gauḍapāda.

The texts in the present section offer the following themes. It is wrong to object against the doctrine of Non-Duality that, in face of the experience of duality, non-duality cannot be eternal and must be something that supervenes and only comes into being after the world has ceased. The world never came into existence, any more than a snake imagined by error in place of a rope came into existence, and since it never came into existence it can never cease from existence either. Similarly, one should not object against the Advaitin that his doctrine is contradicted by the fact that the Vedic texts speak of transformations undergone by the Absolute. For they also speak of the Absolute as partless, and nothing that has no parts can undergo real transformation, though it can appear to undergo transformation through illusion (māyā). In these passages, Śaṅkara uses the term 'māyā' not so much in the sense of the divine creative power of the Lord as in the sense of a bare illusion, and he even defines it in the Buddhist manner as 'a name for something that does not exist'.[46] And as already noted,[47] Śaṅkara elsewhere reduces the 'divine creative powers' (māyā, plural) of Indra to the false cognitions of the individual soul, through which alone the world-appearance takes place.

Extracts 3 and 4 present a rare feature in Śaṅkara's writing, namely abstract dialectical argumentation in favour of the non-duality and transcendence of the Self. The first attacks the whole notion of causality as indefensible. The second uses abstract arguments of an Eleatic kind to show that nothing can come into being. The Sanskrit text of Extract 4 is difficult, and, as Professor Mayeda has shown, even the traditional Indian commentators are not agreed over the meaning. The present translation should be accounted merely exploratory and provisional. Extract 5 argues that Yāska's 'six states of becoming' do not apply to the Self, so that it suffers no 'birth' as the world and consequently no destruction or withdrawal. Extracts 6 and 7 argue that the Self, being purely spiritual, is relationless, actionless and not subject to modification.

TEXTS ON 'NOTHING CAN COME INTO BEING'

1. One might wonder how non-duality could be the real truth when the world is still continuing and when enlightenment can only arise through the cessation of the world. To answer this question the author of the Kārikās (Gauḍapāda) argues as follows.

The objection would apply if the world really existed. But as it is only imagined like a snake in a rope, it does not exist. If it existed, it could no doubt cease. But the case with an imaginary vision is different. A snake erroneously imagined in a rope is not a really existent entity that ceases to exist when it is distinguished from the rope. The case with a magician's hypnotic display is similar. When the spell is removed from the spectator's eyes, we cannot say that any existent reality has ceased to be. And similar again is the case with this mere illusion of duality called the world. All that really exists is the non-dual reality (the Self), comparable to the rope (in the rope-snake illusion) or the magician. Hence the meaning is that no world either comes into being or ceases.[48]

❖

2. It has been said (in Gauḍapāda's Kārikā III.18) that duality is a modification of non-duality. From this people might conclude that duality was real, just like non-duality has been said to be. To answer this objection (which implies that there is a contradiction in the teaching) the author of the Kārikās proceeds with further argumentation as follows.

When it is said that the non-dual reality undergoes modification through *illusion* (māyā) this means that it does so like the moon appearing as many to the one afflicted with the disease called timira, or like the misperceived rope appearing as a snake or a trickle of water. For there are no parts (or plurality) in the Self when it is viewed from the standpoint of the ultimate truth. It is only that which has parts that can undergo modification, because there can be differences among the various parts, as occurs, for instance, when clay undergoes transformation into various different pots and other objects. From this we should conclude that that which is partless and unborn (like the Absolute) cannot undergo real change or modification in any way whatever.

Indeed, if there were any real modification, there would be the absurdity that that which is by its very nature immortal, unborn and non-dual would become mortal, as if fire could become cold. No one can accept this, as it contradicts sound canons of knowledge to suppose that a thing can go contrary to its own nature. The Self, the unborn indestructible principle of reality, undergoes modification through illusion (māyā) only and not in the real sense. Hence duality is not in the ultimate sense real.[49]

❖

3. (The Teacher Gauḍapāda asks:) 'How can those who hold that the cause originates from the effect, and the effect from the cause, maintain that cause and effect form a beginningless series?' Such theorists maintain that the originating cause of good and bad action is the body and its organs, which are themselves the effect of good and bad action. And they regard good and bad action as the cause of the body and organs, taken as effect. Hence they maintain that the cause and the effect originate one another mutually. But how can they affirm that cause and effect form a beginningless series? It is a contradiction, because the eternal changeless Self cannot consist in a series of causes and effects.

Next he (the Teacher Gauḍapāda) explains in what sense their doctrine is contradictory. 'Those who hold that the cause of the cause is the effect are speaking as if a father could be born from his son'. That is, those who hold that a cause originates from an effect that itself originates from a cause are making the same contradiction as if they were saying a son were born from his father.

If the opponent persists in claiming that there is no contradiction, the Teacher proceeds further: 'If cause and effect come into being, you will have to decide which comes into being first. If they both came into being at the same time, they would not be causally inter-related, any more than the two horns (of a cow) are'.

That is..., you will have to investigate how the cause comes first and the effect comes later. For if cause and effect originated simultaneously, they could not be causally inter-related, any more than the left and right horns of a cow are, which originate simultaneously.

Why would they not be inter-related? The Teacher explains further: 'The cause, as conceived by you, proceeds from the effect. But (on your conception) it would not truly exist. And how could a non-existent cause in turn produce an effect?'

The effect by nature has to be produced. It has no independent nature (ātman) of its own. No cause could truly originate from an effect that was itself as unreal as the horns of a hare. And since the cause, as you conceive it, itself has no independent nature and does not truly exist, how could it in turn produce an effect? No causal relation, or any other kind of relation, is ever found to subsist between two things that are mutually dependent *if both are as unreal as the horns of a hare*. That is the Teacher's meaning.

Again the Teacher asks: 'If, on your view, a cause can only exist in virtue of an effect and an effect in virtue of a cause, then which of the two is established first, in dependence on which the other proceeds?' We have already shown that the notion that cause and effect originate one another is unfounded, on the ground that, as you conceive them, they cannot be inter-related. If you still persist in maintaining that the effect can truly bring the cause into existence and the cause can truly bring the effect into existence, then we ask of you which of the two was established first, that the establishment of the other could follow from it.[50]

If you cannot answer, then this impotence is a proof of your ignorance. Or else the alternative is that the sequence you laid down, whereby the cause is established by the effect and the effect by the cause in immediate succession, is broken and shown not to hold. Because thinkers of different schools are able to pick holes in each others' theories of causation in this way, it follows that no cause and effect can really stand to one another in any causal relation, and from this follows the impossibility of anything coming into being.

At this point our opponents will perhaps rejoin as follows. When we said that cause and effect were real and stood in a real mutual causal relation, they will say, you just pounced on the words we used, without considering the sense in which we were using them, and raised various quibbles about a father being sired by his son and absence of causal relation between the two horns of a cow. Of course we never intended to say that any effect could be established through a cause that had not itself been established or that a cause could be established as an effect of an effect that itself had not been established. Our view is that the cause and effect relation is (something that has to be accepted as real and stretching back as a beginningless series because it is familiar as such in experience) just like that of seed and sprout.

To this the author of the Kārikās replies as follows. Regarded from my standpoint, the example of seed and sprout begs the question.[51] You will ask whether it is not evident that there is a beginningless relation of mutual causality between seed and sprout. But the answer is that it is not evident. For one has to admit that each previous link in the chain must have a beginning, just as the present one has. As the new sprout, just produced, originated from a seed, so will any new seed have originated from a sprout, and both will have originated because they belong to a series. Every previous sprout and every previous seed will have had a beginning in just the same way. And as every single seed and every single sprout will have had a beginning, nothing (in the series) can be beginningless. (So the opponent, who has appealed to a 'beginningless' cycle 'as in the case of the seed and the sprout', cannot lay his finger on anything that is beginningless.) What is true of seed and sprout is also true of cause and effect in general.

Perhaps you will say that, even though no single seed or sprout is beginningless, the series as a whole is beginningless. But this idea is wrong too, as no such thing as a series can be established as constituting a single entity. The philosophers who claim that the seed and the sprout and the cause and the effect are beginningless do not themselves accept the existence of a *series* of seeds as a real entity over and above the seeds and sprouts themselves.[52] So our question 'How can they speak of cause and effect as without a beginning?' was only too well justified. Nor should our earlier arguments have been dismissed as quibbles, as the meanings we assigned to the words were not arbitrary but reasoned out from the fact that any different meaning would have been impossible.

Nor, proceeds the author of the Kārikās, do trained logicians use question-begging arguments to prove their theses. By 'question-begging arguments' here he means 'question-begging examples',[53] as it was the mere presence of this example (of the beginningless cycle formed by seed and sprout) occurring in uncritically accepted empirical experience that was supposed (by the opponent) to have probative force.

But what was meant by saying above 'From this follows the impossibility of anything coming into being'? The author of the Kārikās answers as follows. The impossibility of our understanding how cause and effect could follow one another in a beginningless cycle was the evidence for the impossibility of anything coming into being. How could one possibly apprehend an effect coming into being (i.e. with the full knowledge that it *was* an effect) without having previously apprehended its cause? He who apprehends anything being generated cannot but apprehend the generating cause, for the generated and its generator are inseparably linked. It was for this reason that it was said that from the impossibility of our understanding how real causes and effects could follow one another in a beginningless series there flowed the impossibility of anything really coming into being at all.

But there is another reason why nothing can really come into being. Nothing can be conceived as originating either from itself or from something different or from both these together, and this holds true whether we conceive such an effect to be existent, non-existent or both existent and non-existent. Nothing can originate from itself any more than a pot could originate from that very pot, for such a conception would imply that an effect was proceeding from a cause that was not itself yet in complete existence. Nor can anything originate from anything else of a different nature, any more than a cloth can originate from a pot or even from a different cloth. Nor can anything originate from itself and something else taken together, for this is contradictory. We do not find a new pot or a new cloth emerging from a pot and a cloth taken together.

But do we not find that (some things originate from others of like kind, as when) a pot originates from clay and a son from a father? It is true that naïve persons speak and think of effects as 'existing' and 'originating'. But the critically minded will want to examine the words 'exist' and 'originate' and the notions for which they stand when used in this context to see whether they are valid or invalid. But it becomes clear under critical scrutiny that any effect such as a pot or a son referred to or conceived through a word is itself no more than a word. For we have the Vedic text which says that every modification is a mere effect of speech.[54]

What is existent does not originate, from the mere fact of being already existent. It is (if the language of causality be used, not an effect but only a cause) like the clay and the father in the standard examples of causality. What is not existent does not originate either, from the mere fact of being non-existent, like the horn of a hare. What is existent-and-non-existent does not originate, as contradictories cannot form a unity. Hence it stands proved that nothing originates.

As for those (Buddhist realists of the Sarvāstivādin schools) who (deny the existence of any permanent material cause and) attempt to assert that origination is something real while reducing it to a momentary event in which the act, its factors and results are all taken as one, their position is unjustifiable to a degree. For they do not admit that anything lasts from one instant till the next so that its nature could be determined as 'this is such and such'. And a theory which makes experience of anything definite impossible (because nothing persistent exists) fails to account for memory (so that it is implausible when it tries to account for the appearance of objects having stability and permanence on the basis of 'memory' and 'similarity' and the like).

Furthermore, anyone like yourself who maintains that cause and effect are beginningless can be forced to admit that they can never come into being at all. The author of the Kārikās proceeds to explain why. A cause cannot arise from an effect that is beginningless (i.e. that itself never originated). You would not yourself admit that a cause could owe its origin to an effect that itself had not originated. Nor can you claim that an effect could arise naturally and without the aid of any external instrument from a cause that was beginningless.[55] Hence, by maintaining that cause and effect are without a beginning, you virtually admit that they never come into being at all. For it is a general rule that that which has no beginning does not come into being. Only that which has a cause can come into being, not that which does not have a cause.[56]

❖

4. About that which has no beginning (and is consequently eternal) there can be no false imaginations such as 'real' or 'other', so one cannot say that it does not exist. That which is presupposed by the power to imagine, that from which imagination proceeds, cannot itself be imagined. Whatever you see as duality is unreal.[57] But the Self is not seen (as an

object) and therefore cannot be dismissed as non-existent. That from which all imaginations such as 'real' and 'unreal' proceed, together with the power to think and reflect, is itself non-dual and (in the highest sense) real. Even though your conception of existence (as duality) is imaginary, you accept existence. If this duality were negated through reflection, then reflection itself would be negated and existence would remain unaffected. If it is not accepted that reflection is negated, then existence is affirmed all the more clearly (since it is accepted that reflection exists). If you say that the real so conceived (i.e. taken as transcendent) is as good as unreal because (being changeless and actionless) it is without practical bearing on life, like (the chimera of) a man with a horn,[58] we reply that absence of practical bearing on life is not a proof of non-existence, any more than its presence is a proof of real existence (since a dream or hallucination, for instance, may depress a man and affect his waking experience). Thus your position is undermined by (the fact that the Self exists as) the cause of reflection. Therefore duality is just projected[59] by illusion (māyā). The Veda, Smṛti and reason alike confirm this. Indeed, on this theory all becomes clear, and no other conclusion is tenable.

The Veda says that the Self is different in nature from what is imagined. It is already present as the principle and base of all imagination. When the Veda negates all that is imagined, in the text 'Not thus, not thus',[60] its purpose is to affirm the existence (of the Self as) that which is not imagined. Those who imagine empirical being or non-being in that which is not imagined, which is unborn, non-dual and imperishable, proceed from birth to death, their continued transmigratory existence arising from the delusions of their mind.

If one cannot logically establish that duality can arise, it cannot be real. But in fact it cannot (logically) come into being either from the real or the unreal. For if duality arose from the real, the latter would (undergo transformation and so) be unreal. And if duality arose from the unreal, the latter would be (its material cause and so) real. Hence action and its factors and results do not (from the standpoint of the highest truth) exist. Only the one unborn Self exists.

If you say that duality can be produced without action, then (you are left in the absurd position that) anything could produce it. If you say that action is required to produce duality, then whatever acts must be either real or unreal (and we have seen that duality can arise neither from the real nor from the unreal).[61] If you say (that in order to produce duality) the real becomes unreal and the unreal real, it will be like the rising and falling of scales on a balance, and it will not be possible to say where causality lies.[62]

If it is not accepted that either the real or the unreal can undergo a change of nature, then how can anything come into being? The real and the unreal just stay eternally as they are. They are ever distinct. And so, O my mind, how can anything (from the standpoint of the highest truth) ever come into being? Even if, to please you, I admit for argument's sake that things could come into being, you still cannot confer any advantage on me or cause any injury. For since profit and loss do not exist in the Self, they cannot be introduced into it from without. And even if I (went even further to please you and) admitted that profit and loss existed in the Self, then, because profit and loss already existed in my own Self, none of your actions could (introduce them and) affect me. The eternal and transient are unrelated, and it is impossible to establish that any effect could emerge from their congress. So nothing is related to anything else, and the supreme Reality is beyond the realm of speech.[63]

❖

5. The Self undergoes no modification in the form of birth, nor does it undergo final modification or destruction. When the text adds 'never' it means that, as the Self is never born and never suffers destruction, it never undergoes any modification whatever. Having never 'come into being', the Self will never 'pass out of existence' either. This is another ground for its not suffering destruction, as that which, having once existed, later passes out of existence is what is said in the world to 'suffer destruction'. The words meaning 'neither' in the text also imply that this Self is not anything like the body, which, having first not existed, later comes into existence. Thus the Self is not born. For that which comes into existence after at first not existing is said in the world to be born....

If the first (birth) and the last (destruction) of the six modifications of empirical being (recognized by Yāska) are negated, it follows that all the intervening ones are negated too. Still, one might think that the intervening stages ought to be mentioned by name, so the author of the Gītā negates the intervening modifications implicitly in the words beginning 'eternal' (śāśvata). Eternality negates the modification 'decay'. The Self does not fall away from its own true nature as it has no parts, and it does not lose any empirical qualities, as it had none to start with. And the word 'ancient' in the text negates the opposite modification to decay, namely growth. That which accumulates new parts grows and is said to be 'something new' (i.e. *not* ancient). But this Self, because partless, was already something new in ancient times and is also called 'ancient' because it is not subject to increase.[64]

When the text speaks of the 'being slain' of the body the reference is to the development of the body. The Self does not develop while the body develops. Destruction has to be interpreted as development to avoid exposing the text to the charge of self-repetition.

In this verse the 'six states of becoming', through which the objects of the empirical existence pass, are negated of the Self. The meaning of the text is, 'The Self is without modification of any kind'.[65]

❖

6. The body and organs have a gross form and have contact only with that which has a gross form. Such contact is an invariable condition of action. Nothing that does not have a gross form is ever found to act. The Self, however, does not have a gross form, which is why it is called relationless (asaṅga). Because it is relationless, it is not permanently connected with what is experienced in dream.[66] So it cannot in any way be an agent. For agency is possible only through being connected with a body and organs, whereas the Self has no connection or relation with anything. Hence the text proceeds, 'This Spirit (Self) is relationless'. Hence it is immortal.[67]

7. But is it not a proof that the Self engages in action in conjunction with the five factors of action[68] if the text has to speak of 'looking upon the Self alone as the agent'?[69] This difficulty does not arise, because the Self is not subject to modification, and hence cannot enter into conjunction with a vehicle (body) and the other factors of action. Only that which is subject to modification can enter into conjunction with other things and be an agent in conjunction with them. But the Self is without modification and cannot enter into conjunction or become an agent. So when the text spoke of the Self as 'alone' it referred to the natural state of the Self.

That the Self is not subject to modification is clear from the Veda, the Smṛti and reason alike. It has been more than once taught in the Gītā itself, as in such texts as 'The Self is said not to be subject to modification',[70] 'Actions are brought about by the constituents alone'[71] and 'Though seated in the body, He does not act....'[72] While from the standpoint of reason, it is as plain as the king's highway that the Self as a metaphysical principle is partless, not subject to action from outside and not subject to modification.

Even if it were admitted that the Self were subject to modification, it would have to be a modification originating from itself. The Self could not be the agent of the acts of the body and the other factors of action. The action of one person cannot belong to another who did not do it, and that which only belongs to someone through nescience could not belong to him in reality, any more than the silver-nature attributed in error to a piece of nacre belongs to it in reality, or any more than the impurities attributed to the ether of the sky by the naïve really belong to it. And in the same way, the modifications occurring to the body and other factors of action belong to them and not to the Self.[73]

3. The Argument from Dream

The group of Extracts assembled below circles round the theme 'Dream-experience is known in the light of waking experience to have been unreal, but all the characteristic features of waking experience are reproduced in dream, so that it follows that waking experience is as false as dream and that the whole world of waking experience can be seen to have been unreal on awakening to the true nature of the Self, just as the dream-world is rejected as unreal on emergence into the waking state'.

In the first two Extracts below, responsibility for the illusory distinction between subject and object is attributed to our ignorance of the true nature of the mind. As long as we do not realize that the mind is pure undefiled Consciousness in its true nature, it goes on throwing up the appearance of a division into subject and object and supplying us with the experiences we call waking and dream. From the waking standpoint the waking world seems real and the dream-world seems to have been subjective and illusory. But a distinction between the objective and the subjective is also found within the experiences of the dream-state, and Śaṅkara suggests that waking and dream, though distinguishable, are fundamentally the same in kind. In the second Extract, which has already appeared above in a different context,[74] it is argued that the common-sense view that dream experience is *caused* by waking experience does not stand critical examination.

One of the prime distinctions between the waking and the dream-world is that although *both* are private and mental, the time of the dream-objects is private to the individual dream, while the objects of the waking world owe allegiance to more than one private time-system. They are not the less imaginary for that, and are imagined by souls which are themselves but imaginations of the Lord. Objects like the Cosmic Vital Energy (prāṇa), which appear to constitute a common public world, are in fact reducible to the co-ordinated imaginations of individual souls, the co-ordination being explicable because the individual souls themselves are but imaginations of the Lord, the one Self (Extract 6, below).

The Extracts close with a piece from an upanishadic commentary which might be said to form some sort of bridge between the 'subjectivist' doctrine of the Commentary on the Kārikās of Gauḍapāda, in which objects are reduced to 'oscillations' of mind (citta), and the thought-world of the commentaries on the Upanishads and Brahma Sūtras, where the external world is frequently said to be set up by the Lord working through cosmic divinities and powers, and not directly through the imaginations of the individual souls. In this passage, causality is accepted and attributed to the impressions of waking experience, which is here said to cause dream-experience. However, the external world of waking experience is itself set down as mental, being 'thought' directly by the Lord. Everything, it is averred, is in its true nature the Absolute, and *as* the Absolute is perfectly real. But until enlightenment, all waking experience must be accepted as real in its province, even as a dream is accepted as real until the onset of the waking state.

TEXTS ON THE ARGUMENT FROM DREAM

1. The text means that the appearance of a subject and an object is like the appearance of straight and curved lines which results when a flaming torch is set in motion. Here it is consciousness that is set in motion, which means *apparently* set in motion, through nescience. For there is no real motion in motionless consciousness. It has already been declared to be unborn and motionless.

But when that very same flaming torch is held motionless, it does not suffer 'birth' into straight and curved lines, produces no false appearances and is 'unborn'. In the same way, Consciousness is set in motion only through nescience, and when the latter ceases, Consciousness ceases its apparent motion. It will then produce no more false appearances as if it were undergoing birth and the like....

When that flaming torch is in motion, the appearances of straight and curved lines do not come to the torch from any external source. Nor, when that torch is held motionless, do they leave it and depart elsewhere. They do not issue out from the torch as if from a house, as they are bereft of all substantial being. They are not real entities. Only a real entity can enter a place (or leave it), not an unreal one. It is the same with the appearances of birth, etc., in Consciousness. They, too, (do not issue from or enter back into Consciousness, for they) are appearances in just the same way.

The case with Consciousness is exactly parallel with that of the torch, except that Consciousness is in fact ever motionless. What then produces these appearances of birth and the rest in motionless Consciousness? The author of the Kārikās replies that because causality does not (in the true sense) exist, there can be no production of anything. Since nothing can be produced, these appearances are of the nature of non-existence. They are ever incomprehensible.

The overall meaning is that in the case of the appearances of straight and curved lines, we have the mere *notion* of straight and curved lines when there is really only the torch, and that, in just the same way, when there are appearances of birth, etc., in Consciousness, we have nothing but the false *notion* of birth, etc., though there is really nothing but Consciousness.[75]

❖

2. An illusory snake, imagined in a rope, turns out to be the reality when perceived in its true nature as the rope. Similarly, the mind turns out to be a reality when perceived in its true nature as the Self, of the nature of true knowledge. In dream, however, the mind oscillates as subject and object to produce an appearance of duality through illusion, like the false appearance of a snake arising in a rope. And in the waking state, also, it oscillates as subject and object to produce the appearance of subject and object in exactly the same way.

In the case of dream, there can be no doubt that the mind assumes a mere appearance of duality, while remaining non-dual in its true nature as the Self, just as the erroneously imagined snake remains throughout real in its true nature as the rope. For in dream there are in reality neither the elements which are beheld as objects nor the eyes and other sense-organs which 'perceive' them. There is nothing but consciousness. And our argument is that it is exactly the same in waking experience too. There, too, the only reality is consciousness, so that from this point of view there is no difference between the states of waking and dream.

It has been affirmed that it is verily the mind that assumes the form of duality, itself (i.e. the mind) a mere imagination like a snake imagined in a rope. What is the proof of this? The sage Gauḍapāda replies that it is an inference based on the method of agreement and difference,[76] and proceeds to analyse it as follows.

The proposition to be proved is, 'This whole duality seen by the imagined mind is itself nothing but mind'. The reason advanced is that when the mind is present, duality is also present (agreement, anvaya), and when the mind is not present, duality is not present (difference, vyatireka). For duality is not perceived when the mind has reached the state known technically as 'no-mind', that is to say when its movements have been suppressed through the practice of discriminative insight and dispassion,[77] nor is duality perceived when the mind is dissolved in dreamless sleep, like the snake dissolved in the rope. From this we conclude that duality is unreal.[78]

❖

3. The proposition to be proved is, 'The objects of the waking state are unreal'. The universal principle involved is, 'Because they are seen'. The example adduced is, 'like the objects seen in a dream'. The demonstration that the universal principle (technically called the 'reason', hetu) applies to the subject of the proposition runs, 'Just as the objects seen in a dream are unreal, so are the objects seen in the waking state.

For in both cases they are perceived'. And the conclusion of the argument is, 'Therefore the objects of waking experience are also false'.

The objects seen in dream are different from those seen in the waking state in point of existing within the body and being spatially confined. They are non-different from them in point of being seen and unreal.

Because of the well-known reason that the characteristic distinctions (into subjective and objective factors) are common to both states, the wise have called the waking and dream states one.[79] This is but the conclusion to be drawn from the earlier inferences.

Similarly, the falsity of all distinctions pertaining to the waking state follows from their non-existence before and after manifestation.[80] It is a settled principle in the world that whatever is non-existent both before the beginning and after the end of manifestation is also non-existent between, as, for example, a mirage. The same is the case with these distinctions seen in the waking state. They are non-existent both before and after manifestation, and are hence on a par with the mirage and other illusions. They are therefore false, but are taken to be real by deluded persons who do not know the Self.

Objection: This view that the objects seen in waking are unreal like the objects seen in dream is wrong. For the objects seen in waking serve a purpose. Food and drink and vehicles and the like afford comfort by appeasing hunger and thirst and enabling us to travel. But this is not the case with the objects of dream-experience. So this idea that the objects seen in the waking state are unreal like those seen in a dream is a mere fancy.

Answer: Not at all. Food and drink and the like are useful in the waking state, but this may be contradicted in dream. For one who has eaten and drunk his fill in the waking state may very well find himself suffering from hunger and thirst after a day and a night's fast as soon as he falls asleep (and begins to dream). And, conversely, one who has eaten and drunk his fill in dream may wake up to find himself unsatisfied and hungry. So there is an actual contradiction of what is seen in the waking state with what is perceived in dream. Our view therefore is that there cannot be any doubt that the objects seen in the waking state are unreal, just like those in dream. Since the objects both of the waking and the dream states have a beginning and an end, they are both said to be false.

Objection: Your argument that, because the distinctions of waking and dream are the same in kind, the distinctions seen in waking must be false is not right. Why? Because the example does not apply. How so? These distinctions we see in dream are not the same as those we see in waking. You ask in what way? Well, a man sees altogether unprecedented things in dream. For example, he might see himself with eight arms riding on an elephant with four tusks. And one sees many other such wonders in dream. One cannot equate these things with ordinary illusions. So they must be real. Hence the example you quoted did not apply. So it was not right to say that waking is as unreal as a dream.

Answer: No. For the things seen in dream that you regard as unprecedented are not self-evident realities: their manifestation is conditioned by the fact that the one to whom they manifest is *in a particular state*, to wit, the dream-state. Just as those who inhabit heaven have special qualities like the possession of a thousand eyes, so do those in the dream-state assume private characteristics peculiar to that state. Such visions are not independent self-evident realities as the Witnessing Consciousness that witnesses them is, in its true nature. The latter, assuming a particular conditioned state and becoming the dreamer, goes to the dream-world and sees unprecedented things like those just mentioned, which are but imaginations of the mind. It is like a cultured person here in this world on his way to another country, who goes to reach that country on a particular path and notices the objects peculiar to that locality as he passes them by. The rope-snake and the mirage, too, (though unprecedented), are but private characteristics of someone in a particular state (that of defective vision in the waking state), and these are acknowledged to be unreal. And in the same way, the unprecedented things seen in the dream-state are also but private characteristics of a person in a particular state. So to take the example of dream-experience as something unreal was perfectly justified.

The text (i.e. the Kārikās of Gauḍapāda) has disposed of the objection that the objects seen in dream cannot be unreal since they are unprecedented. It now proceeds to explain further how the distinctions perceived in the waking state are on a par with those seen in dream.

In the dream-state, too, that which is (even in the dream-state itself regarded as being) imagined and as mere fancy in the mind is unreal, as it is no longer seen when the fancy ends; whereas that which (in the dream-state) is seen through the eyes and other senses, like a pot, appears to the mind in dream to be something external to it, and is (from the standpoint of the dream) real. So even within that (i.e. the dream-state) which is all determined (after waking up) to have been unreal, a distinction is perceived between real and unreal. (From the waking standpoint) it is seen that in dream both the objects 'inside' the mind and 'outside' it were imagined and unreal, (so that the mere fact that we distinguish between unreal mental fancy and real external fact in the waking state is no proof that the objects perceived as external to the mind in the waking state are real).[81]

❖

4. We conclude that there is no real travelling to other places in dream, because the laws of time and space that govern travelling about in the waking state are not found there. Moreover, conversation with friends and the reception of money and the like, which occurred in dream, are found not to have occurred on waking. So this is another ground for disbelieving in real spatial travel in dream. And the body that is seen (in dream) as roving about is itself unreal, for on waking up we are aware of quite a different body still remaining at the place where it was at the time of going to sleep. Just as the body seen in dream is unreal, so are all objects seen by the mind in the waking state unreal, from the mere fact of being seen by the mind. The whole burden of the present passage is to show that waking experience is unreal because it is on a par with dream.

And here the Teacher proceeds further to explain how the objects of waking experience are unreal. Because dream-experience is perceived as divided into subject and object like waking experience, it is taken to have waking experience as its cause. It is because of this fact that a man's waking experience seems real to him when he has awoken from dream, just like the dream did before he had awoken from it. But even a man's waking experience is not anything real to another man.

To the dreamer himself, and to him alone, the dream-experience seemed (during the dream) like a reality known to all. And therefore his waking experience, too, being taken for its cause, seems to him like a reality known to all. But in fact it is not a reality known to all, any more than the dream was. That is the meaning of the Teacher's words.

Now, it might be argued that the waking experience, though the cause of dream-experience, is not an unreality like the latter. For dream-experience is fleeting, while waking experience proves durable. This is true enough from the standpoint of those who lack the power to discriminate. But those who possess the power of discrimination do not recognize that anything real can come into being. Wherefore the Teacher proceeds to argue further as follows.

Because the coming into being of all this world-appearance is not admitted as a true fact, the Upanishads declare, in the text 'He includes all that is without and all that is within and is unborn',[82] that all is 'unborn', meaning by that that all is really the Self. And though you may think that the dream-experience springs from a waking experience that is real, this view is wrong. It is not generally admitted that anything unreal can spring from anything real. Nothing that is totally unreal like the horn of a hare is found to spring from anything.

But did I not myself say that dream-experience sprang from waking experience? How then can I now say that it does not spring from it? Listen and hear how we conceive this (supposed) relation of cause and effect. First the soul perceives in the waking state objects that are perfectly unreal, as unreal as a snake erroneously imagined in a rope. Under the influence of this experience, he has imaginary visions in dream, divided into subject and object like waking experience. Having seen these unreal visions in dream, he no longer sees them after waking up and no longer imagines them. The word 'and' in the text shows that, just as he no longer sees the dream-objects in the waking state, so he no longer sees the objects of the waking world once he has entered the world of dream, though he saw them formerly. Therefore what we said was that waking experience could be viewed as in some sense a cause of dream-experience, but that (it was not a cause in the true sense because) it was not itself real.[83]

❖

5. Thus, while name, form and action can be shown to be unreal imaginations, the principle of pure Being and Consciousness[84] is not imaginary. It is the *prius* of all knowledge and also that which has to be known (in its true nature through the destruction of ignorance). All other than it is imaginary. In dream, where that primordial knower has experience through illusion (māyā), that by which He knows is called knowledge (in the empirical sense). That by which He sees is called sight, that by which He hears is called hearing... And it is the same with taste, touch and the mind and all the other organs. Thus distinctions are introduced into Consciousness, which is essentially one, through imagined adjuncts, just as the one homogeneous crystal seems to be of different colours according to where it is placed.

And just as in dream, so also in waking, the distinctions in his Consciousness are imaginary. Action springs up in Him through desire on account of nescience, and his light manifests the object as it lies in the intellect. Just as in dream, so also in waking, the external object and internal idea arise as relative conceptions, like the written and spoken word.[85] And when the soul imagines a distinction, it becomes desirous of it and acts to obtain it.[86] And what it desires and acts to obtain, that it gets. All this proceeds from nescience, hence all this world is unreal. It is seen only by him who is afflicted by nescience and is not seen in dreamless sleep. The Veda has characterized knowledge and nescience as vision of unity and vision of difference respectively, and hence it has recommended us with the utmost emphasis to pursue knowledge.[87]

❖

6. An objector might ask: 'If the distinctions of dream-experience and waking experience are illusory, who is it who cognizes these internal and external imaginations? And who is the one who creatively imagines them?' The meaning of the question is, 'What is the basis of memory and knowledge? And if there is no support for them, would not the fallacy of denying the Self result?'[88]

The Self, the great divine luminous principle (deva), Himself imagines Himself in Himself as having the distinctions to be described below, as a snake is falsely imagined in a rope, and it is He Himself, likewise, who cognizes these distinctions. This is the upanishadic doctrine. There is no substratum (āśraya) of empirical memory and knowledge other than this. Empirical knowledge and memory, however, do not proceed without a substratum, as the Nihilists claim.[89]

How does He proceed, then, in this imagining? The Lord, the Self, differentiates out the external objects of the world, such as the (five) great elements beginning with sound, and also others located internally in the mind-stuff (citta) as unmanifest impressions (vāsanā). And with mind (citta) directed outwards He projects the earth and other objects that obey constant laws, and with mind directed inwards He projects daydreams and other spontaneous phenomena (such as errors and hallucinations), limited to the time when they are imagined.

But if you claim that all is imagined by a mind as in a dream, then the following doubt presents itself. Is there not a radical difference between what is merely imagined by the mind, and undergoes conditioning imposed purely by the mind alone, and external objects, which limit one another mutually? Can such a theory explain this distinction?

This doubt, however, is not justified. In some cases, the length of time a phenomenon exists is conditioned solely by one mind, and such phenomena are said to exist in 'mental time'. They exist, that is, only when a single mind imagines them. But external objects belong to two times, to two different time-systems which condition each other on the pattern of 'He stays while he milks the cow'. As long as he stays he milks the cow, and as long as he milks the cow he stays. External distinctions (experienced in the waking state) condition one another mutually in the form 'as long as this, so long that'. Internal phenomena, therefore, belong to mental time, external phenomena to two times. But all are equally imagined. The special distinction that external phenomena (appear to) have of belonging to two times itself has no other cause but being imagined. Here, too, the significant example is dream.[90]

It is true that the haziness that things have when they are internal and manifest as mere impressions and the clarity they have when they are external and in contact with the faculty of sight and other senses constitutes a distinction (between external and internal or purely mental phenomena in the waking state). But this distinction is not introduced by the *real existence* of the (external) phenomena, for the same distinction is found in dreams. What does introduce it then? Difference in the organ through which the phenomenon is perceived. Thus it is shown that the external objects experienced in the waking state are imaginary just like those of dream.

What is the mechanism of this imagination whereby external and internal phenomena appear to stand in the relation of effect and cause? First of all the Lord imagines the individual soul, who belongs to the realm of cause and effect, and thinks, in regard to his own true (actionless) Self, 'I do such and such' or 'I am affected by such and such a joy or such and such a sorrow', whereas his Self is really pure and of a totally different nature. All this is false imagination, like the false imagination of a snake in a rope. Then, for the sake of the individual soul, the Lord imagines the Cosmic Vital Energy and then (as modifications of it) all the other phenomena of the world in all their variety, both external and internal, and differentiated into action, its factors and results.

But how is this imagining actually done? It is the individual soul, imagined by the Lord, who does all this work of imagination. What he formerly projected, that he later remembers. Because he imagined a cause formerly, he proceeds now to imagine an effect. Then he remembers cause and effect and later imagines them again in the same way, and imagines also the act, together with its factors and results, which brought them about.[91] Having imagined all this, he again remembers it, and from this memory arise new imaginations. And in this way he imagines the internal and external phenomena in all their variety as if they were cause and effect.

In this connection, it has been said that the individual soul is the root of all other imaginations. He (the Teacher Gauḍapāda) now proceeds to show through an example the necessary previous condition for the imagination of the individual soul. In worldly experience it happens that in poor light a rope is not clearly known for what it is, and then false imaginations of various kinds arise in regard to it and people think 'Is it a snake?', 'Is it a trickle of water?', 'Is it a stick?' The pre-condition (nimitta) for all this is non-perception of the rope in its true form; for if the rope were already known in its true form, there could not be alternative suppositions regarding it, such as snake, water and stick, any more than one can have alternative suppositions about the fingers of one's own hand. And the conclusion of the entire upanishadic teaching is that different false suppositions arise in regard to the Self in exactly the same way, and that it is falsely imagined under distinctions as all the endless phenomena, beginning with the individual soul and the Cosmic Vital Energy. In its true nature, the Self is quite different from the evil empirical world of cause and effect. But it is not recognized in its true form as pure Consciousness and pure non-dual Being.[92]

❖

7. *Objection:* The objects seen in dream are just forms assumed by the latent impressions (vāsanā) of waking experience. One does not see actual men and women in dream.

Answer: Your statement is true, but does not go far enough. The objects of waking experience, too, proceed from mental impressions, as the objects of the world consist (according to the Chāndogya Upanishad) of the elements fire, water and earth (lit. food) which were brought forth through the 'taking thought' of Being.[93] Moreover, it has been taught that the worlds are rooted in will in the text, 'Heaven and earth were willed'.[94] And the texts in general teach that the rise and dissolution of the world proceed from the inmost Self and that their maintenance takes place there also, as in such passages as, 'Even as the spokes are fastened in the hub'.[95] Thus mental impressions and external objects cause one another mutually, like seed and sprout. Though external objects spring from mental impressions and mental impressions from external objects (so that both, as such, have a mere conditioned and relative existence and do not exist as independent realities), yet neither of them are false *as* the Self.

Objection: But are not the objects beheld in dream found to be unreal by a person when he wakes up?

Answer: True. But they are only false from the standpoint of waking experience, not false in their true nature as the Self. And similarly, the objects of waking experience are false in relation to dream experience, but not in their own true nature (as the Self). It is the determinate form of all things, and that only, which is caused by false notions (mithyā-pratyaya). Therefore the text (at an earlier point of the Chāndogya

Upanishad) said, 'A modification, being only a suggestion of speech, is false, only the three elements (*viz.* fire, water and earth) are real'.[96]

Even these three elements are false when considered in isolation as particular forms, though real in their intrinsic nature as pure Being. Before one awakens to the Self as reality, everything is real in its own realm, as the objects seen in a dream (are real during the dream). So there is no contradiction in our doctrine.[97]

❖

NOTES TO CHAPTER VII

References to Extracts are in bold type

1 Sac, *Sugamā*, 99.

2 Sac, M.V. 667ff.

3 For the exegetical doctrine of 'topics', see Vol.V, Chap.XIII, section 4, below.

4 Cp. U.S. (verse) XVII.9.

5 Chānd. VI.viii.4.

6 G.K. III.15.

7 I.e. as opposed to knowledge about creation, which is a mere aspect of the world-appearance.

8 Taitt. II.1.

9 Chānd. VII.i.3.

10 Śvet. III.8.

11 B.S.Bh. I.iv.14.

12 See Ait. I.iii.12.

13 Ait. I.i.1.

14 Ait. I.i.3. The Aitareyas were a school of Ṛg Vedic priests, so the tradition may well go back to R.V. X.90.

15 Ait. I.ii.1.

16 *Ibid.*

17 The references to all these wonders can be found in the Ait. Up.

18 'Eulogistic' passages in the Veda are those which are concerned, like oratory, not with truth but with persuasion. Mythological passages about creation, according to Śaṅkara, are not literally true but are aids to help the mind reach out towards

the one Absolute, the ground of all.

19 The point in question here is that all the details of the world-appearance are explicable, within the world-appearance, only as proceeding from one conscious controller, while the world-appearance itself is not self-existent but presupposes a self-existent ground.

20 Cp. the example cited above Chap.V, section 5, of telling children that taking milk will make their hair grow, and the reference given there at Note 145.

21 Ait. Bh. II.i.1 (introduction).

22 G.K. III.10.

23 G.K. III.9. The ether, being subtle, undergoes no real differentiation when apparently enclosed, for instance, within different pots.

24 Chānd. I.ii and Bṛhad. I.iii.

25 For the teaching that meditation is a means to unite oneself with the object of one's meditation, see Vol.VI, Chap.XIV, section 1, below.

26 G.K.Bh. III.15.

27 The term kūṭastha, of Sāṅkhya origin, is not found in the classical Upanishads, but occurs at Bh.G. VI.8, XII.3 and XV.16 and frequently in the philosophical portions of the M.Bh.

28 And hence could not have been the meaning intended by any Vedic text, for all the Vedic texts minister directly or indirectly to the good of man.

29 Bṛhad. IV.ii.4. **B.S.Bh. II.i.14.**

30 Especially as a reflection of the intellect. **Bṛhad. Bh. I.iv.7.**

31 Īśa 7.

32 Bṛhad. IV.iv.19.

33 Chānd. VI.viii.3.

34 B.S.Bh. IV.iii.14.

35 We have already encountered the story as reproduced in a slightly different form by another Ācārya, above Vol.I, Chap.I, section 6.

36 The desire for a son, for wealth and for the attainment of an exalted 'world' at death, the first two being valued not only for themselves but also as a means to the last. Cp. Bṛhad. III.v.1.

37 Bṛhad. II.i.20 (under comment) and also Muṇḍ. II.i.1.

38 Bṛhad. IV.v.13.

39 Bṛhad. IV.iv.19, cp. Kaṭha II.i.10.

40 Bṛhad. Bh. II.i. 20.

41 Bṛhad. II.iii.6, III.ix.26, IV.ii.4, IV.iv.22.

42 Bṛhad. Bh. IV.iv.25.

43 G.K. III.15, cp. Extract 3 above.

44 G.K. Bh. IV.42.

45 Hacker, 'Śaṅkara der Yogin', 127ff.

46 G.K. Bh. IV.58, *ad fin*.

47 Above, Chap.V, section 5, Extract 16, with references at Note 199.

48 G.K. Bh. I.17.

49 G.K. Bh. III.19.

50 Nikhilānanda Swāmī observes: 'If the priority of the one cannot be established, then it cannot be proved that one is dependent on the other for its existence'.

51 That is, the thing we want to know is not whether seed and sprout are observed to follow one another in a cycle which must be assumed to be beginningless, but whether they can be rationally established as realities standing in a real causal relation, and not mere appearances.

52 On the Buddhist sources from which Gauḍapāda derived the arguments at present under comment, see V.S. Bhattacharya, Ā.Ś.G. 115-129. The schools under criticism are Buddhist realists of the Hīnayāna tradition.

53 That is, of the seed and sprout, which only illustrates real causality, so to speak, if it does illustrate real causality, i.e. if it can be shown to be itself a genuine case of causality.

54 Chānd. VI.i.4.

55 Because if it could arise from a beginningless cause at all without the support of an external instrument or auxiliary, it would be eternally arising. Sac, M.R.V. 344f.

56 G.K. Bh. IV.14-23.

57 Argumentation in support of this statement will be found in the next section.

58 The stock example of something never perceived and therefore without practical bearing on life. The opponent here is a Buddhist who, as such, makes 'practical efficiency' the test of the real, whereas for the Advaitin non-contradictability in past, present and future is the test of reality.

59 Reading prasṛtam with Mayeda and Gokhale.

60 Bṛhad. III.ix.26, etc.

61 The presence of the disjunctive judgement 'Whatever acts must be either real or unreal' suggests that Śaṅkara did not accept the category 'neither real nor unreal' for anything except the Absolute. Cp. the words of his pupil Troṭaka, Ś.S.S. verses 149-150.

62 If the real becomes unreal (or vice-versa) simultaneously with the rise of duality, then, like the rising and falling of the scales of a balance, neither event will be able to occur without the other, and it will not be possible to say whether the duality arose because of the change of the real into the unreal, or whether the real changed into the unreal as the result of a spontaneous rise of duality. (On the balance, cp. Jacob, *Handful*, Section II, 59.) And (according to the commentator Rāma Tīrtha) the view that duality could arise *after* the fall of reality from its nature would involve infinite regress. The fall of the real from its nature would have to take place in time (being an event) and so be a result, and this result would have to have a cause situated in time and be a result, and this cause would have to have its cause in turn and so to infinity. Similar reasoning would apply if duality were supposed to come into being as a result of the unreal becoming real.

63 U.S. (verse) XIX.13-24. Commentators and interpreters disagree over the meaning of these difficult verses.

64 For a similar juxtaposition of the two ideas of antiquity and freshness, cp. the famous lines of St. Augustine, *Confessions*, X.xxvii: 'Too late am I come to love thee, O thou Beauty, so ancient and withal so fresh'.

65 Bh.G.Bh. II.20. The 'six states of becoming' are birth, existence, growth, transformation, decline and destruction.

66 The context is that of illustrating from dream the relationlessness and actionlessness of the Self. Cp. Bṛhad. Bh. IV.iii.15, below, Vol.III, Chap.IX, section 1, Extract 5.

67 Bṛhad. Bh. IV.iii.15.

68 On this technical term, see Bh.G.Bh. XVIII.14-16, Vol.V, Chap. XII, section 1, Extract 1, below.

69 Referring to Bh.G. XVIII.16.

70 Bh.G. II.25.

71 Bh.G. III.27.

72 Bh.G. XIII.31.

73 Bh.G.Bh. XVIII.17.

74 Above Vol.I, Chap.III section 4, Extract 1, *ad init.*

75 G.K.Bh. IV.47-52.

76 In order to draw a secure inference you need a universal law. Universal laws (vyāpti) are discovered empirically by noting cases where things are invariably concomitant (anvaya) and not concomitant (vyatireka). Smoke is a sign or 'reason' (hetu) of fire. This is known because smoke is invariably accompanied by fire (anvaya) and there are no instances of smoke without fire (no vyatireka).

77 The doctrine that the motions of the mind are to be suppressed altogether (citta-vṛtti-nirodha) through discrimination based on spiritual practice (abhyāsa) allied to dispassion (vairāgya) may be traced to Vyāsa's Commentary on Yoga Sūtra I.12, which is probably the basis for Śaṅkara's juxtaposition of the same three ideas in the present passage. Elsewhere Śaṅkara is careful to differentiate Vedanta doctrine from Yoga doctrine, and particularly to insist that the Yoga of Patañjali cannot of its own lead to the final liberation and immortality taught in the Upanishads. Cp. Bṛhad. Bh. I.iv.7, trans. Mādhavānanda, 91, and B.S.Bh. II.i.3, trans. Gambhīrānanda, 306. On this topic, cp. Sac, *Misconceptions*, 110-113 and 117f. Professor Hacker has argued, with characteristic attention to terminological detail, that Śaṅkara may have passed, as it were, by stages from Yoga to Vedanta, and that the Commentary to Gauḍapāda was a relatively early work which retains features of the Yoga Śāstra that were later rejected. Cp. 'Śaṅkara der Yogin', 125ff.

78 G.K.Bh. III.28-31.

79 'The wise' probably includes Gauḍapāda here, cp. below, Vol.III, Chap.IX, section 3, Extract 4, also *ibid.* Chap.VIII, section 1, Extract 4, which is from Ait.Bh. I.iii.12. But the words 'the wise' derive from Gauḍapāda's own text (G.K.III.16), and are evidence of earlier authors thinking on the same lines.

80 There is a contrast between this view and the Sat-kārya Vāda developed in the Upanishad and Brahma Sūtra commentaries where it is maintained, against the Vaiśeṣikas and Buddhists, that the effect pre-exists in the material cause before its manifestation. But we have also seen (above, Chap.VI, section l, introduction) that Śaṅkara really only *used* the Sat-kārya Vāda doctrine as a springboard for going beyond the idea of causality altogether and rising to the standpoint of Gauḍapāda, that of the highest truth.

81 G.K.Bh. II.4-9.

82 Muṇḍ. II.i.2.

83 G.K.Bh. IV.34-39.

84 sac-cin-mātram. On the inclusion of sat and cit coupled with the omission of ānanda, cp. above, Vol.I, Chap.IV, section 4, introduction.

85 The notions of an object that is 'external' and an idea that is 'internal' are false relative conceptions. Relative to a written character, there arises a false idea in the reader's mind of some sound for which it is conventionally agreed to stand. Communication through reading and writing is a useful and profitable exercise, but it involves taking the written characters for heard sounds when they are not in fact sounds. What the written character calls up is in fact not even an external sound, it is a mere impression, a mere 'internal' idea. This 'internal' idea is again expressed 'externally' through written characters when the reader proceeds later to write. Whatever significance

reading and writing have is relative to each other. They are not related naturally but only through conventional attribution. Similarly, the notions of external object and mental idea are significant relative to each other only and not in relation to truth. Cp. above Chap.VI, section 2, Extract 15.

86 Cp. Bṛhad. IV.iv.5.

87 U.S. (verse) XVII.13-21.

88 Any doctrine advanced in the course of explaining the Upanishads that logically implies the non-existence of the Self is wrong, as it contradicts their central teaching. Moreover, it betrays common cause with the arch-enemy of the Veda, the Buddhist.

89 By 'Nihilists' Śaṅkara usually means the Mādhyamika school of Buddhists, whose teaching will be discussed at Vol.IV, Chap.I, section 5, below. The Mādhyamika declares both the world and the individual soul to be illusions, but refuses to affirm Being or any other permanent principle as their base. The Advaitin claims it is impossible to account for empirical knowledge or memory on this basis.

90 Just as in waking, so in dream, conditioning in time and place occurs according to the (admittedly 'wilder') rules of the dream. In many dreams, some of the phenomena appear to belong to two times and so to be causally conditioned from without, and also to be permanent and real. But it is agreed that all dream-experience is imagined. The fact that some phenomena of waking experience appear to be causally conditioned, permanent and real, is therefore no argument to show that waking phenomena are not imagined. Sac, M.R.V. 179.

91 What he imaginatively creates is 'external' and 'clear'. But as it is imagined, it lasts only during the period of being imagined. It is, however, 'remembered'. That is, it leaves a deposit, as it were, of memory, and this is the seed or potentiality of new

creative imagination. As memory, it is 'internal' and 'obscure', but it issues in further imagination.

92 **G.K.Bh. II.11-17.**

93 Chānd. VI.ii.3.

94 Chānd. VII.iv.2.

95 Chānd. VII.xv.1.

96 Chānd. VI.iv.1. The term rendered 'is false' (anṛtam) is inserted by Śaṅkara to bring out the full force of the meaning.

97 I.e. our doctrine explains the texts proclaiming non-duality as the final truth while at the same time explaining how all things are real as perceived before enlightenment. **Chānd. Bh. VIII.v.4.**

LIST OF GENERAL ABBREVIATIONS

In principle, works are referred to under their authors' names throughout the Notes, and the abbreviations occasionally used to distinguish between an author's different works should not cause any difficulty. Except for the two entries R.T. and Sac, the following list comprises those abbreviations that are used independently of any author's name. The list excludes the names of Upanishads on which Śaṅkara wrote commentaries, which are listed under his name in the Bibliography and readily identifiable there.

A.B.O.R.I.	*Annals of the Bhandarkar Oriental Research Institute*, Poona
Ā.D.S.	*Āpastamba Dharma Sūtra*
Ā.Ś.G.	*Āgama Śāstra of Gauḍapāda*
Ā.S.S.	Ānanda Āśrama Sanskrit Series, Poona
Ā.Ś.S.	*Āpastambīyam Śrauta Sūtram*, Mysore University
A.V.	*Atharva Veda*
B.B.V.	*Bṛhadāraṇyakopaniṣad Bhāṣya Vārtika* (Sureśvara)
B.B.V.S.	*Bṛhadāraṇyakopaniṣad Bhāṣya Vārtika Sāra* (Vidyāraṇya)
Bh.	*Bhāṣya* (i.e. Commentary)
Bh.G.	*Bhagavad Gītā*
Bh.G.Bh.	*Bhagavad Gītā Bhāṣya* (Śaṅkara)
B.S.	*Brahma Sūtras*
B.S.Bh.	*Brahma Sūtra Bhāṣya* (Śaṅkara)
B.Sid.	*Brahma Siddhi* (Maṇḍana Miśra)
C.P.B.	*The Central Philosophy of Buddhism* (T.R.V. Murti)
G.I.P.	*Geschichte der indischen Philosophie* (Frauwallner)

G.K.	*Gauḍapāda Kārikās*, included in Gambhīrānanda, *Eight Upanishads*, Vol.II
G.K.Bh.	*Gauḍapāda Kārikā Bhāṣya*
G.O.S.	Gaekwad's Oriental Series, Baroda
G.P.	Gītā Press, Gorakhpur
I.H.Q.	*Indian Historical Quarterly*
I.I.J.	*Indo-Iranian Journal*
J.A.	*Journal Asiatique*
J.A.O.S.	*Journal of the American Oriental Society*
J.B.O.O.S.	*Journal of the Bihar and Orissa Oriental Society*
J.O.I.B.	*Journal of the Oriental Institute*, Baroda
J.O.R.M.	*Journal of Oriental Research*, Madras University
J.R.A.S.B.B.	*Journal of the Royal Asiatic Society of Great Britain and Ireland, Bombay Branch*
J.U.B.	*Jaiminīya Upanishad Brāhmaṇa*
M.Bh.	*Mahābhārata* G.P. Mūla-mātra Ed., 4 Vols.
M.K.	*Mādhyamika* (or *Mūlamādhyamika*) *Kārikās* of Nāgārjuna
M.R.V.	*Māṇḍūkya Rahasya Vivṛtiḥ* (Saccidānandendra Svāmin)
M.V.	*Method of the Vedanta* (Saccidānandendra Svāmin)
N.S.	Nirṇaya Sāgara Press
N.Sid.	Naiṣkarmya Siddhi (Sureśvara)
N.Sū.	*Nyāya Sūtras*
P.D.	*Pañcadaśī* (Vidyāraṇya)

P.E.W.	*Philosophy East and West*, Honolulu
P.M.	Pūrva Mīmāṃsā
P.P.	*Pañcapādikā* (Padmapāda)
R.T.	Rāma Tīrtha (17th century commentator)
R.V.	*Ṛg Veda*
Sac.	Saccidānandendra Svāmin (modern author d.1975)
Ś.B.	*Śatapatha Brāhmaṇa*
S.B.E.	Sacred Books of the East Series, Oxford University Press, Oxford (reprinted by Motilal Banarsidas, Delhi)
Ś.Ś.P.B.	*Śuddha-Śaṅkara-Prakriyā-Bhāskara* (Saccidānandendra Svāmin)
Ś.V.	*Mīmāṃsā Śloka Vārtika* (Kumārila Bhaṭṭa)
T.S.	*Taittirīya Saṃhitā*
T.B.V.	*Taittirīya Bhāṣya Vārtika* (Sureśvara)
U.S.	*Upadeśa Sāhasrī* (Śaṅkara)
V.P.	*Viṣṇu Purāṇa*
V.V.S.	*Viśuddha Vedānta Sāra* (Saccidānandendra Svāmin)
W.Z.K.S.O.	*Wiener Zeitschrift für die Kunde Süd- und Ostasiens*
Y.D.	*Yukti Dīpikā*
Y.S.	*Yoga Sūtras* (Patañjali)
Z.D.M.G.	*Zeitschrift der Deutschen Morgenländischen Gesellschaft*
Z.I.I.	*Zeitschrift für Indologie und Iranistik*
Z.M.R.	*Zeitschrift für Missionswissenschaft und Religionswissenschaft*, Münster/Westfalen

BIBLIOGRAPHY

I. Texts of Śaṅkara

Aitareya Upaniṣad Bhāṣya, G.P. Ed., n.d. See Venkataramiah, D.

Bhagavad Gītā Bhāṣya (Bh.G.Bh.), ed. D.V. Gokhale, Poona, 1931. See also Śāstrī, A. Mahādeva.

Brahma Sūtra Bhāṣya (B.S.Bh.), ed. with the *Ratna Prabhā Ṭīkā* of Govindānanda, the *Nyāya Nirṇaya Ṭīkā* of Ānandagiri and the *Bhāmatī* of Vācaspati, by Mahādeva Śāstrī Bākre, N.S. Press, Bombay, 1934. See also S.S. Sūryanārāyaṇa Śastrī.

Bṛhadāraṇyaka Upaniṣad Bhāṣya, ed. H.R. Bhāgavat, Ashtekar Company, Second Ed., Poona, 1928. Also consulted: Ā.S.S. Ed. of the same work, with the *Ṭīkā* of Ānandagiri.

Chāndogya Upaniṣad Bhāṣya, Ā.S.S. Ed., Poona, 1890. Also consulted: H.R. Bhāgavat's Ed., Ashtekar Co., Poona, 1927.

Īśa Upaniṣad. See Saccidānandendra, *Īśāvāsya*. Also consulted: G.P. Ed. of Śaṅkara's *Īśa Bhāṣya*.

Kāṭhaka (usually referred to as *Kaṭha*) *Upanishad*, ed. with Shri Shaṅkara's Commentary and Sanskrit Notes by Saccidānandendra Svāmin, Adhyātma Prakāśālaya, Holenarsipur, South India, 1962. Also consulted: G.P. Ed. of same work.

Kena Upanishad, with the *Pada* and *Vākya* Commentaries of Shri Shaṅkara, ed. with Sanskrit Notes by Saccidānandendra, Holenarsipur, 1959. Also consulted: G.P. Ed.

Māṇḍūkya Upaniṣad and Gauḍapāda Kārikā Bh.(G.K.Bh.), G.P.Ed., n.d.

Muṇḍaka Upanishad, ed. with Shri Shaṅkara's Commentary and Sanskrit Notes by Saccidānandendra, Holenarsipur, 1960. Also consulted: G.P. Ed.

Praśna Upaniṣad Bhāṣya, G.P.Ed., n.d.

Taittirīya Upaniṣad. See Sac, *Taittirīya Upanishad Shikshāvallī* and *Ānandavallī-Bhṛguvallī*, with Shaṅkara's Commentary and Editor's Notes and Commentary. Also consulted: G.P. Ed. of *Taittirīya Bhāṣya*.

Upadeśa Sāhasrī with gloss of Rāma Tīrtha, ed. D.V. Gokhale, Bombay, 1917. Also consulted: *Upadeśa Sāhasrī* with Hindi trans. of Munilāla, Banaras, 1954. See also Jagadānanda, Mayeda and Alston.

Vivaraṇa on the *Adhyātma Paṭala* of the *Āpastamba Dharma Sūtra* in H.R. Bhāgavat, *Minor Works of Śrī Śaṅkarācārya*, 2nd Ed., 1952 (422ff).

(Attributed) *Vivaraṇa* on *Yoga-Bhāṣya* of Vyāsa on Patañjali's *Yoga Sūtras*, Madras Government Oriental Series, 1952.

For TRANSLATIONS of Śaṅkara's work, see under: Alston, Deussen, Gambhīrānanda, Hacker, Jagadānanda, Jhā, Leggett, Mādhavānanda, Mayeda, Nikhilānanda, A. Mahādeva Śāstrī, Thibaut and Venkataramiah.

II. List of other authors and works quoted

('trans.' denotes English translation unless otherwise stated.)

ABHINAVAGUPTA, *Īśvara Pratyabhijñā Vimarśinī*, 2 vols, Bombay, 1919 and 1921.

AITAREYA ĀRAṆYAKA: see Keith, A.B.

AITAREYA BRĀHMAṆA: ed. Aufrecht, Bonn, 1879.

ALSTON, A.J. (trans.), *The Thousand Teachings of Śaṅkara* (*Upadeśa Sāhasrī*), Shanti Sadan, London, 1990.

— , *Realization of the Absolute* (*Naiṣkarmya Siddhi* of Sureśvara), Shanti Sadan, London, 2nd. Ed. 1971.

BIBLIOGRAPHY

ĀNANDABODHENDRA: see *Yoga Vāsiṣṭha.*

ĀNANDAGIRI: standard sub-commentaries (ṭīkā) on Śaṅkara's commentaries and Sureśvara's Vārttikas consulted in Ā.S.S. Ed.

ĀNANDAPŪRṆA, *Nyāya Kalpa Latikā*, ṭīkā on B.B.V., Tirupati, Vols.I and II, 1975.

ANANTAKṚṢṆA ŚĀSTRĪ (ed.), *Two Commentaries on the Brahma Siddhi*, Madras, 1963. (Being the *Bhāvaśuddhi* of Ānandapūrṇamuni and the *Abhiprāya Prakāśikā* of Citsukha).

ANNAMBHAṬṬA, *Tarka Saṅgraha*, ed. and trans. Athalye, 2nd ed., Bombay, 1930.

ĀPA DEVA, *Mīmāṃsā Nyāya Prakāśa*, ed. (with comm.) V. Abhyankar, Poona, 1937. Ed. and trans. F. Edgerton, New Haven (Yale), 1929.

ĀPASTAMBA DHARMA SŪTRA: See Cinnaswāmī Śāstrī, Bühler, and Bhāgavat, *Minor Works.*

ĀRYA DEVA, *The Catuḥśataka*, ed. V. Bhattacharya, Calcutta, 1931.

ASHTEKAR: see Bhāgavat, H.R.

ĀTMĀNANDA, Swāmī, *Śaṅkara's Teachings in his own Words*, Bombay, 2nd. Ed., 1960.

AUGUSTINE, St., *Confessions*, trans. Sir Tobie Matthew, Loeb Ed., London, 1923.

— , *De Trinitate*, text and French trans. Mellet, Desclée de Brouwer, 2 vols, 1955.

BELVALKAR, S.K., *Lectures on Vedānta Philosophy*, Part I, Poona, 1929.

— , *The Brahma Sūtras of Bādarāyaṇa*, Poona, 2 vols, 1923 and 1924.

BERGAIGNE, A., *La Religion Védique* (3 volumes), Paris, 1883.

BHĀGAVAT, H.R., *Upaniṣadbhāṣyam* (of Śaṅkara) Vols I and II, Ashtekar Company, Poona, 1927 and 1928.

—, *Minor Works of Śrī Śaṅkarācārya*, Poona, 2nd Ed. 1952.

BHĀMATĪ: See Śaṅkara, *Brahma Sūtra Bhāṣya*.

BHĀRAVI, *Kirātārjunīyam*, ed. with Mallinātha's comm. and Hindi trans., Śobhita Miśra, Banaras, 1952.

BHARTṚHARI, *Vākyapadīya*, complete text ed. K.V. Abhyankar and V.P. Limaye, Poona, 1965.

BHĀSKARA, *Brahma Sūtra Bhāṣya*, Banaras, 1915.

BHATT, G.P., *Epistemology of the Bhāṭṭa School of Pūrva Mīmāmsā*, Varanasi, 1962.

BHATTACHARYA, V.S., *Āgama Śāstra of Gauḍapāda*, Calcutta, 1943, (Abbreviated Ā.Ś.G.).

BIARDEAU, M., *La définition dans la pensée indienne*, J.A., 1957, 371-384.

— , (Contribution on Indian philosophy to) *Encyclopédie de la Pléiade, Histoire de la philosophie*, I, Paris, 1969.

—, *La philosophie de Maṇḍana Miśra*, Paris, 1969.

—, *Quelques réflexions sur l'apophatisme de Śaṅkara*, I.I.J., 1959, 81-100.

—, *Théorie de la connaissance et philosophie de la parole dans le brahmanisme classique*, Paris and the Hague, 1964.

— , *La démonstration du Sphoṭa par Maṇḍana Miśra*, Pondichéry, 1958.

BOETZELAER, J.M. van, *Sureśvara's Taittirīyopaniṣad Bhāṣyavārttika*, Leiden, 1971.

BÖHTLINGK, O., *Sanskrit-Wörterbuch*, 3 vols, St Petersburg, 1879-89, reprinted Graz, 1959.

BUDHAKAR, G.V., '*Is the Advaita of Śaṅkara Buddhism in Disguise*?', Quarterly Journal of the Mythic Society, Bangalore, several parts, *incipit* Vol. XXIV, 1933: 1-18, 160-176, 252-265, 314-326.

BÜHLER, G., (trans.) *Āpastamba Dharma Sūtra*, S.B.E.

BUITENEN, J.A.B. van and DEUTSCH, E., *A Source Book of Advaita Vedānta*, Hawaii, 1971.

CAMMANN, K., *Das System des Advaita nach der Lehre Prakaśātmans*, Wiesbaden, 1965.

CANDRAKĪRTI: see Nāgārjuna.

CHATTERJI, S.K., *Indo-Aryan and Hindi*, 2nd Ed., Calcutta, 1960, reprinted 1969.

CHATTOPADHYAYA, D.P., *History of Indian Philosophy*, New Delhi, 1964.

CINNASWĀMĪ ŚĀSTRĪ (ed.) *Āpastamba Dharma Sūtra*, Banaras,1932.

CITSUKHA, *Abhiprāya Prakāśikā* (Comm. on Maṇḍana's *Brahma Siddhi)*, see Anantakṛṣṇa Śāstrī.

CRESSON, A., *Les courants de la pensée philosophique française*, Vol. 2, Paris, 1927.

CURTIUS, G., *Principles of Greek Etymology*, trans. A.S. Wilkins, London, two vols, 1875 and 1876.

DAKṢIṆĀMŪRTI STOTRA, ed. A. Mahādeva Śāstrī and K. Raṅgācārya with Sureśvara's *Mānasollāsa* and explanatory ṭīkās by Svayamprakāśa and Rāmatīrtha, Mysore Oriental Library Publications, 6, 1895.

DAṆḌIN, *Daśakumāra Carita*, ed. and trans. M.R. Kale, 3rd Ed., Bombay, 1925, reprinted Delhi, 1966.

DARŚANODAYA: see Lakshmīpuram Srīnivāsāchār.

DAS GUPTA, S.N., *History of Indian Philosophy*, Vol. V, Cambridge, 1955.

DE, S.K., *Aspects of Sanskrit Literature*, Calcutta, 1959.

DEUSSEN, P., *Erinnerungen an Indien*, Kiel and Leipzig, 1904.

— , *The Philosophy of the Upanishads*, trans. Geden, 1906, reprinted New York, 1966.

— , *Sechzig Upanishad's des Veda*, Leipzig, 3rd Ed. 1921, reprinted Darmstadt, 1963.

— , *Die Sūtra's des Vedānta*, Leipzig, 1887, reprinted Hildesheim, 1966.

— , *The System of the Vedānta*, Chicago, 1912. Abbreviated D.S.V.

— , and Strauss, O., *Vier Philosophische Texte des Mahābhāratam*, Leipzig, 1906.

DEUTSCH, E., *Advaita Vedānta*, Honolulu, 1969. See also van Buitenen, J.A.B.

DEVARAJA, N.K., *An Introduction to Śaṅkara's Theory of Knowledge*, Delhi, 1962.

DEVASTHALI, G., *Mīmāṃsā*, Vol. I, Bombay, 1959.

— , *Śaṅkara's Indebtedness to Mīmāṃsā*, J.O.I.B., 1951-2, 23-30.

DHARMAKĪRTI, *Pramāṇa Vārttikam*, ed. Dvārikādāsa Śāstrī, Varanasi, 1968. See also Prajñākara Gupta.

DĪGHA NIKĀYA, ed. Rhys Davids and Carpenter, Vol. II, Pali Text Society, London, 1966 (reprint).

DOWSON, J., *A Classical Dictionary of Hindu Mythology*, reprinted London, 1968.

ECKHART, Meister, *Sermons and Treatises*, ed. and trans. M. O'C. Walshe, Vol. II, Watkins, London, 1981.

EDGERTON, F., *Buddhist Hybrid Sanskrit Grammar and Dictionary*, Yale University, 1953, two vols. Reprinted Delhi 1970 and 1972.

FRAUWALLNER, E., *Geschichte der indischen Philosophie*, Vols I and II, Vienna, 1953 and 1956. Abbreviated G.I.P.

— , *Materialien zur ältesten Erkenntnislehre der Karma-mīmāṃsā*, Vienna, 1968.

— , *Die Philosophie des Buddhismus*, Berlin, 1958.

GAIL, A., *Bhakti im Bhāgavata Purāṇa*, Wiesbaden, 1969.

GAMBHĪRĀNANDA, Swāmī (trans.), *Brahma-Sūtra Bhāṣya of Śaṅkarācārya*, Calcutta, 1965.

— (trans.), *Chāndogya Upaniṣad with the Commentary of Śaṅkarācārya*, Calcutta, 1983.

— (trans.), *Eight Upaniṣads with the Commentary of Śaṅkarācārya*, Calcutta, two vols 1957 and 1958. (Vol.I comprises Īśa, Kena, Kaṭha, Taitt: Vol.II, Ait., Muṇḍ., Māṇḍ.with G.K. and Praśna.)

GARBE, R., *Die Sāṅkhya Philosophie*, Leipzig, 1917.

GAUTAMA DHARMA SŪTRA, trans. G. Bühler, S.B.E.

GELDNER, K.F., *Der Rigveda*, Harvard, four vols, 1951-57.

GHATE, V. S., *Le Vedānta*, Paris, 1918.

GLASENAPP, H. von, *Entwicklungsstufen des indischen Denkens*, Halle, 1940.

—, *Die Philosophie der Inder*, Stuttgart, 1949 (abbreviated as '*Einführung*')

—, *Stufenweg zum Göttlichen*, Baden Baden, 1948.

GOKHALE, D.V. see under Texts of Śaṅkara (above), *Bhagavad Gītā Bhāṣya* and *Upadeśa Sāhasrī*..

GONDA, J., *Inleiding tot het Indische Denken*, Antwerp, 1948.

—, *Les religions de l'Inde*, Vols I and II, Paris, 1953 and 1956.

GOPĪNĀTH, see Kavirāj.

GOUGH, A.E. see *Vaiśeṣika Sūtras*.

GOVINDĀNANDA: see Śaṅkara, *Brahma Sūtra Bhāṣya*.

GROUSSET, R., *Les philosophies indiennes*, two vols, Paris, 1931.

HACKER, P. Most of Paul Hacker's important articles on Advaita Vedanta were assembled in *Kleine Schriften* (see below). These can now be read in English translation in *Philology and Confrontation*, ed. and trans. Wilhelm Halbfass, State University of New York Press, 1995.

— , *Eigentümlichkeiten der Lehre und Terminologie Śaṅkaras*, Z.D.M.G., 1950, 246ff. (Halbfass, 57ff).

— , *Die Lehre von den Realitätsgraden im Advaita-Vedānta*, Z.M.R., 1952, 277ff. (Halbfass, 137ff).

— , *Jayanta Bhaṭṭa und Vācaspati Miśra, ihre Zeit und ihre Bedeutung für die Chronologie des Vedānta* included in *Beiträge... Walter Schubring dargebracht* (see Schubring) 160-169.

— , *Kleine Schriften*, herausgegeben von L. Schmithausen, Wiesbaden, 1978.

— , *Prahlāda*, Wiesbaden, 1960.

— , *Śaṅkara der Yogin und Śaṅkara der Advaitin*, W.Z.K.S.O. 1968/1969, 119ff. (Halbfass, 101ff).

— , *Śaṅkarācārya and Śaṅkarabhagavatpāda*, New Indian Antiquary, April-June 1947. Preferably consulted in the corrected version in *Kleine Schriften*, 41ff. (Halbfass, 41ff).

— , *Untersuchungen über Texte des frühen Advaita Vāda*, I, Wiesbaden, 1951. (abbreviated 'Texte').

— , *Upadeshasāhasrī, Gadyaprabandha* (Prose Section) übersezt und erläutert, Bonn, 1949.

— , *Vedānta Studien* I, Die Welt des Orients, Wuppertal, 1948, 240.

— , *Vivarta*, Wiesbaden, 1953.

HALBFASS, W. (ed. and trans.), *Philology and Confrontation*, State University of New York Press, 1995. (See above, under Hacker)

HAUER, J.W., *Der Yoga*, Stuttgart, 1958.

HAZRA, R.C., *Studies in the Purāṇic Records*, Dacca, 1940.

HEIMANN, B., *Studien zur Eigenart indischen Denkens*, Tübingen, 1930.

HIRIYANNA, M., *Essentials of Indian Philosophy*, London, 1949.

— , *Outlines of Indian Philosophy*, London, 1932.

HUME, R.E., *The Thirteen Principal Upanishads*, 2nd Edition of 1931, reprinted Madras (O.U.P.), 1958.

INGALLS, Daniel H.H., *Śaṅkara on the Question 'Whose is Avidyā?'* in P.E.W. 1953, 68ff.

—, *Śaṅkara's Arguments against the Buddhists*, in P.E.W., 1954, 291-316.

ĪŚVARA KṚṢṆA, *Sāṅkhya Kārikās* with *Tattvakaumudi* Commentary of Vācaspati Miśra, text and trans. Gaṅgānātha Jhā, ed. H.D. Sharma, Poona, 1934.

IYER, K.A. Subramania, *Bhartṛhari*, Poona, 1969.

JACOB, Col. G.A., *A Handful of Popular Maxims*, in three Parts, Bombay, 1900, 1902 and 1904.

—, *A Concordance to the Principal Upanishads and Bhagavad Gītā*, 1891, re-issued Delhi, 1963.

— see also under Sadānanda and Sureśvara.

JAGADĀNANDA, Svāmī, *A Thousand Teachings* (the *Upadeśa Sāhasrī* of Śaṅkara), text and trans., Madras, 2nd Ed. 1949.

JAIMINI: see under Śabara.

JASPERS, K., *The Way to Wisdom*, London, 1951.

JAYA DEVA, *Gītagovinda Kāvyam*, ed. Nārāyaṇa Rāma Ācārya, Bombay, 9th Ed., 1949.

JHĀ, Gaṅgānātha, *Pūrva Mīmāṃsā in its Sources*, Banaras, 1942.

—, *Chāndogya Upanishad and Śrī Śaṅkara's Commentary* (2 volumes), Madras, 1899

— see also under Īśvara Kṛṣṇa, Kumārila Bhaṭṭa, Śabara, Praśastapāda.

JHALAKĪKARA, B.J., *Nyāya Kośa*, Bombay, 3rd Ed., 1928.

JOHNSTON, E.H., *Early Sāṅkhya*, London, 1937.

JOSHI, L.M., *Studies in the Buddhistic Culture of India*, Delhi, 1967.

JOŚĪ, T.L. (= Jośi, Tarkatīrtha Lakṣmaṇaśāstrī), *Vaidika Saṃskṛti kā Vikāsa* (Hindi trans. from the Marathi), Bombay, 1957.

—, *Dharma Kośa Upaniṣat Kāṇḍa*, Wai (Maharashtra), 1950.

KAṆĀDA: see Vaiśeṣika Sūtras.

KAVIRĀJ, Gopīnāth, *Bhūmikā* (Introduction to Acyuta Grantha Mālā Ed. of Śaṅkara's B.S.Bh.), Banaras, 1937.

KEITH, A.B. (ed. and trans.), *Aitareya Āraṇyaka*, Oxford, 1909.

—, *A History of Sanskrit Literature*, Oxford, 1920.

—, *The Karma-Mīmāṃsā*, Calcutta, 1921.

—, *The Sāṃkhya System*, Calcutta, 1924.

—, (trans.) *Taittirīya Saṃhitā*, Harvard Oriental Series, 2 vols, 1914.

KṚṢṆA MIŚRA (ed. and trans.), *Prabodha Candrodaya*, Sita Krishna Nambiar, Delhi, 1971.

KṚṢṆA YAJVAN, *Mīmāṃsā-Paribhāṣā*, text and trans. Mādhavānanda, Calcutta, 1948.

KULLŪKA: see under Manu Smṛti.

KUMĀRILA BHAṬṬA, *Mīmāṃsā Śloka Vārttika* (abbreviated Ś.V.), Banaras, 1898-1899; trans. Gaṅgānātha Jhā, Calcutta, 1900-1908.

—, *Tantra Vārttika*, ed. Gangādhara Shāstrī, Benares, 1882-1903; trans. Gaṅgānātha Jhā, Bibliotheca Indica, Calcutta, 1903-24.

KUNJUNNI RAJA, K., *The Date of Śaṅkarācārya and Allied Problems*, Brahma Vidyā (= Adyar Library Bulletin) Vol. 24, 1960, 125-48.

—, *Indian Theories of Meaning*, Adyar, Madras, 1963.

KŪRMA PURĀṆA, Bombay, 1927.

LACOMBE, O., *L'Absolu selon le Védanta*, Paris, 1937.

LAKSHMĪPURAM SRĪNIVĀSĀCHĀR, *Darśanodaya*, Mysore, 1933.

LEGGETT, T., *The Chapter of the Self* (translation and exposition of Śaṅkara's *Vivaraṇa* on Praśna I, Paṭala 8 of *Āpastamba Dharma Sūtra)*, London, 1978.

LEHMANN, A., *Aberglaube und Zauberei*, 3rd Ger. Ed., Stuttgart, 1925.

MĀDHAVĀNANDA, SVĀMĪ (trans.), *The Bṛhadāraṇyaka Upanishad with the Commentary of Śaṅkarācārya*, Calcutta, 6th Ed., 1985.

MADHUSŪDANA, see Sarvajña Muni.

MĀGHA, *Śiśupālavadham*, Chowkamba Vidyā Bhavan, Banaras, 1955.

MAHĀBHĀRATA: G.P. Ed. (Mūlamātra). Also consulted, critical Ed. of V.S. Sukthankar, Poona, 1933-72. See also Deussen and Strauss.

MAHADEVAN, T.M.P., *Gauḍapāda*, Madras, 1952.

—, (ed.) *Word Index to the Brahma-Sūtra Bhāṣya of Śaṅkara*, Madras, two Parts, 1971 and 1973.

MAHĀNĀRAYAṆA UPANISHAD, ed. and trans. J. Varenne, Paris, 1960.

MAṆḌANA MIŚRA, *Brahma Siddhi* (abbreviated B.Sid.), ed. Kuppuswami Shastri, Madras, 1937. See also Anantakṛṣna Śāstrī, Biardeau, Schmithausen and Vetter.

MANU SMṚTI, with Comm. of Kullūka, Bombay, 1902.

MATICS, Marion L., *Entering the Path of Enlightenment*, trans. of *Bodhicaryāvatāraḥ*, London, 1970. See also Śānti Deva.

MAYEDA, S., *The Authenticity of the Upadeśa Sāhasrī*, J.A.O.S., 1965, No.2, 178-196.

— , *On the Authenticity of the Māṇḍūkya and the Gauḍapādīya Bhāṣya*, Brahma Vidyā (= Adyar Library Bulletin), 1967-8, 74ff.

— , *On Śaṅkara's Authorship of the Kenopaniṣadbhāṣya*, I.I.J., X (1967), 33-35.

—, *The Authenticity of the Bhagavadgītābhāṣya ascribed to Śaṅkara*, W.Z.K.S.O. IX (1965), 155-197.

— , *Śaṅkara's Upadeśa Sāhasrī*, critically edited with Introduction and Indices, Tokyo, 1973.

— , *A Thousand Teachings, The Upadeśasāhasrī of Śaṅkara*, trans. with Introduction and notes, Tokyo, 1979.

MONIER-WILLIAMS, Sir M., *Sanskrit-English Dictionary*, Oxford, 2nd Ed., 1899.

MORICHINI, G., *Early Vedānta Philosophy* (being a short summary of H. Nakamura's work on that subject) in the periodical *East and West* (Rome), 1960, 33-39.

MÜLLER, Max, *Sacred Books of the East* (abbreviated S.B.E.), Vol. XV, Oxford, 1884. Reprinted Delhi.

MURTI, T.R.V., *The Central Philosophy of Buddhism* (abbreviated C.P.B.), London, 1955.

— , *The Two Definitions of Brahman in the Advaita*, in *Krishna Chandra Bhattacharya Memorial Volume*, Almaner, 1958, 135-150.

MUS, P., *Barabadur*, Hanoi, 1935.

NĀGĀRJUNA, *Mūlamādhyamika Kārikās*, ed. with *Prasannapadā* Commentary of Candrakīrti by de La Vallée Poussin, St. Petersburg, 1903-1913.

NAKAMURA, H., *A History of Early Vedanta Philosophy*, Part One, New Delhi, 1983.

— , *The Vedānta Philosophy as was Revealed in Buddhist Scriptures*, in Dr. Maṇḍan Miśra (ed.), *Pañcāmṛtam*,Delhi, 1968, pp 1-74.

—, *Vedanta Tetsugaku No Hatten (Development of Vedānta Philosophy)*, in *Indian Philosophical Thought, Vol. III*, Tokyo, 1955.

— see also Morichini, G.

NARENDRADEVA, *Bauddha-Dharma-Darśana*, Patna, 1956.

NIKHILĀNANDA, *The Māṇḍūkyopaniṣad with Gauḍapāda's Kārikā and Śaṅkara's Commentary*, Calcutta, 4th ed., 1955.

OLDENBERG, H., *Die Lehre der Upanishaden und die Anfänge des Buddhismus*, Göttingen, 1923.

— , *Die Weltanschauung der Brāhmaṇa-Texte*, Göttingen, 1919.

ÖPIK, E.J., *The Oscillating Universe*, Mentor Books, N.Y., 1960.

OTTO, R., *Mysticism East and West*, N.Y., 1932.

PADMAPĀDA, see PAÑCAPĀDIKĀ

PADOUX, A., *Recherches sur la symbolique et l'énergie de la parole dans certains textes Tantriques*, Paris, 1964.

PAÑCAPĀDIKĀ (abbreviated P.P.), a work attributed to Padmapāda, ed. S. Shrīrāma Shāstrī and S.R. Krishnamūrthi Shāstrī, Madras, 1958. For trans. see Venkataramiah.

PANDEY, S.L., *Pre-Śaṅkara Advaita Philosophy*, Allahabad, 1974.

PĀṆINI, *The Ashṭādhyāyī of Pāṇini*, ed. and trans. S.C. Vasu, two vols, 1891, reprinted Delhi, 1962.

PARAMĀRTHA SĀRA: ed. with the *Vivaraṇa* of Rāghavānanda by S. N. Śukla, Banaras, 1933. For trans., see S.S. Śāstrī, below.

PASSMORE, J., *A Hundred Years of Philosophy*, Pelican Books, Harmondsworth, 1968.

PATAÑJALI, *Yoga Sūtras* with Comms. of Vyāsa and Vācaspati, Bombay, 1892.

—, (trans.) J.H. Woods, Harvard, 1914, reprinted Delhi, 1972.

— : see also Śaṅkara for (attributed) *Vivaraṇa* on Vyāsa's Comm. (Bhāṣya) to *Yoga Sūtras*.

POTTER, Karl, *Bibliography of Indian Philosophies*, Delhi, 1970.

PRAJÑĀKARA GUPTA, *Pramāṇa Vārtika Bhāṣyam*, ed. Rāhula Sāṃkṛtyāyana, Patna, 1953.

PRAKĀŚĀTMAN, *Vivaraṇa*, ed. S. Shrīrāma Shāstrī and S.R. Krishnamūrthi Shāstrī, Madras, 1958. See also Cammann, above.

PRAŚASTAPĀDA, *Praśastapāda-Bhāṣya* (or *Padārthadharma Saṅgraha*), with *Nyāyakandalī* of Shrī Dhara, Banaras, 1895. Eng. trans. Gaṅgānath Jhā, Banaras, 1916.

PŪRVA MĪMĀṂSĀ SŪTRAS: see under Śabara.

RADHAKRISHNAN, Sir S., *Indian Philosophy*, London, two vols, 1927.

—, *The Principal Upanishads*, London, 1953.

RĀGHORĀM, B. Shivprasād: (Publisher) *Hundred and Eight Upanishads*, Banaras, 1938 (Sanskrit text only).

RĀMA DEVA: see Jaiminīya Upanishad Brāhmaṇa.

RĀMĀNUJA, *Śrī Bhāṣya*, ed. Vāsudeva Śāstrī Abhyaṅkar, Bombay, 1914.

RATNAPRABHĀ: see Śaṅkara, *Brahma Sūtra Bhāṣya*.

RENOU, L., *Grammaire et Védanta*, in J.A., 1957, 121-132.

RENOU and FILLIOZAT, *L'Inde Classique*, two vols, Paris and Hanoi, 1947 and 1953.

ṚG VEDA, Rig Veda (Abbreviated R.V.): see also Geldner.

— , *Ṛg Veda Saṃhitā*, with Comm. of Sāyana, Vedic Research Institute, Poona, 5 vols 1933-51.

RITTER, H., *Das Meer der Seele*, Leiden, 1955.

RŪMĪ, Jalālu'ddīn, *Mathnawī*, trans. R.A. Nicholson, London, Vol.I, 1926.

RÜPING, K., *Studien zur Frühgeschichte der Vedānta Philosophie*, Wiesbaden, 1977.

ŚABARA, Jaimini's *Pūrva Mīmāṃsā Sūtra Bhāṣya*, Calcutta, two vols, 1873 and 1887. Trans. Gaṅgānātha Jhā, G.O.S., 3 vols, 1933, 1934 and 1936. See also Frauwallner.

SACCIDĀNANDENDRA SVĀMIN (abbreviated as Sac.) All Sac's works are published by the Adhyātma Prakāśa Kāryālaya, Holenarsipur, Karnataka, India, unless otherwise stated.

—, *Brahmavidyā Rahasya Vivṛtiḥ*, 1969.

—, *Gītā-Śāstrārtha-Vivekaḥ*, 1965.

—, *Intuition of Reality*, 1973.

— , *Īśāvāsya Upaniṣad* with Śaṅkara's Bhāṣya and author's Sanskrit *tīkā* (written under the lay name of Y. Subrahmanya Śarmā), 1937.

—, *Māṇḍūkya Rahasya Vivṛtiḥ*, 1958.

— , *The Method of the Vedanta* (abbreviated M.V.), London, 1989 (Translation by A.J. Alston of *Vedānta Prakriyā Pratyabhijñā*, q.v.).

—, *Misconceptions about Śaṅkara*, 1973.

—, *Śaṅkara's Clarification of certain Vedantic Concepts*, 1969.

— , *Śuddha-Śaṅkara-Prakriyā-Bhāskara* (abbreviated Ś.Ś.P.B.), quoted from Sanskrit Ed. in 3 parts, 1964. Available in English, 3 parts 1965-1968, subtitled *Light on the Vedantic Method according to Śaṅkara*.

—, *Sugamā* (Sanskrit exposition of Śaṅkara's Adhyāsa-bhāṣya), 1955.

—, *Taittirīya Upanishad Shikshāvallī,* ed. with Shaṅkara's Commentary and editor's Sanskrit notes, 1961.

— , *Taittirīya Upanishad Ānandavallī-Bhṛguvallī,* ed. with Shaṅkara's Commentary and editor's *Bhāṣyārtha Vimarśinī* sub-commentary, 1962.

— , *Vedānta Prakriyā Pratyabhijñā*, 1964. For an English translation of this work, see *The Method of the Vedānta*, previous page.

— , *Viśuddha Vedānta Sāra*, 1968. (Abbreviated V.V.S.)

SADĀNANDA, *Vedānta Sāra*, ed. with two commentaries, Col. G.A. Jacob, 5th revised Ed., 1934.

— , text of *Vedānta Sāra* with Eng. trans. Nikhilānanda Svāmin, Calcutta, 1947.

SADĀNANDA YATI, *Advaita Brahma Siddhi*, Calcutta, 1888-90.

ṢAḌVIṂŚA BRĀHMAṆA, ed. K. Klemm, Gütersloh, 1894. Trans. W.B. Bollée, Utrecht, 1956.

SAHASRABUDDHE, M.T., *A Survey of Pre-Śaṅkara Advaita Vedānta*, Poona, 1968.

SĀṄKṚTYĀYANA, Rāhula, *Darśana Dig-Darśana*, Allahabad, 2nd Ed., 1947. (Hindi).

ŚĀNTI DEVA, *Bodhicaryāvatāraḥ*, ed. P.L.Vaidya, Darbhanga, 1960. See also M.L. Matics.

SARVAJÑA MUNI, *Saṅkṣepa Śārīrakam* with the Commentary of Madhusūdana, Banaras, 1924.

Sarvajñātman and Sarvajñātma Muni: alternative forms of the above name.

ŚĀSTRĪ: sometimes interchanged with Shāstrī, q.v.

ŚĀSTRĪ, A. Mahādeva, *The Bhagavad-Gītā with the Commentary of Śaṅkarācārya*, Madras, 1897. Reprinted, Madras, 1977.

— , *Dakshiṇāmūrti Stotra of Śrī Śaṅkarāchārya*, Madras, 3rd Ed., 1978. Contains Sanskrit text and Eng. trans. of the *Mānasollāsa Vārttika* attributed to Sureśvara. See also entry under *Dakṣiṇāmūrti*

Stotra above for Sanskrit edition of text and commentaries.

ŚĀSTRĪ, Maṅgaladeva, *Bhāratīya Saṃskṛti kā Vikāsa*, Part II, *Aupaniṣada Dhārā*, Banaras, 1966 (Hindi).

ŚĀSTRĪ, Rāmānanda Tivārī, *Śrī Śaṃkarācārya kā ācāra darśana*, Allahabad, 1950 (Hindi).

ŚĀSTRĪ, S.S. Sūryanārāyaṇa, *The Paramārtha Sāra of Ādi Śeṣa*, Bombay, 1941.

— and C.K. Rājā, *The Bhāmatī: Catussūtrī*, Adyar, Madras, 1933.

ŚATAPATHA BRĀHMAṆA, trans. Eggeling, S.B.E. (in 5 parts).

SCHMITHAUSEN, L., *Maṇḍana Miśras Vibhrama Vivekaḥ*, Vienna, 1965.

SCHUBRING, W. (Festschrift) *Beiträge zur indischen Philologie... Walther Schubring dargebracht*, Hamburg, 1951.

SHARMA, L.N., *Kashmir Śaivism*, Banaras, 1972.

SHĀSTRĪ : sometimes interchanged with Śāstrī, q.v.

SHASTRI, Hari Prasad: see Vālmīki and Vidyāraṇya.

SILBURN, L., *Instant et Cause*, Paris, 1955.

SOGEN, Yamakami, *Systems of Buddhistic Thought*, Calcutta, 1912.

ŚRĪ HARṢA, *Śrī Harṣa's Plays*, ed. and trans. Bak Kun Bae, Bombay, 1964.

SRĪNIVĀSĀCHARĪ, P.N., *The Philosophy of Bhedābheda*, Madras, 1934.

STAAL, J.F., *Advaita and Neoplatonism*, Madras, 1961.

STCHERBATSKY, Th., *The Conception of Buddhist Nirvāṇa*, revised and enlarged edition by Jaidev Singh, Bhāratīya Vidyā Prakāśana Edition, Banaras, n.d.

— , *Buddhist Logic*, Vol. II, Leningrad, 1930.

— , *Central Conception of Buddhism*, London, 1923.

— , *La théorie de la connaissance et la logique chez les Bouddhistes tardifs*, Paris, 1926.

STRAUSS, O., *Indische Philosophie*, Munich, 1925. See also Deussen.

SŪRA DĀSA, *Sūra Sāgara*, ed. Vājapeyī, Vārāṇasī, 2 vols, 1953 and 1956.

SUREŚVARA, *Bṛhadāraṇyaka Bhāṣya Vārttikam* (abbreviated B.B.V.) ed. with Ānandagiri's ṭīkā in the Ā.S.S. Ed., three vols, Poona, 1892-1894. See also Ānandapūrṇa.

—, (Attributed) *Mānosollāsa*. Commentary on *Dakṣiṇāmūrti Stotra*, q.v.

—, *Naiṣkarmya Siddhi* (abbreviated N.Sid.), ed. with Jñānottama's Commentary, by Col. G.A. Jacob and revised by M. Hiriyanna, Bombay,1925. Trans. by A.J. Alston as *The Realization of the Absolute*, Shanti Sadan, 2nd Ed. 1971.

—, (Attributed) *Pañcīkaraṇa Vārttika* in *Panchīkaraṇam of Shree Shankarāchārya*, Edited with six commentaries, Gujarati Printing Press, Bombay, 1930.

—, *The Sambandha Vārttika*, text and Eng. trans. T.M.P. Mahadevan, Madras, 1958.

—, *Taittirīya Bhāṣya Vārttika* (abbreviated T.B.V.), Ā.Ś.S. Ed. with ṭīkā of Ānandagiri, 1911. For Eng. trans. see Boetzelaer, above.

TAITTIRĪYA ĀRAṆYAKA, Ā.S.S., Poona, Vol. I, 1926.

TAITTIRĪYA BRĀHMAṆA, ed. Rājendralāl Mitra, Calcutta, 1870.

TAITTTIRĪYA SAṂHITĀ: see Keith, above.

THIBAUT, G., *The Vedānta Sūtras with the Commentary of Śaṅkarācārya* (= Brahma Sūtra Bhāṣya, B.S.Bh.), Eng. trans., Parts I and II.

TROṬAKA (or Toṭaka), *Śruti Sāra Samuddharaṇa*, ed. Kevalānanda Svāmin, Ā.S.S. Ed., Poona, 1936.

UDDYOTAKARA, *Nyāya Vārttikam*, ed. Dvivedin and Dravid, Benares, 1916-7.

UI, Hakuju, *Vaiśeṣika Philosophy according to the Daśapadārtha-śāstra,* Chinese Text with English translation and notes, Banaras, 1962.

UPĀDHYĀYA, Baladeva, *Śrī Śaṃkarācārya*, Allahabad, 1950. (Hindi).

— , *Śrī-Śaṃkara-Dig-Vijaya*, Sanskrit text with Hindi trans., Hardwar, 1944.

UPĀDHYĀYA, B.S., *Bauddha Darśana tathā anya Bhāratīya Darśana*, 2 vols, Calcutta, 1954 (Hindi).

UPĀDHYĀYA, Rāmajī, *Bhārata kī Saṃskṛti-Sādhanā*, Allahabad, 1967. (Hindi).

VĀCASPATI MIŚRA: see under Texts of Śaṅkara, *Brahma Sūtra Bhāṣya, Bhāmatī sub-commentary*. See also Īśvara Kṛṣṇa.

VAIŚEṢIKA SŪTRAS, with Comm. of Śaṅkara Miśra, ed. and trans. A.E. Gough, Benares, 1873, reprinted New Delhi, 1975.

— , ed. Jīvānanda, Calcutta, 1886.

VALLABHĀCĀRYA, *Aṇu Bhāṣya*, text and *Bālabodhinī* commentary, two vols, Bombay, 1921 and 1926.

VĀLMĪKI, *The Ramayana of Valmiki* (trans. H.P. Shastri), three vols., London, 2nd revised Ed. of Vol. I, 1962.

VĀSIṢṬHA *Dharma Sūtra*, trans. G. Bühler, S.B.E.

VĀTSYĀYANA, *Nyāya Sūtra Bhāṣya*, Poona, 1939. Eng. trans. Gaṅgānāth Jhā, Poona, 1939.

VENKAṬANĀTHA, *Tattva Muktā Kalāpaḥ* with *Sarvārtha Siddhi* and *Bhāva Prakāśa*, Mysore, Vol. II., 1940.

VENKATARAMIAH, D., *The Pañcapādikā of Padmapāda*, G.O.S., Baroda, 1948.

— , *Aitareyopaniṣad with Śaṅkarācārya's Bhāṣya*, text and Eng. trans., Bangalore, 1934.

VETTER, T., *Maṇḍana Miśra's Brahmasiddhiḥ, Brahmakāṇḍaḥ* only, annotated German trans., Vienna, 1969.

— , *Zur Bedeutung des Illusionismus bei Śaṅkara*, W.Z.K.S.O. 1968/69, 407-423.

— , *Erkenntnisprobleme bei Dharmakīrti*, Vienna, 1964.

VIDYĀRAṆYA, *Bṛhadāraṇyaka Bhāṣya Vārttika Sāra* (B.B.V.S.), Acyuta Grantha Mālā Ed., Banaras, two vols, 1941 and 1943.

— , *Panchadashi* (= Pañcadaśī, abbreviated P.D.), text and trans. by H.P. Shastri, 2nd revised Ed., London, 1965.

VIJÑĀNA BHIKṢU, *Sāṃkhya Pravacana Bhāṣya*, ed. R. Garbe, Cambridge, Mass., 1895.

VIMUKTĀTMAN, *Iṣṭa-Siddhi*, ed. Hiriyanna, G.O.S., Baroda, 1933.

VIṢṆU PURĀṆA: G.P. Ed. with the Hindi trans. of Śrī Munilāla Gupta, 1937.

VIVARAṆA: see Prakaśātman.

VYĀSA: see Patañjali.

WARDER, A.K., *Outlines of Indian Philosophy*, New Delhi, 1971.

WOODS, J.H: see Patañjali.

YĀJÑAVALKYA SMṚTI, with Mitākṣarā Commentary and Hindi trans., Umesh Chandra Pandey, Banaras, 1967.

YAMAKAMI, S: see under Sogen, Y.

YĀSKA, *Nirukti*, Calcutta, 4 vols, 1882-91.

YOGA VĀSIṢṬHA, with the Commentary of Ānandabodhendra, two vols, Bombay, 1937.

YOGA SŪTRAS: see Patañjali.

YUKTI DĪPIKĀ, ed. Ram Chandra Pandeya, Banaras-Delhi, 1967.

The Śaṅkara Source-Book

A Conspectus of the Contents of the Six Volumes

Volume I — Śaṅkara on the Absolute

I. SOURCES OF ŚAṄKARA'S DOCTRINE: HIS LIFE & WORKS

1. A Doctrine of Transcendence
2. Vedas: Saṃhitās, Brāhmaṇas, Upanishads
3. The Smṛti: Viṣṇu worship and Śiva worship
4. The Bhagavad Gītā
5. The Brahma-Sūtras and their Background: Bhartṛprapañca
6. The True Tradition: Gauḍapāda, Draviḍa, Brahmanandin, Sundara Pāṇḍya
7. Doctrine of Illusion before Śaṅkara: Māyā Vāda and Avidyā Vāda
8. Śaṅkara's Date, Life and Works
9. Śaṅkara's School

II. THE DOCTRINE OF NESCIENCE

1. The Nature and Results of Nescience
2. Nescience as Non-Comprehension and False Comprehension
3. The Self and the Not-Self: Non-Discrimination and Mutual Superimposition
4. The Standpoint of Nescience and the Standpoint of Knowledge

CONTENTS OF THE ŚAṄKARA SOURCE BOOK

III. KNOWLEDGE OF THE ABSOLUTE

1. The Absolute is already known in a general way
2. The Absolute is not known as an object
3. The Path of Negation
4. Going beyond the Mind

IV. THE ABSOLUTE AS BEING, CONSCIOUSNESS AND BLISS

1. The Definition of the Absolute as 'Reality, Knowledge, Infinity'
2. The Absolute as the Self-Existent Principle
3. The Absolute as the Self-Luminous Principle
4. The Absolute as Bliss

Volume II — Śaṅkara on the Creation

V. THE ABSOLUTE AS CREATOR AND CONTROLLER

1. The Absolute as Creator and Controller of the World
2. The Absolute as the Lord
3. The Absolute as the Material and Efficient Cause of the World
4. The Absolute as Inner Ruler
5. The Absolute as the Lord of Māyā

VI. THE WORLD AND ITS PRESIDING DEITIES

1. Sat-kārya Vāda
2. Name and Form: Indeterminability
3. World-periods and Theory of the Elements
4. The Presiding Deities

VII. THE ACOSMIC VIEW

1. The Creation-texts as a Device to teach Non-Duality
2. Nothing can come into being
3. The Argument from Dream

Volume III — Śaṅkara on the Soul

VIII. THE SOUL AND ITS ORGANS AND BODIES

1. The Soul as the Self viewed under External Adjuncts
2. The Organs and Bodies of the Soul
3. The Light that illumines the Soul
4. The Soul and the Lord are not distinct

IX. THE 'STATES' OF THE SOUL AND THEIR TRANSCENDENCE

1. Dream
2. Dreamless Sleep
3. Turīya

Volume IV — Śaṅkara on Rival Views

X. REFUTATION OF INADEQUATE BRAHMINICAL DOCTRINES

1. Refutation of Liberation through Action
2. Refutation of Liberation through Knowledge and Action Conjoined
3. Refutation of Bhedābheda Vāda
4. Refutation of the Pāśupatas and Pāñcarātras
5. Refutation of Sphoṭa Vāda

XI. REFUTATION OF NON-VEDIC WORLD-VIEWS

1. Dialectic (tarka): its Purpose and Rules
2. Refutation of Materialism
3. Refutation of the Sāṅkhyas
4. Refutation of the Vaiśeṣikas
5. Refutation of the Buddhist Schools
6. Refutation of the Jainas

Volume V — Śaṅkara on Discipleship

XII. ADOPTING THE PATH

1. The Wheel of Transmigration
2. The Injunction to Adopt the Path
3. Preliminary Qualifications for the Path
4. Spiritual Qualities to be cultivated on the Path

XIII. THE VEDA AND THE TEACHER

1. The Self can only be known through the Veda
2. The Veda, the Smṛti and Reason
3. The Approach to the Teacher
4. The Teacher and the Texts

Volume VI — Śaṅkara on Enlightenment

XIV. THE INDIRECT PATH

1. Meditation in the Context of the Vedic Ritual (upāsanā)
2. Realization of Identity with Hiraṇyagarbha
3. The Path of the Flame
4. Supernormal Powers on the Indirect Path

XV. THE DIRECT PATH

1. Adhyātma Yoga
2. Devotion (bhakti)
3. Communication of 'That Thou Art'
4. Meditation (dhyāna) and Repeated Affirmation (abhyāsa)
5. Meditation on OM

XVI. THE ENLIGHTENED MAN

1. Enlightenment is not a change of state

Two books by A M Halliday that present the teachings of Advaita Vedanta in a contemporary setting

Yoga for the Modern World

As modern man strives to meets the challenges of the new millennium, his life is more than ever dominated and shaped by the influence of science and technology. Yet only the deeper values, upheld by the great spiritual traditions, can ensure that the outer progress rests on a corresponding inner progress in peace, goodwill and enlightenment.

The Vedanta tradition, in practical application, has always emphasized personal enquiry and experiment, and, like science, seeks to realize the deeper truth behind phenomena. Its inner discoveries in the field of self-knowledge should be of no small interest to those currently investigating the nature of consciousness.

These nineteen lectures consider various aspects of contemporary life, and show how the ancient wisdom of the Upanishads and the Bhagavad Gita, pregnant with valid and practical insights, has the power to infuse modern life with meaning and purpose.

402pp paperback 0-85424-051-9

Freedom Through Self-Realisation

These eighteen lectures place the teachings of the Bhagavad Gita and the Upanishads in a modern setting, and show the way to an inner development open to everyone.

'All the talks deal with timeless, enduring themes and they are still very relevant to contemporary life. The author, a pupil of the late Hari Prasad Shastri, enlivens his text with well-chosen passages from the writings of philosophers, poets and mystics.... The book offers clear, practical advice from a Vedantic viewpoint, on techniques of meditation and good living.'

Yoga and Health

225pp Paper 0-85424-040-3

Advaita Vedanta texts translated into English

by A J Alston

THE THOUSAND TEACHINGS OF ŚAṄKARA
Upadeśa Sāhasrī

The *Upadeśa Sāhasrī* is the one independent work accepted by all authorities as undeniably written by Śaṅkara, most of whose known writings are concerned with commenting on and interpreting the words of the great classical texts of the Upanishads, Brahma Sutras and Bhagavad Gita. It gives an unconstrained exposition of Advaita Vedanta by India's greatest philosopher. The practising student of Yoga will find in this classic a wealth of insight and a powerful aid to spiritual self-examination (*viveka*). Includes transliterated Sanskrit text.

438pp Paper 0-85424-041-1

REALIZATION OF THE ABSOLUTE
Naiṣkarmya Siddhi of Sureśvara

Sureśvara was an enlightened disciple of Śaṅkara and a brilliant exponent of Advaita Vedanta in its purest form. His *Naiṣkarmya Siddhi* establishes the Upanishadic doctrines on a strictly rational basis. At the same time, it introduces the reader to the course of discipline and meditation required for practical realization of his identity with the Absolute. Sureśvara called the work 'a compendium containing the essence of the entire Upanishadic teaching'. Transliterated Sanskrit text and explanatory notes are included.

285pp Cloth 0-85424-021-7

THE HEART OF SHRI SHANKARA
by Śrī Swāmī Satchidānandendra

A translation of a work first published in 1929 under the title *Refutation of Root Ignorance* or *The Heart of Shri Shankara*. It considers the philosophical view that there is a root-ignorance that creates the phenomenal world and which in some sense really exists. The Swami sets out to show that this view arose among Advaitins after Shankara and is contrary to his true teaching.

226pp A4 comb-bound. 0-85424-050-0

THE CREST JEWEL OF WISDOM
Viveka Chūḍāmaṇi

A classic of Advaita Vedanta

The commentary by Hari Prasad Shastri demonstrates the practical validity of the teachings of Adhyatma Yoga, while the translation by A J Alston puts the verses into approachable English, faithful to the Sanskrit original, which is included in romanised script. The text covers some sixty key Vedanta topics ranging from the qualifications of the enquirer to his final enlightenment.

336pp Paper 0-85424-047-0

Classical texts translated by Hari Prasad Shastri

ASHTAVAKRA GITA

AVADHUT GITA

DIRECT EXPERIENCE OF REALITY
Aparokshānubhūtī

PANCHADASHI
A 14th Century Vedāntic Classic

THE RAMAYANA OF VALMIKI
in three volumes

TEACHINGS FROM THE BHAGAVAD GITA

TRIUMPH OF A HERO
Vīra Vijaya of Swami Mangalnāth

VERSES FROM THE UPANISHADS
with commentary

WORLD WITHIN THE MIND
Teachings from the Yoga Vāsishtha

Book catalogue available from Shanti Sadan
29 Chepstow Villas, London W11 3DR
www.shantisadan.org